To Walt,
with deep appreciation
for your teaching and mentoring
that has had such a lasting
impact on my life.

Hal Knight
February, 2014

ANTICIPATING HEAVEN BELOW

Anticipating Heaven Below

—

Optimism of Grace
from Wesley to the Pentecostals

HENRY H. KNIGHT III

CASCADE *Books* · Eugene, Oregon

ANTICIPATING HEAVEN BELOW
Optimism of Grace from Wesley to the Pentecostals

Cascade Books
An Imprint of Wipf and Stock Publishers
199 W. 8th Ave., Suite 3
Eugene, OR 97401

www.wipfandstock.com

ISBN 13: 978-1-62032-960-3

Cataloguing-in-Publication Data

Knight, Henry H., 1948–

    Anticipating heaven below : optimism of grace from Wesley to the Pentecostals / Henry H. Knight III.

    xvi + 260 p. ; 23 cm. Includes bibliographical references.

    ISBN 13: 978-1-62032-960-3

    1. Wesley, John, 1703–1791. 2. Wesley, Charles, 1707–1788. 3. Theology, Doctrinal. I. Title.

BX8495.W5 K55 2014

Manufactured in the U.S.A.

To Theodore Runyon
and
Walter J. Lowe

in gratitude for their teaching
and friendship
which has meant so much

Contents

Acknowledgments

I HAVE BENEFITTED IMMEASURABLY from the suggestions given, issues raised, and encouragement offered by many of my colleagues in teaching and ministry. D. William Faupel, Diane Leclerc, Stephen W. Rankin, Chris E. W. Green, Dennis C. Dickerson, and Harold E. Rasor read all or much of the manuscript; Randy L. Maddox and Steven J. Land examined the earlier chapters, and William C. Kostlevy read those that came later. Their advice and insight contributed significantly to the content and argument of the book. I am also indebted to several theologically gifted pastors who provided helpful commentary on the manuscript, including Kathy Bray, John Collins, Laura Guy, Philip Hamner, Rodney McNeall, and Rusty L. Husted. Their advice, support, and prayers throughout this project mean more to me than I can adequately express.

This work contains some of my own deepest concerns and hopes, not only for the Wesleyan stream of Christianity, but for the gospel of Jesus Christ. I am grateful to Wipf and Stock for enabling me to share them with a wider audience.

Introduction

Thy nature, gracious Lord, impart;
Come quickly from above;
Write thy new name upon my heart,
Thy new, best name of love!
—CHARLES WESLEY[1]

WESLEYANISM IS A MOVEMENT marked by profound hope. It is inherently discontented with hearts bound by sin, lukewarm churches, and unjust societies. It holds to the promise not only of a future new creation that will put an end "to sin, and misery, and infirmity, and death," and reestablish "universal holiness and happiness,"[2] but also new creation in this present age, of a holiness that transforms hearts, renews churches, and brings hope to the world. The animating core of this holiness is the love of God in Jesus Christ.

It was out of discontent with their own lives that John and Charles Wesley began the spiritual search that led to a new Protestant vision of salvation. Certainly they shared much with the Calvinists who dominated the eighteenth-century awakening: salvation by grace alone, justification by faith, and the new birth. Yet the Wesleys insisted there was more to the Christian life than this, that the gospel promised for this life a full salvation from sin and a fullness of love in the heart.

Their discontent spread to the condition of their own Church of England. The Wesleys were living in a highly churched society, in which virtually everyone thought of himself or herself as a Christian. But the Wesleys distinguished between being a churched society and a Christian

---

1. Hymn 334, *Wesley's Works* 7: 491.
2. John Wesley, "The General Spread of the Gospel," 27, *Wesley's Works* 2:499.

society. A churched society simply expects persons to go to church, assent to belief in the Christian God, and live morally respectable lives. To be a Christian, they argued, implies something far deeper than that—it implies a life transformed by love.

This theme is found in *An Earnest Appeal to Men of Reason and Religion*. There John Wesley says his Methodists are "grieved at the sight" of "on every side, either men of no religion at all, or men of a lifeless, formal religion." They would, he says, "greatly rejoice in convincing some that there is a better religion to be attained, a religion worthy of God that gave it. And this we conceived to be no other than love: the love of God and of all mankind; the loving God with all our heart and soul and strength, as having first loved us, as the fountain of all the good we have received, and of all we ever hope to enjoy; and the loving every soul which God hath made, every man on earth, as our own soul."[3]

Being a Christian, then, is much more than many in Wesley's day supposed. It was not that there were more requirements to being a Christian than they thought—a longer checklist of things to do. It was that the salvation God promises is more wonderful than they imagined.

In this salvation, we not only know *about* God—we come to *know* God, to experience the living reality of God. Salvation is not only what God has done *for* us through Jesus Christ, but what God does *in* us through the Holy Spirit. Salvation includes not only justification—the forgiveness of our sins—but sanctification, the gift of new hearts and lives motivated and governed by love. Salvation is not only about our ending up in heaven after we die. It is about our having heaven in our hearts in the present. It is, in a term favored by Charles Wesley, about "heaven below."

Charles Wesley used "heaven below" to describe the Christian life, and most especially holiness or sanctification. As we shall see, for the Wesleys sanctification begins with a new birth, marked by fruit of the Spirit such as faith, hope, and love. As we grow in sanctification, we seek for God to fill us with love, so that it governs both our hearts and lives. This they called Christian perfection, or entire sanctification, a second instantaneous work of God. The entire process, both the gradual growth and the instantaneous transformation, was by the power of the Holy Spirit. It is what salvation *is*.

3. John Wesley, *An Earnest Appeal to Men of Reason and Religion*, in *Wesley's Works* 11:45.

In one sense Christian perfection is a *restoration*. We were created in God's image, and God is love. We were therefore created to love as God loves. But the fall into sin corrupted that image. God's goal is not only to forgive us but to restore us to that image in which we were created. But "heaven below" is an eschatological term. It extends the meaning of Christian perfection, and indeed sanctification as a whole, to that of a present *anticipation* or *realization* of the new creation to come. Through the power of the Holy Spirit, the life of the coming kingdom is already breaking into the present, beginning in human hearts, and spreading from there to families, communities, and nations.

To think eschatologically involves recognizing a tension between the "already" and the "not yet." This tension, found within the New Testament, can be summarized in this way: already some of the realities of the future kingdom of God are being experienced and realized in the present age. Yet Jesus has not returned, and the fullness of the kingdom has not arrived. We live between the times—after Easter, after Pentecost, but before the second coming. This much is common to many theologies. What is in dispute is how much of the "already" we may expect. How much of the new creation do we experience or realize in the present?

For John Wesley it is clear: there is a great deal of the already that we can experience and realize. This is due to his "optimism of grace," his emphasis on the presence and power of the Holy Spirit. Thus, in addition to proclaiming what God has done in Jesus Christ, Wesley was also proclaiming the promise of a fullness of life in Christ through the power of the Spirit, a perfection of the heart in love.

This theology of "heaven below" launched a new Protestant tradition that, while flourishing in England, crossed the Atlantic to grow enormously in nineteenth-century America, and then exploded globally in the twentieth century, especially in the Southern Hemisphere. Methodism, the Holiness movement, and Pentecostalism all have the promise of "heaven below" encoded in their spiritual DNA.

The eschatological orientation so pervasive in the Wesleys' theologies is not always so explicit in their theological descendants. But their common focus on the promise of holiness and the power of the Holy Spirit contained within it the content of heaven below: a present realization of the life of heaven, which is centered in love. Their optimism of grace evoked an expectant hope, which indelibly marked their spirituality.

In the chapters that follow we will examine this optimism of grace in its many diverse manifestations. As we do, we will give attention to theological issues that often divided the proponents of heaven below and that continue to deserve careful attention today. My hope is that by examining these issues, those of us in this extended Wesleyan family will be enabled in our day to faithfully proclaim the promise of heaven below, and to do so with the balance of realism and hope that marked our predecessors at their best.

The first chapter provides a broad picture of Wesleyan theological identity, and then argues that anticipating heaven below is essential to that identity. This sets the stage for the chapters to follow.

Chapters 2 through 4 examine the foundation and shape of this theology of heaven below as found in John and Charles Wesley and their colleague John Fletcher. The focus of chapter 2 is the tension between an optimism of grace and a pessimism of nature, showing its linkage to the eschatological tension between the "already" and the "not yet." Maintaining this tension is crucial to any credible theology of heaven below. Chapter 3 demonstrates how pervasive the understanding of salvation as a foretaste of heaven is in the theologies of these first Wesleyans. The fourth chapter makes the Trinitarian argument that for all three of these theologians, the life, teachings, and death of Christ is the norm for the content of heaven, and the Holy Spirit is the agent who brings it to reality in the present.

The very heart of heaven below is holiness, or Christian perfection, the subject of chapters 5 through 8. In chapter 5 the theology of Phoebe Palmer, the mother of the Holiness movement, is introduced and compared to that of John Wesley. This brings to the fore the relation of instantaneous and gradual sanctification, and the related issue of presumptive and expectant faith. Chapter 6 continues the comparison, now focused on the relation of human and divine agency, and the related issues of God's faithfulness and freedom in relation to God's promises. Chapter 7 extends the discussion of these issues to the theologies of non-Methodists Charles Finney, William Boardman, A. B. Simpson, and William Durham, along with examining their more christological approach to holiness in comparison to Wesley's Trinitarianism. Here we will see how different understandings of optimism of grace and pessimism of nature lead to different portrayals of the promise of sanctification. Chapter 8 turns to the critical issue of the relationship of holiness to power, the issue that more than any other divided the Holiness movement from Pentecostalism. There we compare the reality of empowerment in Wesley's movement, especially with regard to the ministry of women, with the contrasting theological understandings of Phoebe Palmer and early Pentecostals like Charles Parham and William Seymour. These various perspectives have much to tell us about the purpose, extent, and spiritual grounding of enduement with power by the Holy Spirit.

Chapters 9 through 14 extend the vision of heaven below beyond personal salvation and empowerment to church and society. In chapter 9 we examine the presence of God as both mediated and manifest in church and awakenings, as well as in everyday lives. Chapters 10 and 11 examine healing, with the first focused on Wesley and the second on the divine healing movement that emerged in the nineteenth century. For many in Holiness and Pentecostal movements, divine healing is as important a theological claim as holiness or power, and it raises profound issues for understanding divine sovereignty and human faith. The focus of chapter 12 is the nature of Christian community, especially in terms of implications of holiness for race, class, and denominationalism. In chapter 13 we look at how the larger society is envisioned when seen through the lens of heaven below, especially with regard to slavery and the poor. Finally, in chapter 14, we examine the difficulty of living as citizens of the kingdom of heaven in a resistant culture, and whether the late nineteenth-century shift to premillennialism in the face of such resistance led to a diminished vision of heaven below. That chapter concludes with a summation of the theological tensions identified throughout the book that must be maintained if our proclamation of the promise of heaven below is to have integrity, and a reflection on sanctification as a catalyst for ecclesial renewal and social change.

Although drawing on history, this book is primarily a work of theological reflection. While there is some attention to primary sources, especially those of John Wesley, I shall be dependent on the work of historians throughout. I will draw upon this historical research to show continuities of thought and practice of the various movements and figures while noting as well their distinctive contributions. My intent is to offer the Wesleyan and Pentecostal traditions a rich and comprehensive theological vision of what it means to proclaim heaven below. This book is a call to recognize anticipating heaven below as essential to their identity as well as their gift to the church universal, and to proclaim it with theological integrity.

PART ONE

The Beginning of Heaven

CHAPTER 1

Wesleyan Identity

Love Divine, all loves excelling
Joy of heaven, to earth come down ...

—CHARLES WESLEY[1]

TRADITIONS ARE COMPLEX. IF Alasdair MacIntyre is correct in describing a living tradition as "an historically extended, socially embodied argument" focused on "the goods which constitute that tradition,"[2] then a tradition cannot continue to exist without a diversity of voices in conversation. Yet as MacIntyre also shows, traditions have goals and concerns that give them their distinctive shape. Their identity comes from the goal or central good that those in the tradition seek, a communal narrative that both identifies and describes the goal, and a common set of practices that enable persons to cultivate the virtues necessary to attain the goal while avoiding being drawn away by temptations or distraction.

Christianity is itself a complex tradition that exhibits these characteristics. It is shaped by the gospel narrative (here understood as the story of God's creative and redemptive activity culminating in Jesus Christ and the coming of the Holy Spirit), focused on salvation and mission, and embodied in a wide range of communities and practices that shape the lives of participants. There is over two thousand years of ongoing argument over the nature of God, salvation, church and mission, which at its

1. Hymn 374, *Wesley's Works* 7:645.
2. MacIntyre, *After Virtue*, 207.

best has given the tradition theological vibrancy (and at its sometimes violent worst, betrayed in practice the very gospel it professed).

Wesleyanism is a distinctive tradition within Christianity. It has its own way of telling the gospel story, specifying the nature and goal of salvation, and providing communities and practices to aid persons in attaining that goal. But attempting to identify just what it is that makes this tradition "Wesleyan" in its theology and practice has itself produced a vigorous and insightful conversation from the mid-twentieth century to the present.

This book is a contribution to that discussion. My intent is not to challenge the work that has gone before; indeed I will presuppose it and build upon it. What I hope to do is to make explicit a way of thinking—a kind of theological vision—that permeates John Wesley's theology and is an essential component of its "Wesleyan" identity. Moreover, I want to show that this way of thinking, which I've labeled (drawing on Charles Wesley) "anticipating heaven below," continues to shape the theological vision of early Methodism, the Holiness movement, and the Pentecostal tradition.

As preparation for that argument, let us first identify some of the key insights already advanced concerning Wesleyan identity which are foundational for my own proposal.

A Theology of Love and Grace

Most broad descriptions of John Wesley's theology quickly center on two terms which are at its core: love and grace. Mildred Bangs Wynkoop emphasized the first. "To be Wesleyan," she wrote, "is to be committed to a theology of love."[3]

The centrality of love in Wesley's theology can hardly be understated. It governs both the character of God and the content of salvation. While many of Wesley's Calvinist contemporaries made sovereignty central to the divine nature, Wesley instead insisted that "God is often styled holy, righteous, wise but not holiness, righteousness, or wisdom in the abstract, as He is said to be love: intimating that this is . . . His reigning attribute, the attribute that sheds an amiable glory on all His other perfections."[4] For Charles Wesley, "Love Divine" was a frequent synonym for God in his hymns.

3. Wynkoop, *Theology of Love*, 101.
4. John Wesley, 1 John 4:8. *Explanatory Notes*, 914.

Because humanity was created in the image of this God, and for the Wesleys the goal of salvation is to restore us to the image in which we were created, love is the content and goal of salvation. They emphatically opposed reducing salvation to a kind of simplified version of justification, where the point was to be forgiven through Christ in order to attain a happy afterlife. Salvation "is a present thing"[5] John Wesley insisted; justification is the doorway to sanctification wherein the Christian receives and grows in a new life marked by fruit of the Spirit and governed by love.

Sanctification, then, is the goal of salvation, and Christian perfection is the goal of sanctification. Christian perfection (or entire sanctification), said Wesley, "is neither more nor less than pure love—love expelling sin and governing both the heart and life of a child of God."[6]

The Wesleys understood salvation to be by grace alone. Hence Thomas A. Langford could argue that "the grace of God, as the redeeming activity of divine love, is the center of Wesley's theology."[7] Here Langford coordinates the two terms, understanding the graciousness of God as itself an expression of God's love.

Grace indeed permeates the theology of both Wesleys, and does so in the most thoroughgoing Protestant fashion. Their disagreement with Luther and Calvin was not over the priority and necessity of grace, but over the extent of grace and the manner in which it works.

Randy L. Maddox has described in some detail the nature of grace in John Wesley's theology. He argues that Wesley has a "practical theology" governed by an "orienting concern" for "responsible grace." Maddox understands a "practical theology" to be centered on shaping the worldview of Christians in order to further spiritual growth and faithful discipleship. (This is a more precise way of stating what Wesley himself means when he describes his theology as a "practical divinity.") The "orienting concern" is a central perspective that gives guidance in theologically addressing diverse contexts and changing situations. "Responsible grace," as the orienting concern, refers to both grace enabling us to respond to God (and without which we could not due to sin) and, having been so enabled, our responsibility to do so.[8] (My own language for this is that

---

5. John Wesley, "The Scripture Way of Salvation" I.1., *Wesley's Works* 2:156.

6. John Wesley, Letter to Walter Churchey, February 21, 1771, *Wesley's Works* (Jackson) 7:482.

7. Langford, *Practical Divinity*, 1:20.

8. Maddox, *Responsible Grace*, 16–19.

"grace both enables and invites us to participate in an ongoing personal relationship with God."[9])

What sets Wesley at odds with the great Protestant reformers was his insistence on this relational understanding of grace plus the universality of grace. No one is without a measure of prevenient (or preventing) grace, thus everyone has a divinely-given capacity to respond to God, according to the revelation they have. This universality of grace is directly linked to the universality of God's love.

Kenneth L. Collins has further developed these lines of thinking. He argues that the "axial theme" of Wesley's practical theology is both "holiness *and* grace," where holiness is understood as "holy love" and grace as both free and co-operant.[10] Each combination of terms illumines central aspects of Wesley's theology. "Holiness" implies separation and purity, while "love" is self-giving, embracing, and inclusive. It is their "conjunction" in holy love that describes both the character of God and the content of Christian salvation. Grace is understood both as freely given *and* co-operant, involving divine and human cooperation in the process of salvation. This maintains both the priority of and empowerment by grace without losing its relationality.

Collins identifies the conjunctive nature of Wesley's theology as itself one of its central features. While not using that term, others have noted the same characteristic. Paul Wesley Chilcote, for example, describes Wesley as having a "both/and" theology, understanding "salvation as *both* Christ's work for us *and* the Spirit's work in us; as *both* freedom from sin *and* freedom to love."[11]

Our Doctrine and Discipline

Early Methodists on both sides of the Atlantic frequently spoke of "doctrine and discipline." Thus Wesleyan identity is not simply theological in the narrow sense. It involves not only a gospel-based set of teachings that identify the content and goal of divine redemption and renewal, but as with any tradition, a set of practices through which persons both experience and participate in that redemption and renewal. Both terms had distinct meanings within the early Wesleyan movement.

9. Knight, *Presence of God*, 8; see also 9–10.

10. Collins, *Theology of John Wesley*, 6–18.

11. Chilcote, *Recapturing the Wesleys' Vision*, 12.

"Doctrine" was considered to be primarily "practical divinity," in contrast to "speculative divinity." That is, doctrine had to do with salvation, discipleship, mission and the like. In one essay, having first described the character of a Christian, Wesley then proceeds to discuss Christianity as "a scheme or system of doctrine" in this way: "First. It describes this character in all its parts, and that in the most lively and affecting manner. The main lines of this picture are beautifully drawn in many passages of the Old Testament. These are filled up in the New, retouched and finished with all the art of God. . . . Secondly. Christianity promises this character shall be mine, if I not rest till I attain it. . . . Christianity tells me, in the Third place, how I may attain the promise: namely, by faith."[12] As we will see, Wesley has a much larger theological vision than personal salvation, although it was clearly the focus of his "practical divinity."

The "discipline" of early Methodism was what today would be called a set of spiritual disciplines. "Nothing can be more simple, nothing more rational than the Methodist discipline," wrote Wesley. "Any person determined to save his own soul may be united . . . with [the Methodists]. But this desire must be evidenced by three marks: avoiding all known sin, doing good after his power, and attending all ordinances of God."[13] Early Methodists were held accountable to attempting to live by this discipline at a weekly class meeting, which was also an occasion to gain clarity as to what faithful discipleship meant concretely in day to day life.

The discipline aided both in faithfully living out a Christian life and engaging in those practices God uses to effect Christian growth. With regard to the first, the discipline encouraged Methodists not only to refrain from sin but to positively engage in works of mercy toward their neighbor and works of piety toward God. Thus whether prior to justification or in the process of growing in sanctification, the discipline provided direction for living out what the heart was coming increasingly to desire.

With regard to the second, such works of piety and works of mercy were means of grace used by God to enable persons to grow in faith, hope, and love. That is, as we serve our neighbor, and as we pray, study Scripture, worship, attend the Lord's Supper, and converse together, the Holy Spirit works to continue to transform our lives. I have argued elsewhere that this distinctive pattern of spiritual discipline, small group meetings, and means of grace is essential to Wesleyan identity because

12. John Wesley, "Letter to the Rev. Dr. Conyers Middleton occasioned by his late 'Free Inquiry'" IV. II.5, *Wesley's Works* (Jackson) 10:72–73.

13. John Wesley, "On God's Vineyard" III.1, *Wesley's Works* 3:511.

it constitutes the central practices through which we receive grace and attain salvation.[14]

To speak of "doctrine" and "discipline" in this manner has resonance with two other terms that have come to prominence in late twentieth-century theology: orthodoxy and orthopraxis. "Orthodoxy" is of course a much older term, and is usually defined as "right belief," although its root meaning is more "right praise" (*ortho doxa*). "Orthopraxis" designates the kind of practice that shapes our beliefs as well as itself being shaped by belief. To put it in the most general terms, orthopraxis implies we may learn much about God and God's mission in the world through faithful Christian practice—in worship, devotional life, and acts of compassion and justice.

In the Wesleyan tradition orthodoxy and orthopraxis mutually shape one another. But as Richard B. Steele notes, a number of Wesleyan and Pentecostal scholars have found this correlation helpful but inadequate. What is missing is a third element often called "orthopathy" ("right affections" or "right experience") or "orthokardia" ("right heart").[15] This three-way integration has the happy tendency to enable persons and communities to avoid several dangers to the Christian life. The emphasis on orthopathy and orthopraxis (in Wesleyan terms, holiness of heart and life) prevents Christianity from becoming a dead orthodoxy. Orthopathy, focused as it is on the changed heart, counters the tendency for Christianity to devolve into simply a set of duties, a kind of dead formalism. And orthodoxy and orthopraxis aid in avoiding what in Wesley's day was called the danger of enthusiasm, that is, the constant seeking of religious experience understood as having certain religious feelings.

What we learn from this brief survey is that Wesleyan identity is indeed complex. Not only are there a number of core terms—love and grace, doctrine and discipline, holiness of heart and life—but each term has a distinctive Wesleyan definition. Moreover, the dynamic of the tradition is found not simply in the terms themselves but in their interrelationship. What we also learn is that each term or relationship provides us an angle of vision from which to interpret Wesleyan identity. While

---

14. Knight, *Presence of God*.

15. Steele, *"Heart Religion,"* xxxiii. In addition to Steele, the term "orthopathy" is used by Land, *Pentecostal Spirituality*; Knight, *Presence of God*; and Runyon, *New Creation*. "Orthokardia" is used by Clapper, *Religious Affections*, and Green, *Reading Scripture*.

each illumines central features of the tradition, none by itself portrays the tradition in all of its richness.

My goal in this book is to provide yet another angle of vision on the Wesleyan tradition. What I hope to illumine is an aspect of the tradition that is central to its Wesleyan identity, such that without it the tradition could hardly be called Wesleyan at all. I do not believe this is the only central element of the tradition that remains to be explicated. There is, for example, an implicit and explicit Trinitarianism that many have noted as constitutive of Wesleyanism and remains to be explored in much greater depth.[16] But my task is to develop another essential feature of the Wesleyan tradition, that of anticipating heaven below.

In doing this I am especially building on a proposal by Theodore Runyon that "the new creation" be considered a Wesleyan distinctive, indeed "one of the most basic Wesleyan distinctives." On the personal level Runyon links new creation to Christian perfection understood as renewal of the image of God, an image that is relational and centered in love. More broadly, new creation means "the very real transformation in the creature and the world that salvation brings about." This theme "of hope and expected transformation virtually sings its way through many" of Wesley's later sermons.[17]

Randy Maddox has argued that it was Wesley's embrace of the conviction that "we are ultimately inclined and enabled to love others only as we experience being loved ourselves" that enabled him to envision new creation as presently available. This "marked the beginning of a trajectory in Wesley's theological development" that led him to describe new creation first in spiritual terms, and later in his ministry in socio-economic and cosmic terms.[18] Thus new creation is focused on but not limited to the renewal of persons. These are all themes I will explore in the chapters ahead.

My concern is not with which term—new creation or heaven below—should be used to name the distinctive to which they both point.

16. For a proposal to develop the Trinitarian insights of John and Charles Wesley, see Colyer, "Trinitarian Evangelical Theology." For a discussion of the Wesleys' Trinitarianism, see Wainwright, "Why Wesley Was a Trinitarian." For the implications of their Trinitarianism for Christian formation, see Matthaei, "Transcripts." On Charles Wesley's Trinitarian theology and its implications, see Vickers, "Charles Wesley."

17. Runyon, *Exploring the Range of Theology*, 174 (in a chapter originally published as "The New Creation").

18. Maddox, "Nurturing the New Creation," 27.

Whichever term is used, I want to point to an eschatological way of thinking that not only shapes John Wesley's theology, but explicitly or implicitly much of the tradition he births. Indeed, new creation has a more biblical resonance than heaven below. The advantage of "anticipating heaven below" is not only as an apt description of the hope that marks this theological tradition, but that it also denotes the spiritual yearning it evokes and missional vision it enables.

Heaven Below

"Heaven below" was a term used by Charles Wesley to describe knowing Jesus and his love, as well as its salvific effects. While often focused on the initial encounter with the love of Christ and the pardon that brings, he also used "heaven below" to describe sanctification, Christian perfection, and even the final eschatological renewal of creation.

Here is a stanza from one well-known Wesley hymn, in which the speaker is Jesus:

> With me, your chief, ye then shall know,
>> Shall feel your sins forgiven;
> Anticipate your heaven below,
>> And own that love is heaven.[19]

The linkage between "heaven below" and love is made explicit. Another hymn, this time spoken to Jesus, links the term with grace:

> Jesus, I bless thy gracious power,
> And all within me shouts thy name;
>> Thy name let every soul adore,
> Thy power let every tongue proclaim;
>> Thy grace let every sinner know,
> And find with me their heaven below.[20]

Charles Wesley used the term around twenty times in his published hymns. He also used a number of similar terms, each with about the same prevalence. "Antepast of heaven" seems especially to refer to pardon or justification and the peace that accompanies it. "Heaven on earth" ranges in reference from Jesus' love and justification, to new birth, sanctification,

---

19. Hymn 1, *Wesley's Works* 7:81.
20. Hymn 198, ibid., 329.

Christian perfection, and following Jesus.[21] For example, he describes the new birth in this way:

> When thou dost in my heart appear,
> And love erects its throne,
> I then enjoy salvation here,
> And heaven on earth begun.[22]

He uses the same language to describe following Jesus:

> Happy the souls to Jesus join'd
> And sav'd by grace alone,
> Walking in all thy ways we find
> Our heaven on earth begun.[23]

My intent here is not to do an intensive study of Wesleyan hymnody but to demonstrate a way of thinking. Knowing the love of Christ and receiving and growing in salvation is regularly described in terms of heaven; that is, in eschatological terms. More particularly, this is an *inaugurated eschatology*, in which the life of the kingdom of heaven that has not come in fullness is nonetheless already breaking into the present through Christ and in the power of the Holy Spirit.

Inaugurated eschatology has been recognized by many as a feature of John Wesley's theology as well. John did not use "heaven below" or the other terms so characteristic of his brother's hymns. But he did use his own eschatologically-charged language: "the beginning of heaven," "walking in eternity," and "tasting the powers of the world to come." Similar language can also be found in the writings of the Wesleys' friend and colleague John Fletcher, including the term "heaven below": ". . . the love of God shed abroad in a *believer's* heart by the Holy Ghost given unto him, is salvation itself; this love being the tree on which all good works grow, and making our gracious heaven below, as it will make our glorious heaven above."[24]

21. This is based on my own survey of Charles Wesley's Published Verse as compiled by the Center for Studies in the Wesleyan Tradition, Duke Divinity School.

22. Charles Wesley, "Rejoicing in Hope" [Romans xiii.12], in *Hymns and Sacred Poems* (1742), 182, Published Verse.

23. Hymn 96, *Hymns on the Lord's Supper* (1745), in Rattenbury, *Eucharistic Hymns*, 225.

24. John Fletcher, "Salvation by the Covenant of Grace," Second Head, in "An Equal Check to Pharisaism and Antinomianism," Part First, *Works* 1:69.

The use of these eschatologically laden terms to refer to a range of soteriological loci points to a deeper and more pervasive feature of the theologies of the Wesley brothers and Fletcher. These theologies can be seen from one angle as essentially inaugurated eschatologies, linking present salvation in all its aspects with the life of the world to come. My use of "anticipating heaven below," then, extends further than Charles Wesley's explicit usage. In this book I'm using it as an apt metaphor for a way of thinking that characterizes not only this trio of theologians at the root of the Wesleyan movement, but implicitly or explicitly much of the tradition they produce. To be Wesleyan *is* to anticipate heaven below, or to put it differently, it is to yearn for, seek, and expect for God's will to be done on earth, in the present, as it is in heaven.

The term "heaven below" does reappear from time to time in the later tradition. American Bishop Francis Asbury, writing to one of his preachers in the early nineteenth century, links it to Christian perfection: "O purity! O, Christian perfection! O, Sanctification! It is heaven below to feel all sin removed. Preach it, whether they will bear or forbear. Preach it. . . . Our Pentecost is come, in some places, for sanctification."[25]

Phoebe Palmer, the leading theologian of the Holiness movement that emerged in Methodism in the 1830s, describes the advantage of personal holiness this way: "My experience continually attests the truth of the assertion, that the life of the believer is a heaven below. The divine tranquility; the deepened communion with the Father, Son, and Holy Spirit; and the accompanying increase of love, faith, light, and humility; make it such . . ."[26] In similar language Palmer praises God for entire sanctification in her well-known hymn, "The Cleansing Stream":

> I see the new creation,
> I hear the speaking blood;
> It speaks! Polluted nature dies!
> Sinks! 'neath the cleansing flood.

> I rise to walk in heaven's own light
> Above the world and sin,
> With heart made pure, and garments white,
> And Christ enthroned within.

25. Asbury, "Letter to Henry Smith," *Journal and Letters*, 3:440.
26. Palmer, *Faith and Its Effects*, 38

Amazing grace! 'tis heaven below
To feel the blood applied;
And Jesus, only Jesus know,
My Jesus crucified.[27]

"Heaven below" was used in other ways as well. William Watters, the first American-born Methodist preacher, used it to describe coming together for worship and the sharing of testimonies at a 1780 Love Feast: "I was in a little Heaven below, and believe Heaven above will differ more in quantity than in quality."[28] Over 125 years later, in 1906, a Pentecostal described the Azusa Street revival this way: "We have no need of organs or pianos, for the Holy Ghost plays the piano in all our hearts. . . . It is so sweet. It is heaven below."[29]

But as with the Wesleys, this occasional use of the term bespeaks a more profound theological understanding. The God who in the end will make all things new is even now, through the Spirit, transforming the hearts and lives of persons in love, manifesting the divine presence in worship and their life together, and then enlisting them in a present work of renewing both church and society. Even now, God is bringing heaven below.

27. Palmer, "Cleansing Wave," stanzas 2–4.
28. Cited in Ruth, *Little Heaven Below*, 154.
29. *The Apostolic Faith*, December 1906, cited in Wacker, *Heaven Below*.

CHAPTER 2

An Optimism of Grace

To use the grace we have, and now
to expect all we want, is the grand secret.[1]

—JOHN WESLEY

WESLEY WROTE THESE WORDS to a female band leader in 1765. Bands were small groups especially designed for those who were growing in sanctification and earnestly seeking Christian perfection. So it is no surprise that much of his correspondence with her, which ranged from 1760 to 1777, sought to present a carefully nuanced understanding of Christian perfection to enable her to be a faithful guide to her little flock.

What Wesley says in this correspondence does not differ from his more straightforward theological writings of this period, including his important *A Plain Account of Christian Perfection*, which compiled and summarized his thinking on the matter from 1725 to 1767 (and was amended in subsequent editions through 1777). The need for clarification that prompted the *Plain Account* is also evident in these letters. What implicitly governs both is this question: To what extent may we hope to be renewed in love in this life?

The Fullness of Salvation

Early on in this correspondence Wesley affirms the instantaneous nature of Christian perfection and our need to cultivate an expectant faith:

1. John Wesley, Letter to a Member of the Society CCL, October 13, 1765, *Wesley's Works* (Jackson) 12:281–82.

> Every one, though born of God in an instant, yea, and sanctified
> in an instant, yet undoubtedly grows by slow degrees, both after
> the former and the latter change. But it does not follow from
> thence that there must be a considerable tract of time between
> one and the other. A year or a month is the same with God as
> a thousand. . . . Much less is there any necessity for much suf-
> fering: God can do his work by pleasure as well as by pain. It is
> therefore undoubtedly our duty to pray and look for full salva-
> tion every day, every hour, every moment, without waiting till
> we have either done or suffered more. Why should not this be
> the accepted time?[2]

Here Wesley is sorting out a number of practical issues for those seeking
the promise of perfection in love. Does it come gradually or instantaneously? Wesley says both: sanctification is indeed a gradual, day-by-
day process of growth, but Christian perfection itself (also called entire
sanctification or full salvation) is instantaneous, and followed by further
growth. Are there conditions we have to first meet—more we must do, or
suffering we must undergo? No, says Wesley, it is by grace alone, and although the timing belongs to God, we should nonetheless look to receive
it at any moment with hopeful expectancy.

Now it may be that Wesley is affirming these points because of the
perfectionist controversy that had rocked the Methodist movement in
the early 1760s. Thomas Maxfield and George Bell were promoting a
version of Christian perfection that emphasized the instantaneous over
the gradual, that was evidenced more by extraordinary spiritual experiences than love, and from which one could no longer be tempted or fall.[3]
In reaction to these embarrassing excesses of perfectionist enthusiasm,
Charles Wesley was moving in the opposite direction, denying the instantaneous work until the time of death, and insisting on suffering as a
necessary element for growth in sanctification. John Wesley is charting a
middle course between the presumptuous expectations of the perfectionists and what he considered the too limited expectations of his brother.
Thus he encourages his correspondent to "never be afraid of expecting
too much": "O what heights of holiness," he exclaims, "are to come."[4]

2. John Wesley, Letter to a Member of the Society CCXL, June 27, 1760, ibid.,
275–76.

3. For a detailed account of the controversy, see Gunter, *Limits of "Love Divine"*,
211ff.

4. John Wesley, Letter to a Member of the Society CCXLIII, June 17, 1761, *Wesley's
Works* (Jackson) 12:277.

There is in these letters, then, a powerful affirmation of what the Holy Spirit can do, truly an optimism of grace. And if brother Charles had become a bit less optimistic than John on Christian perfection, the difference is only in degree. Compared to most of their contemporaries in the evangelical awakening, both affirm a robust realization of sanctification in this life, a form of "heaven below."

Claims that we can be sanctified to this extent are never spiritually simple, as both brothers knew. Distinctions must be made to clarify just what is entailed in a promise of sanctification or Christian perfection. So unsurprisingly we find John Wesley carefully describing what Christian perfection means and does not mean to his correspondent: "They that love God with all their heart, and all men as themselves, are scripturally perfect. And surely such there are; otherwise the promise of God would be a mere mockery of human weakness. Hold fast to this. But then remember, on the other hand, you have this treasure in an earthen vessel.... Hence all your thoughts, words, and actions are so imperfect ... that you may well say, till you go to Him you love,—'every moment, Lord, I need the merit of thy death.'"[5]

So yes, says Wesley, there really is a scriptural Christian perfection, one in which love fully governs our motivation, disposition, and desires. But at the same time our thoughts and actions remain imperfect. We are finite creatures in a fallen world, and that inevitably leads us to fall short of the perfect will of God (what he elsewhere calls "involuntary transgressions"). Wesley writes this in 1763, and returns to the subject again in a 1770 letter.

In 1768 he discusses a related issue. There he speaks of "innumerable degrees in both a justified and a sanctified state," and warns that, while desiring the fullness of Christian perfection, "nothing would be more likely to hurt the soul than undervaluing the grace already received."[6] In expecting more, one should not think less of what God has already accomplished (which was yet another error of perfectionists like Maxfield and Bell).

Such distinctions are necessary if you are encouraging people to seek and expect something like Christian perfection in this life. An optimism of grace must be both hopeful and realistic at the same time: hopeful to encourage an expectant and receptive faith; realistic about both the

5. John Wesley, Letter to a Member of the Society CCXLVI, April 7, 1763, ibid., 278–79.

6. John Wesley, Letter to a Member of the Society CCLIL, March 14, 1768, ibid., 283.

conditions and content of the promise expected. It comes with the territory of an inaugurated eschatology, which, to be sound, must maintain a tension between the "already" and the "not yet." The Wesleys insist God has promised a bit more of the "already" in this present life than most other Protestant traditions, and that the promise extends to a much larger group (namely all believers) than most Christians, Protestant or otherwise, had usually assumed. Yet the Wesleys must maintain this in tension with the "not yet" if they are to avoid falling into the sorts of errors made by the extreme perfectionists. As we shall see, adequately maintaining this tension is also an issue for subsequent traditions that proclaim God has promised a significant dose of "heaven below" in this life.

Maintaining the Tension

The phrase "optimism of grace" to describe John Wesley's theology was first used in an essay by Gordon Rupp in 1952. Drawing on the insights and terminology of the Catholic historian Rondet, Rupp argues that over several centuries, culminating with the seventeenth, a "pessimism of nature" dominated the thinking of Protestant and Catholic alike. Their common conclusion was that God in the end would save only a small portion of sinful humanity. In contrast with this view was the "rational doctrine of progress, as it was expounded by the perfectibilian philosophers" of the Enlightenment, an "optimism of nature" that "denied the fact of sin . . . repudiated the need for grace and of redemption," and trusted reason to free humanity from the chains of religion, superstition, and ignorance, and lead it to ever-increasing progress in this world.[7]

Different from both of them was the evangelical Arminianism of John and Charles Wesley, which proclaimed an "optimism of grace." Unlike the philosophical proponents of an optimism of nature, the Wesleys firmly held to a doctrine of original sin. Indeed, they believed in total depravity, which holds that human nature in its fallenness is deeply and fundamentally flawed, marked by "positive rebellion, mutiny, hostility to God, a restless egoism, a perseverance in idolatry by which" humanity puts "itself on the altar and worships the creature"[8]

---

7. Rupp, *Principalities and Powers*, 91–92. Others have cited this phrase from Rupp, including Runyon, *New Creation*, 26, and Williams, *Wesley's Theology Today*, 54. Williams cites Rupp extensively throughout his book.

8. Rupp, *Principalities and Powers*, 94. John Wesley preferred the term "total corruption."

So the Wesleys believed in original sin every bit as strongly and thoroughly as Luther and Calvin. But to a much greater extent than their Protestant forbears, the Wesleys saw that "the depth of this tragedy must be attached with the heights of grace." Thus for them, "Total depravity is set in the context of total grace, of the great salvation."[9] And the Wesleys took their message to all persons, believing all, not just a few, were eligible recipients of that salvation.

Rupp insists that Wesleyan theology "has a shape and a coherence,"[10] a uniqueness centered on the linkage of "justification by faith, which is the beginning and groundwork of salvation, to the hope of perfect love, which is the horizon."[11] While Luther had set Christians "looking eagerly toward the horizons with an eschatology of faith," Wesley in the eighteenth century "gave them an eschatology of love" and called Christians, as Rupp put it, "to be always seeking, eagerly and expectantly, new horizons of Christian experience . . . which the bountiful Giver is always more ready to bestow than his children to ask."[12]

This Wesleyan optimism of grace stood out in his day as it does in ours. After acknowledging "the limitations and qualifications" John Wesley placed around the doctrine, Rupp makes this telling statement: "Let us be content with the statement that 'given the limitations inherent in existence in a body in a fallen world, we dare set no limit to what the Grace of God can do for a man here and now': That is still a great deal more than was believed by most eighteenth-century Christians and a good deal more than is believed and hoped for by most modern Methodists."[13] In this regard, not much has changed between 1952 when Rupp published this statement and American Methodism in the early twenty-first century.

There is one major divergence between Rupp's argument and the one I am making here. In defending Wesley's optimism of grace, Rupp is dismissive of what he calls "holiness cults which have another origin and another theology than his."[14] While I by no means claim that the various holiness theologies of the nineteenth century are identical to

9. Ibid., 95.

10. Ibid., 97.

11. Ibid., 99.

12. Ibid., 98–99.

13. Ibid., 98.

14. Ibid.

Wesley's, they are clearly "Wesleyan." That is, they are contributors to the conversation that constitutes the Wesleyan tradition, and in the process enlarge and expand the expectation of "heaven below" in the present.

Because these subsequent movements proclaimed an optimism of grace, they, like the Wesley brothers, were faced with the theological task of maintaining the tension between the "already" and "not yet." At the inception of these movements, when this tension was not maintained it was usually due to emphasizing the "already" at the expense of the "not yet." Several generations later, the problem is reversed: expectations for the "already" are minimized, and hope shifts solely to "heaven above" or to the age to come.

But this foreshadows chapters yet to come. Here our remaining task is to return to John Wesley's theology and show in a bit more detail how the dynamic tension between an optimism of grace and a pessimism of nature encourages expectant hope while realistically facing the challenge of sin.

Attainment and Expectation

Clarence L. Bence has described Wesley's theology as a dialectical tension between attainment and expectation. "Throughout his theological system," Bence argued, "Wesley repeatedly counterbalances the attainment of a specific goal with an immediate expectation of a new goal which transcends and at the same time extends that which has already been realized."[15] Each attainment along the way of salvation is actual in itself, but never a stopping point. It is foundational for further growth, which builds upon and enlarges what has gone before. Because the ultimate horizon is eschatological, there is no point in the Christian life where growth is no longer possible or desirable. There is always "more." Hence Wesley urges those who have attained Christian perfection, "When ye have attained a measure of perfect love, when God has . . . enabled you to love him with all your heart and with all your soul, think not of resting there. That is impossible. You cannot stand still; you must either rise or fall. . . . Therefore the voice of God . . . to the children of God, is, 'Go forward!'"[16]

---

15. Bence, "John Wesley's Teleological Hermeneutic," 7.

16. John Wesley, "On Faith (Hebrews 11:6)" II.6, *Wesley's Works* 3:501.

What I want to do is link this insight of Bence with that of Rupp. When we do, we find that the reason that each attainment cannot be a resting point is that, until the eschaton, there is always more "fallenness" to overcome, always more love to receive and live. So there is a double lure to go forward: the persistence of remaining sin, broadly defined (the pessimism of nature), and the eschatological vision of what yet can be (the optimism of grace). And it is the latter that illumines the former.

While Bence emphasizes the day-to-day, gradual Christian growth, I believe the theological dynamic is best seen if we look at key steps along the way, including the instantaneous works of grace within the overall process of salvation.

To begin at the beginning: humanity was created in the image of God (*imago Dei*). Wesley understands the *imago Dei* as actually three images, organically connected. The *natural image* consists of our understanding (including reason), will (the affections and tempers of the heart), and liberty (or freedom). The *political image* is our human capacity and responsibility, as a vice-regent of God, to mediate God's love and care for the earth. Most central is the *moral image*, consisting of righteousness and true holiness, that is, love. Just as God is love, so also were humans created in the image of that love, which governed both the heart and life.[17]

The fall into sin brought the total corruption of the moral image, and with that the distortion of the other images. The effect on the natural image was to dim our understanding, direct our will (that is, our motivations and desires) to things other than God, and to take away our liberty, so that we cannot do otherwise than our will allows. Put differently, the will is now bound to sin; we *are* sinners, and our liberty consists only in being "free" to be who we now are. The political will is likewise damaged. Instead of mediating God's care, our ruling over the earth is now driven by our own interests apart from God, with tragic consequences for both human society and the natural world.

This is a deep pessimism of nature—that is, of fallen human nature. And it is just this condition of total corruption that salvation seeks to heal. As we have seen, for the Wesleys salvation is much more than justification and new birth, and much more than a happy afterlife. And

17. What follows is my own summation of Wesley's "way" or "order" of salvation. For more extensive accounts, see the standard texts: Collins, *Theology of John Wesley*; Maddox, *Responsible Grace*; Runyon, *New Creation*; as well as chapters 2 and 3 of Knight, *Presence of God*.

John Wesley is emphatic on this point: "By salvation I mean, not barely . . . deliverance from hell, or going to heaven; but a present deliverance from sin, a restoration of the soul to its primitive health . . . a recovery of the divine nature; the renewal of our soul after the image of God, in righteousness and true holiness . . ."[18] This is a profound optimism of grace. And there is no theological way to get from a thoroughgoing Protestant understanding of original sin to the restoration of the *imago Dei* in this life except by a Trinitarian understanding of salvation that contains a strong affirmation of the presence and power of the Holy Spirit. As we shall see, that is just what we find in the Wesleys' theologies as well as that of Fletcher.

Salvation for John Wesley encompasses the entire progression from original sin to the full recovery of the image of God in Christian perfection. It begins with prevenient (or preventing) grace, itself a renewing work of God in human lives. Universally given, prevenient grace reverses the effects of original sin in two ways: it restores to our understanding a general sense of right and wrong (giving us a conscience), and hence a moral accountability; and it restores a measure of liberty, enabling us to act in conformity with conscience and contrary to our sinful will.

Prevenient grace is actually prior to and foundational for the dynamic of expectation and attainment. It empowers our response to God through enabling us to respond to conscience, and, upon encountering the message of good news in Christ, to the promise of salvation. Even in this minimal way grace is triumphant over sin. Yet this initial optimism of grace remains in tension with the sin that still holds the will captive.

While prevenient grace can lead to an uneasy conscience and a slight conviction of sin, it is convincing (or convicting) grace that awakens us to our condition as sinners who stand before a just God. Here grace has dissipated the clouds of illusion that covered our understanding, and we recognize the hold sin has over our life. We are given the "faith of a servant," wherein we seek to obey God's law even though it is contrary to the desires of our heart. But the tension with sin remains, as we again and again experience its power over our lives. So having attained this understanding and life of struggle with sin, we also expectantly take hold of the promise of justification, yearning to know our sins are forgiven and for the power of sin over us to be finally broken.

18. John Wesley, *A Farther Appeal to Men of Reason and Religion* I.3, *Wesley's Works* 11:106.

This yearning is fulfilled through the twin gifts of justification and the new birth (or regeneration). Wesley distinguishes them in this way: "God in justifying us does something *for* us; in begetting us again, he does the work in us. The former changes our outward relation to God, so that of enemies we become children; by the latter our inmost souls are changed, so that of sinners we become saints. The one restores us to the favour, the other to the image, of God. The one is taking away the guilt, the other the taking away the power, of sin . . ."[19] Wesley can also speak of this distinction in explicitly Trinitarian terms, wherein justification is "what God does for us through his Son," and sanctification is "what he works in us by his Spirit."[20] We now have the faith of children of God.

The new birth begins sanctification, which consists of growing in love for God and neighbor along with all other accompanying holy tempers. Thus the new birth is the actual beginning of our being restored to the image of God. Justification and new birth, then, are also the beginning of "heaven below," as the experiencing of God's love and the birth of that love in our hearts. And although both occur together, justification is the logical precondition for new birth and sanctification: until our sins are forgiven and we are reconciled to God through the cross of Christ, we cannot have the relationship with God that sanctifies hearts and lives. Justification is the door to sanctification.

Here again is the optimism of grace: our relationship as children of God can be restored, the hold of sin over our lives can be broken, we can be freed to live a new life of love that takes root in our hearts. Yet the tension with the pessimism of nature remains. This new life coexists with the old; while the will is no longer under the power of sin we find that unholy desires and motivations remain. As Wesley says, it is not long before we find "sin was only suspended, not destroyed. Temptations return, and sin revives: showing it was but stunned before, not dead. They now feel two principles in themselves, plainly contrary to each other . . ."[21] Thus the attainment of justification and new birth lays the foundation for growth in sanctification, while the experience of continual inward sin coupled with the promise of God fuels expectation for further workings of grace.

19. John Wesley, "The Great Privilege of Those that Are Born of God" 2, *Wesley's Works* 1:431–32.

20. John Wesley, "Justification by Faith" II.1, *Wesley's Works* 1:187.

21. John Wesley, "The Scripture Way of Salvation" I.6, *Wesley's Works* 2:159.

As we grow in sanctification, love increasingly comes to govern our hearts and motivates our lives. At the same time, inward sin decreases, becoming less of a factor in our lives. But we yearn for love to so fill our hearts that there is no longer room for sin. This is Christian perfection, in which we become fully restored to the image of God.

As we have already seen, Charles Wesley came to reserve the promise of Christian perfection until the end of life, while John encouraged the expectation that it could be attained much earlier. But for both, it was this goal that theologically governed the entire way of salvation, the seemingly final culmination of an optimism of grace. Yet as we have also seen, for John Wesley it was not the end. We can grow in perfection; even this attainment is both a foundation and incentive for new expectation. This is because, even with the absence of intentional sin, involuntary transgressions remain. Thus Wesley states "No one then is so perfect in this life as to be free from ignorance. Nor, secondly, from mistake, which is indeed almost an unavoidable consequence of it; seeing those who 'know but in part' are ever likely to err touching the things which they know not."[22] Nor are they free from "bodily infirmities" such as "weakness or slowness of understanding," nor as well from temptations.[23]

We can grow in perfection as we become less ignorant, more adept at wise judgment, and perhaps even overcoming some bodily limitations. That is, we can become able to live out more faithfully and effectively the love that now governs our hearts. But even so, there is a pessimism of nature that remains in tension with Christian perfection, inciting further growth and evoking the hope for that final eschatological resolution when sin and death shall be no more, God's love will reign over all, and God's will is fully done on earth as it is in heaven. Then heaven and earth will be united; heaven above and heaven below will finally be one.

22. John Wesley, "Christian Perfection" I.4, *Wesley's Works* 2:101–2.
23. Wesley, "Christian Perfection" I.7, 8, ibid., 103–4.

CHAPTER 3

The First Fruits of Heaven

It is your Father's good pleasure yet to
renew the face of the earth.... Be thou part
of the first-fruits, if the harvest is not yet.

—JOHN WESLEY[1]

WE HAVE NOW IDENTIFIED a number of essential features that give shape
to Wesleyan theology and practice. Using "anticipating heaven below" as
a descriptor of both the content and goal of Wesleyan practical divinity,
we have argued that Wesleyan soteriology is oriented toward the restoration of the *imago Dei* in Christian perfection, that it is moved toward that
goal by the related dialectics of an optimism of grace and a pessimism
of nature, and of expectation and attainment, and that this in turn is an
expression of the eschatological dynamic of the "already" and "not yet."
If Wesleyanism understands the promise of the "already"—of heaven below—to be greater than many other Christian traditions, it can only do so
credibly by still maintaining a tension with the "not yet."

What is needed now is to take a closer look at the central content of
heaven itself and the implications of that for Christian life in the present.

The Kingdom of Heaven

Contemporary New Testament scholar N. T. Wright has argued that the
common assumption that heaven is where you hope to go when you

1. John Wesley, "Upon Our Lord's Sermon on the Mount II" III.18, *Wesley's Works*
1:508–9.

24

die is fundamentally unbiblical. Wright frames the issue around two questions: the nature of our "ultimate Christian hope" and our hope for change in the present. "As long as we see Christian hope in terms of "going to heaven," he argues, "of a salvation that is essentially *away from* this world, the two questions are bound to appear as unrelated." But if instead "the Christian hope is for *God's new creation,* for 'new heavens and earth,' and if that hope has already come to life in Jesus of Nazareth, then there is every reason to join the two questions together."[2]

Theologian Howard A. Snyder echoes this critique. The early church, he says, affirmed the biblical understanding that "spirit and matter" are not two different worlds. They are interlaced dimensions of the one world God created in its entirety and intends to redeem, save, liberate, and heal in its entirety.[3] But over time, especially after the Constantinian period, heaven and earth became increasingly separated, so that "by 1500 the divorce between heaven and earth was nearly fixed and final. . . . Now Christianity is seen as a journey from this world to the next. . . . God has dictated the way to heaven, and it is through the church and its sacraments and institutions. . . . Out of the narrative extends a vertical line— up to heaven, as emphasized by the great cathedral spires—rather than a horizontal line that moves forward with the narrative into time, history, and God's reign on earth."[4]

The point for Wright and Snyder is not that Christians for whom "this world is not my home" are necessarily uninvolved in doing good in this life. The issue is much larger. In insisting on the linkage between heaven and earth, they are presenting the central biblical promise that God intends to renew the *entire* creation, transforming and uniting *both* heaven and earth, and has already begun this work in Jesus Christ and through the Holy Spirit. The kingdom of God "in the preaching of Jesus," says Wright, "refers not to postmortem destiny, nor to our escape from this world into another one, but to God's sovereign rule coming 'on earth as it is in heaven.'"[5] This is the teaching that from the medieval period until today has been so often missed.

It was not missed by John Wesley.

2. Wright, *Surprised by Hope*, 5.

3. Snyder and Scandrett, *Salvation Means Creation Healed*, x.

4. Ibid., 17.

5. Wright, *Surprised by Hope*, 18.

Commenting on Jesus' preaching in Matthew 3:2, Wesley explains, "The kingdom of heaven and the kingdom of God are but two phrases for the same thing. They mean, not barely a future happy state in heaven, but a state to be enjoyed on earth; the proper disposition for the glory of heaven, rather than the possession of it."[6] Wesley connects the future kingdom of heaven with salvation in the present, a salvation that both anticipates that future and fits us to live in it. We shall see that in his later writing Wesley extends this linkage of eschatological renewal to the entirety of creation.

What is the kingdom of heaven for Wesley? In his sermon "The Way to the Kingdom," he describes its content as holiness and happiness, where holiness (or righteousness) consists of love for God and neighbor, and happiness of peace and joy through the Holy Spirit. While treating them as synonyms, Wesley does find distinct connotations in the terms "kingdom of God" and "kingdom of heaven": "It is termed 'the kingdom of God,' because it is the immediate fruit of God reigning in the soul. So soon as ever he takes unto himself his mighty power, and sets up his throne in our hearts, they are instantly filled with this 'righteousness, and peace, and joy in the Holy Ghost.' It is called 'the kingdom of heaven,' because it is (in a degree) heaven opened in the soul."[7] The holiness and happiness of salvation now is a foretaste of that in the age to come.

Now, some important matters of terminology: John Wesley's mature theology, in contrast with most of the Western theological tradition from the medieval period on, generally equated "heaven" with the future kingdom of heaven. Salvation was a present manifestation of the life of heaven, or, as Albert Outler put it, "soteriology and eschatology were actually two sides of the same mystery of God's proffered grace" to humanity.[8]

But if heaven describes the age to come, what is the fate of those who die prior to Christ's return? Wesley uses the term "hades" for this intermediate state, which itself consists of two divisions with an unbridgeable gulf between them: one a place of torment for the unrighteous, the other (Paradise) the "place where the souls of the righteous remain from death till the resurrection,"[9] "the porch of heaven."[10] As Charles W. Christian

6. John Wesley, Matt 3:2, *Explanatory Notes*, 22.

7. John Wesley, "The Way to the Kingdom" I.12, *Wesley's Works* 1:224.

8. Outler, in *Wesley's Works*, 3:181.

9. John Wesley, Luke 23:43, *Explanatory Notes*, 294; see also "On Faith (Hebrews 11:1)," *Wesley's Works* 4:187–200.

10. John Wesley, "Of Hell" I.4, *Wesley's Works* 3:35. These distinctions are much

has put it, "at death the soul temporarily separates from the body, existing in a (conscious) state of waiting for the resurrection, when the body and soul are reunited.[11] Wesley affirms embodiment as essential to humanity, and as we shall see he places the eschatological transformation of the body within the larger renewal of all creation.

Thus there is much in John Wesley's theology that should merit the approval of N. T. Wright, and in fact does gain that of Howard Snyder. Brother Charles does not fare as well, however; both take him to task for lines such as "Till in heaven we take our place," which might imply an upward postmortem trajectory rather than a future hope for creation.[12] Likewise Maddox notes that, in continuity with the dominant Western model of "transcendent 'spiritual' Heaven," "it is not surprising to find Charles Wesley's hymns rather consistently treating death as simply our transition to eternal life with God," a life that "will continue long after the destruction of the earthly world."[13]

Yet in fairness to Charles, it might be more accurate to speak as Snyder does of an "ambivalence" or "mixed message" in the hymns, some describing heaven as an escape from earth, and others speaking of new creation and the coming kingdom.[14] John Tyson argues that Charles, like John, understands sanctification and Christian perfection in terms of "the kingdom or reign of God in the life of the Christian," a "'present heaven' established in the heart." Just as faith "brings the eschatological Kingdom into the present life of the Christian," so in the hymns it is described as consummated "either in Christ's return to earth or in the Christian's passage through the veil to be" with, or even within, God.[15]

This ambivalence in Charles Wesley, perhaps leaning in the direction of a spiritualized heaven above, raises a question about "anticipating heaven below" as the theme for this book. After all, "heaven below" has its logical contrast in "heaven above"; "present heaven" might seem more desirable if the contrast is with the future kingdom of heaven. But while

---

clearer in his later writings. For more on this, see the discussions in Maddox, *Responsible Grace*, 248–50, and Collins, *Theology of John Wesley*, 318–20 (including Collins' excellent chart).

11. Christian, "John Wesley's Anthropology," 141.

12. Wright, *Surprised by Hope*, 299; Snyder and Scandrett, *Salvation Means Creation Healed*, 32–33.

13. Maddox, *Responsible Grace*, 247.

14. Snyder and Scandrett, *Salvation Means Creation Healed*, 32.

15. Tyson, *Charles Wesley on Sanctification*, 201.

I find John's mature clarity preferable to Charles' ambiguity, their differences should not obscure their decisive point of commonality. "Heaven below" in the end speaks to the life of God, centered on love, entering our world both personally and socially. The love that characterizes the triune God *is* the life of heaven now, and will be the life that pervades the entirety of creation, heaven and earth, in the kingdom of heaven. While "heaven below" might not be the only terminological option, it remains an apt choice to designate this manifestation of the life of God in the present.

The New Creation

We have spoken of Christian perfection as a restoration to the image of God in which we were created. Used frequently by both the Wesley brothers and Fletcher, this description suggests a recovery of that which is lost, a return to the Edenic condition prior to the Fall. But for all of them Christian perfection is much more than a recovery; it denotes a degree of holiness and happiness beyond what was possible for our first parents, a depth of love to which they could never have attained. The ultimate horizon toward which salvation points is future, not past; eschatological rather than creational.

This insistence that the end is more than the beginning is a promise given not just to humanity but to all creation—a promise, in Paul's words, "that the creation itself will be set free from its bondage to decay and will obtain the freedom of the glory of the children of God" (Rom 8:21). Deliverance, says John Wesley, is not annihilation;[16] rather, it is transformation.

The promise extends to both the inanimate and animate portions of creation, and to both heavens above and earth below. In the new creation, says Wesley, "all the earth shall be a more beautiful Paradise that Adam ever saw."[17] With regard to animals, "The whole brute creation will then . . . be restored, not only to the vigour, strength, and swiftness which they had at their creation, but to a far higher degree of each than they ever enjoyed."[18] And humanity will attain "an unmixed state of holiness and happiness, far superior to that which Adam enjoyed in Paradise."[19] As we

16. John Wesley, "The General Deliverance" III.1, *Wesley's Works* 2:445.

17. John Wesley, "The New Creation" 16, *Wesley's Works* 2:508.

18. Wesley, "The General Deliverance" III.3, *Wesley's Works* 2:446.

19. Wesley, "The New Creation" 18, *Wesley's Works* 2:510.

have seen, the embodied nature of humanity itself will be restored, in the form of glorified bodies.

Thus this claim that the end is greater than the beginning is not a diminution of creation but a strong affirmation. God intends to save and glorify the entirety of creation, all but those moral agents who in their freedom refuse God's grace in Christ. In making this claim, Wesley could have compared the beginning of the biblical narrative to its ending: how in the early chapters of Genesis the waters are depicted as threatening (and indeed prove to be so in the flood) while in the new heaven and earth "the sea was no more" (Rev 21:1); how the sun was created to give light by day and the moon by night, but the New Jerusalem "has no need of sun and moon to shine on it, for the glory of the Lord is its light, and its lamp is the Lamb" (Rev 21:23); how the serpent in the Garden that deceived humanity, "that ancient serpent who is the Devil and Satan" (Rev 20:2), is "thrown into the lake of fire and sulfur" (Rev 20:10) where it can deceive no more. Wesley could have done this but does not; instead he goes to the very heart of the gospel, the cross of Jesus Christ.

Wesley begins his argument by raising a question of theodicy: how could a loving God permit Adam to fall into sin and thereby introduce evil into the world? Wesley's response is "if Adam had not fallen, Christ had not died," and hence "there would have been no room for that amazing display of the Son of God's love" on the cross.[20] Adam knew God's love, but Adam did not know the fullness of God's love as expressed in dying for us on a cross.

As a result, says Wesley, we now have the capacity "of being more holy and more happy on earth" and in heaven than we otherwise could have been.[21] Without the cross there "could have been no such thing as faith in God thus loving the world."[22] Nor could we have loved God the way we can now: "The chief ground of this love . . . is plainly declared by the Apostle: 'We love Him, because He first loved us.' But the greatest instance of his love had never been given, if Adam had not fallen."[23] The same is true for our love for neighbor. If we are to love one another as "God so loved us;—observe, the stress of the argument lies on this very point," then without the cross "we could not then have loved one another

---

20. John Wesley, "God's Love to Fallen Man" [I] 1, *Wesley's Works* 2:425.

21. Ibid., 4, 425.

22. Ibid., [I] 2, 426.

23. Ibid., [I] 4, 427.

in so high a degree as we may now."[24] It is as we live out this love, most especially in acts of sacrificial compassion for our neighbor, that our happiness increases with our holiness, an increase that we carry with us into the eternal kingdom of heaven.

Salvation, then, entails more than a recovery of the image of God that was corrupted by sin. The image restored is more reflective of God's love than was possible for our first parents because that love has been manifested in the incarnate God dying on the cross. This is at the heart of why the eschatological future is itself more than a recovery of creation; it is its transformation into a more glorious arena for the manifestation of God's love.

Tasting the Powers of the World to Come

It is *this* love, unsurpassibly revealed in the cross of Christ, that John Wesley calls "the beginning of heaven,"[25] "a foretaste of heaven now,"[26] "the beginning of that eternal life which God hath given us in his Son."[27] When we first come to know Christ and his love for us, true happiness begins, and "heaven is opened in the soul" as "the love of God, as loving us, is shed abroad in the heart," producing love for all humanity.[28] To experience this love, and the peace and new life that it produces, is (borrowing from Hebrews 6:5) to taste the powers of the world to come.[29]

Thus "heaven below" begins with the peace and assurance of justification and the new birth. As we grow in sanctification, we increase in the knowledge and love of God, so that "by the same degrees, and in the same proportion, the kingdom of an inward heaven must necessarily increase also," until "we fully dwell in Christ, and Christ in us." It is only then, upon attaining Christian perfection, that "we properly experience

---

24. Ibid., [I] 5, 428.

25. John Wesley, "A Word to a Sabbath Breaker," in *Wesley's Works* (Jackson) 11:165; see also "A Word to a Swearer," ibid., 168.

26. John Wesley, "The Important Question" III.14, *Wesley's Works* 3:197.

27. John Wesley, "The Case of Reason Impartially Considered" II.10, *Wesley's Works* 2:600.

28. John Wesley, "Spiritual Worship" 11.5, *Wesley's Works* 3:96.

29. See John Wesley, Heb 6:5, *Explanatory Notes*; "Self-Denial" II.5, *Wesley's Works* 2:246–47; and "The Way to the Kingdom" I.10, *Wesley's Works* 1:223.

what that word meaneth, 'God is love;' and whosoever dwelleth in love, dwelleth in God, and God in him."[30]

We know this love through faith. Drawing on Hebrews 6:1, Wesley defines faith as "a divine *evidence and conviction . . . of things not seen . . .* not perceivable by sight, or by any other of the external senses."[31] It is faith alone that "opens the eyes of the understanding, to see God and the things of God."[32] That is, we see what Wesley calls the "invisible world"— both the "spiritual world" that presently surrounds us and the "eternal world" that to us, in the midst of time, is past and future.[33]

Because faith is a way of knowing unseen reality just as our five senses enable us to know the natural, visible world, Wesley describes faith as our having "spiritual senses."[34] Without this faith, our sense of reality is reduced to the natural world, although through prevenient grace we may have intimations of something more. Faith is itself a gift of God, a work of the Holy Spirit. As Wesley says, "No man is able to work it in himself. It is a work of omnipotence. It requires no less power thus to quicken a dead soul, than to raise a body that lies in the grave. It is a new creation; and none can create a soul anew, but He who at first created the heavens and the earth."[35]

Both Wesleys used a range of imagery to describe the effects of faith, often focused on enabling us to see. Thus Charles Wesley wrote:

> Spirit of faith, come down,
>
>> Reveal the things of God,
>
> And make to us the Godhead known,
>
>> And witness with the blood:
>
> 'Tis thine the blood to apply,
>
>> And give us eyes to see,

30. John Wesley, "Spiritual Worship" II.6, *Wesley's Works* 3:97.

31. John Wesley, "The Scripture Way of Salvation" II.1, *Wesley's Works* 2:160.

32. John Wesley, "On Eternity" 17, *Wesley's Works* 2:368.

33. John Wesley, "The Scripture Way of Salvation" II.1, *Wesley's Works* 2:161.

34. There has been a debate about whether "spiritual senses" are latent capacities in a sinner that need awakening, or new capacities entirely. Wesley has analogies that suggest the former, but also uses language that implies the latter. For a helpful survey of this discussion, see Lee, "Doctrine of New Creation," chapter 4. The most extensive analysis of Wesley's religious epistemology is found in Matthews, "Religion and Reason Joined"; a more recent discussion in the context of Wesley's understanding of experience is Runyon, *New Creation*, 74–81 and 146ff.

35. John Wesley, *An Earnest Appeal to Men of Reason and Religion*, 9, *Wesley's Works* 11:47–48.

> Who did for every sinner die
>
> Hath surely died for me.[36]

While the Wesleys sometimes spoke of faith as either giving us sight or having our eyes opened,[37] another common image is that of removing or rendering transparent what John calls an "impenetrable veil" between us and God.[38] Charles says it this way:

> No man can truly say
>
> That Jesus is the Lord
>
> Unless thou take the veil away
>
> And breathe the living word . . .[39]

John Wesley also can draw an analogy with natural senses: the believer *sees* the glory and love of God "in the face of Jesus Christ," "hears the voice of the Son of God, and lives," "tastes . . . the power of the world to come," feels the presence and love of God.[40]

Faith is implicitly related to "heaven below" in that it is the means we come to know God and become open to receiving the promise of a new life of love. But it is explicitly eschatological in that, as a divinely given evidence "of things not seen" it enables us to know (that is, experience) "past, future, or spiritual things."[41] We saw the past dimension in the hymn cited above, where faith enabled a transformative encounter with the reality of the cross. Faith likewise enables us encounter the promised future as a present reality, and in so doing becomes the ground of hope. In Charles Wesley's words,

> By faith we know thee strong to save
>
> (Save us, a present Saviour thou)
>
> What'er we hope, by faith we have,
>
> Future and past subsisting now.[42]

---

36. Hymn 83:1, *Wesley's Works* 7:182.

37. See, for example, John Wesley, "The New Birth" II.4, *Wesley's Works* 2:192–93.

38. John Wesley, "On Eternity" 17, *Wesley's Works* 2:368–9.

39. Hymn 83:2, *Wesley's Works* 7:183.

40. John Wesley, *An Earnest Appeal to Men of Reason and Religion*, 7, *Wesley's Works* 11:46–47; see also "On Living Without God" 9–11, *Wesley's Works* 4:172–73.

41. John Wesley, "The Minutes: Monday, June 25th, 1744," Q.4, *Wesley's Works* 10:123; also "The Doctrinal Minutes, 1749," Conversation the First, Q.4, ibid., 778–79.

42. Hymn 92:3, *Wesley's Works* 7:194.

Because faith is how we know God, it enables our expectant and receptive participation in means of grace such as Scripture, prayer, and the Lord's Supper. Each of these presents to us who God is, what God has done, and what God has promised, thereby mediating the presence of God through the Spirit in a form united to God's identity.[43]

This role of faith as a means to experientially know past, present, and future is nowhere clearer than in the *Hymns on the Lord's Supper*. Drawing on distinctions by Daniel Brevint (whose work he abridged), John Wesley describes the sacrament as presenting the passion of Christ (past), conveying the first fruits of that passion (as present grace), and assuring us of the glory to come (future).[44] Charles Wesley's accompanying hymns are arranged in accordance with these categories. But while appreciatively appropriating the work of Brevint, in the hymns the Wesleys expand the terms to move into new theological territory.

Daniel B. Stevick has identified emphases in these hymns that Charles Wesley develops in ways strikingly unusual for his time. One related to the past aspect of the Lord's Supper is that of the crucified God. Although this could be found in Isaac Watts' hymns as well, it becomes, Stevick says, a "running theme of *Hymns on the Lord's Supper*."[45] Here are two examples from among many:

> Crucified before our eyes
> Faith discerns the dying God . . .[46]

> O that our faith may never move,
> But stand unshaken as Thy love!
> Sure evidence of things unseen,
> Now let it pass the years between'
> And view Thee bleeding on the tree,
> My God, who dies for me, for me![47]

Although related to the "past" aspect of the Lord's Supper, this theme has eschatological significance as well. As we have seen, the love manifested

43. This is the argument of Knight, *Presence of God*.

44. John Wesley, "The Christian Sacrament and Sacrifice, Extracted from Dr. Brevint" ii/1, in Rattenbury, *Eucharistic Hymns*, 176

45. Stevick, *Altar's Fire*, 81.

46. Hymn 18:2, in Rattenbury, *Eucharistic Hymns*, 200.

47. Hymn 5:3, ibid., 196.

in the incarnate Deity dying for sinners on the cross *is* the central content of the coming kingdom, as well as of our sanctification wherein that kingdom is established in the heart. It is why the eschatological end is greater than the original creation, and the restored *imago Dei* greater than that in pre-fallen humanity.

A second emphasis is explicitly eschatological. Brevint had called the Lord's Supper a "pledge of heaven," an assurance that we will inherit the promised eternal glory. Again the Wesleys use Brevint's terminology, but infuse it with a depth and richness all their own. As Steven T. Hoskins says, "the hymns give wings to the phrases and do not relegate the terms to such pedestrian use" as the "legal relationship between the Lord's Supper and coming kingdom" described by Brevint.[48] In these hymns, Stevick notes, "through the Holy Spirit, the powers of the age to come impinge on a believer's present."[49] And in so doing, as Paul Sanders says: "The Wesleyan Eucharistic hymns . . . revived the eschatological note that had been missing in Western liturgies from earliest centuries."[50]

Important for understanding the "future" aspect of the Lord's Supper are the terms "pledge" and "earnest," used by both Brevint and the Wesleys. John Wesley distinguishes them this way: "There is a difference between an earnest and a pledge. A pledge is to be restored when the debt is paid; but an earnest is not taken away, but completed. Such an earnest is the Spirit. The first fruits we have . . . and we wait for all the fullness."[51] For Brevint, as a pledge the Lord's Supper is a promise or an assurance of the future, which will be taken away when we attain the reality toward which it points. But the benefits received from the sacrament (such as holiness of heart) are an earnest that will be retained forever.[52]

Charles Wesley certainly conveys these meanings in *Hymns on the Lord's Supper*, frequently using the terms "earnest" and "pledge" to do so. Here is a verse containing both terms:

> Title to eternal bliss
>> Here His precious death we find,
> This the pledge, the earnest this,
>> Of the purchas'd joys behind:

48. Hoskins, "Eucharist and Eschatology," 74.

49. Stevick, *Altar's Fire*, 129.

50. Sanders, "Sacraments," 358, cited in Stevick, *Altar's* Fire, 129.

51. John Wesley, 2 Cor 1:22, *Explanatory Notes*, 646.

52. Stevick, *Altar's Fire*, 130.

Here He gives our souls a taste,

> Heaven into our hearts He pours;

Still believe and hold Him fast,

> God and Christ and all is ours![53]

The sacrament is our title to eternal bliss if we believe and hold fast (pledge); but even now through it we are given a taste of the life to come as heaven is poured into our hearts (earnest).

As Stevick notes, "The sacrament is not only a pledge of heaven to come, it brings heaven here and now." This occurs in two ways: "The Supper brings heaven near, and it transports the communicants to heaven itself."[54] Through faith there is the reception of the life of heaven in the present, and a present experience of that which is yet to come.

The earnest theme is evident in these lines:

Happy the souls to Jesus join'd,

> And saved by grace alone;

Walking in all Thy ways we find

> Our heaven on earth begun.[55]

The sense of being transported to the kingdom of heaven while still in this present age (which I see as an especially dynamic and experiential aspect of the sacrament as pledge) can be seen in these words:

By faith and hope already there,

> Even now the marriage-feast we share . . .[56]

Movement in both directions is evident in this verse:

It bears us now on eagle's wings,

> If Thou the power impart,

And Thee our glorious earnest brings

> Into our faithful heart.[57]

What we find in these hymns is an especially powerful presentation of the theme of heaven below. Through the Holy Spirit the faithful participant in the Lord's Supper receives both heaven in the heart, and

53. Hymn 103:2, Rattenbury, *Eucharistic Hymns,* 227.

54. Stevick, *Altar's Fire,* 138.

55. Hymn 96:1, Rattenbury, *Eucharistic Hymns,* 225.

56. Hymn 93:4, ibid.

57. Hymn 94:3, ibid.

experiences heaven yet to come, both foretastes of the full renewal of creation. The Holy Spirit is even now bringing that future life into the present, bringing to birth the love that is revealed in Jesus Christ.

CHAPTER 4

The Power of the Age to Come

This is certain—too much grace cannot be desired
or looked for; and to believe and obey with all the
power we have is the high way to receive all we have
not. There is a day of Pentecost for believers; a time
when the Holy Ghost descends abundantly. Happy they
who receive most of this perfect love.

—JOHN FLETCHER[1]

THE KINGDOM OF HEAVEN consists of holiness and happiness, and at the
heart of holiness is love. To know God's love for us in Christ is a present
foretaste of knowing God face to face in the age to come. To be born
anew and grow in that love is to become part of the first fruits of the new
creation.

In describing this new creation we have been presupposing distinct
yet interrelated roles for Jesus Christ and the Holy Spirit. When we have
spoken of the *content* of the new creation we have focused on the love of
God revealed in Jesus Christ, in his life but most especially in his redemptive death on the cross. Christ concretely embodies what we mean when
we speak of "kingdom of heaven," "new creation," or "heaven below"
especially as it is lived out in terms of this present age. When we have
spoken of the *power* of the age to come as it enters into the present, our
emphasis has been on the Holy Spirit.

1. Fletcher, "The Test of a New Creature," XXI, *Works* 4:469.

While there is complementarity in the work of Christ and the Spirit, there is also an implied tension, which we might describe as the tension between cross and pentecost. The way of the cross is the way of suffering and death, but it is also the way of love. Pentecost has more triumphant connotations: hearts transformed, diseases healed, demons cast out, the gospel spreading across the world. If this tension is resolved in the direction of the cross, the "not yet" supplants the "already," and hope is shifted from this age to the age to come, which will deliver us from this life of sorrow and suffering. If the tension is resolved in a pentecostal direction, the "already" overcomes the "not yet," and hope becomes presumptive and unrealistic, and disconnected from the love which is at the heart of new creation. We saw this in the "perfectionism" of Maxfield and Bell.

Wesleyan theology must speak of both Christ and Spirit, content and power, in such a way as to avoid collapsing one into the other. Doing this requires maintaining a robust Trinitarianism with regard to God's work in the world.

The Way of the Cross

John Wesley was an advocate for a holistic Christology in preaching. Over against those who preach only law or gospel, he insists, "The most effectual way of preaching Christ, is to preach him in all his offices, and to declare law as well as his gospel, both to believers and unbelievers. Let us strongly and closely insist upon inward and outward holiness, in all its branches."[2] This is especially aimed at those who preached the atonement of Christ as a means to heaven above (Christ as priest) while ignoring entirely the point of salvation, holiness of heart and life (Christ as king and prophet). He underscores its comprehensive nature when he defines *"preaching the gospel"* as "preaching the love of God to sinners, preaching the life, death, resurrection, and intercession of Christ," and its benefits; and *"preaching the law"* as "explaining and enforcing the commands of Christ, briefly comprised in the Sermon on the Mount."[3]

Yet Wesley's writings themselves often do not have the balance he advocates, perhaps in part due to the issues he seeks to address or the

2. John Wesley, "The Large Minutes, 1753–63," Q. 47 and "The Large Minutes, 1780–9," 38, *Wesley's Works* 10:860 and 919. These are combined in the quotation, reflecting the published text in its final edition.

3. John Wesley, "Letter on Preaching Christ" (1751), *Wesley's Works* (Jackson) 11:486.

audience he wants to reach. Unsurprisingly, like almost all of Western Christianity, both Wesleys are much more focused on the cross than on the resurrection. It would be the second half of the twentieth century before Western theologians would recover the emphasis on the resurrection of the crucified Jesus that was so natural to early Christianity.[4]

What is more puzzling is their emphasis on the divinity of Jesus, especially in John Wesley's writings. Some have found Albert Outler's comment that Wesley's "Sermon on the Mount I" manifests a "practical monophysitism"[5] to be an apt description of much of Wesley's theology.[6]

I find Jason Vickers' explanation of this to be most persuasive. He notes that John Wesley lives at a time in which proponents of Arian, Socinian, or Deist alternatives to Christian orthodoxy are all, to differing degrees, questioning Jesus' divinity and elevating his humanity. "Given the popularity of these christological heterodoxies," says Vickers, "it is not surprising that Wesley stressed the divinity of Christ. Nor is it especially perplexing that he sometimes downplayed Christ's human nature." In fact, Vickers adds, Wesley was so concerned to counter Joseph Priestley's popular denial of Christ's divinity that he asked John Fletcher to write a response (finally completed after his death by Joseph Benson).[7]

But it should be said that Wesley's focus was not on apologetics but proclamation. In his series of sermons on the Sermon on the Mount Wesley wants there to be no doubt that it is *God* who is giving that sermon. Likewise, he wants to underscore that it is God incarnate who dies for us on the cross. And, as we have seen, Charles Wesley in his hymns will speak in terms of the death of God on the cross.

Vickers is absolutely correct to remind us that Charles Wesley does strongly emphasize the humanity of Jesus in his *Hymns for the Nativity of Our Lord* (1745), such that "the eternal Son of God befriends human persons, becoming their brother."[8] Yet taken together, the Wesleys clearly

---

4. My own modest attempt at this can be found in Knight, *Future for Truth*. Among the major theological voices restoring the resurrection to its place of prominence are Jürgen Moltmann, Wolfhart Pannenberg, T. F. Torrance, and Lesslie Newbigin. This does not mean the Wesleys ignored the resurrection, only that they emphasized the cross. Charles is the author of the great Easter hymn "Christ the Lord Is Risen Today"; see also his *Hymns for Our Lord's Resurrection*.

5. Outler, *Wesley's Works* 1:470.

6. For a fine survey of differing views on this, see Riss, "John Wesley's Christology."

7. Vickers, "Christology," 555–56.

8. Ibid., 558.

place their emphasis on the divinity of Christ. But for all the theological downsides of that focus there is this one enormous advantage: they are able to give unsurpassed expression to what is meant by "God is love," and with that the nature of the kingdom of heaven.

What then does this way of the cross mean for the Christian life? If sanctification in some way shapes us to love as Christ loves, does this mean we suffer as he did? There are passages of Scripture that could be interpreted to mean that we do (Rom 8:17; Heb 12:1–13). Certainly Charles Wesley, as we have seen, understood suffering as necessary to growth in sanctification; we must bear the cross, he would say in his hymns, if we are to one day wear the crown. Not only does this imply perseverance through persecution, but also resignation in the face of suffering and sorrow. Indeed, as Tyson notes, one form of the cross for Charles could be the "rod" of divine punishment or correction, the discipline of a loving Father who seeks to turn "the straying pilgrim back on the pathway to perfection."[9]

Of course, we have seen that John Wesley's response to this linkage of suffering and sanctification was an emphatic "no." He consistently links holiness and happiness. Does this mean, as some have thought, that John totally discounts the pedagogical role of suffering for Christian growth?

To find an answer we must first note the important distinction Wesley makes between "bearing a cross" and "taking up a cross." To bear a cross is to "endure what is laid upon us without our choice, with meekness and resignation." To take up a cross is "to voluntarily suffer what it is in our power to avoid; when we willingly embrace the will of God, though contrary to our own . . ."[10] Bearing a cross *may* have a pedagogical role in our growth in sanctification, but is not at all necessary to it. But taking up a cross, which Wesley equates with self-denial, "is absolutely, indispensibly necessary, either to our becoming or continuing" as Christ's disciples.[11] In this sense, and in this sense alone, is a form of "suffering" necessary to sanctification for John Wesley.

What both Wesleys and John Fletcher all agree upon, however, is that sanctified love is *humble* love. There is considerable overlap in John Wesley's use of the terms "repentance" and "humility" in that both refer to a kind of self-knowledge, that is, an honest and true sense of ourselves

---

9. Tyson, *Charles Wesley on Sanctification*, 267.

10. John Wesley, "Self-Denial" I.11, *Wesley's Works* 2:244.

11. Ibid., 2, 238.

as we stand before God. We can of course grow in this self-knowledge, indeed must if we are to grow in sanctification.

Repentance or humility is thus a necessary precondition for both justification and sanctification in that, by showing us to be sinners unable to cure ourselves, it engenders openness and receptivity to divine grace.[12] But humility is also identified as a fruit of the new birth and the love it creates. Thus Wesley says, "'Love is not puffed up.' As is the measure of love, so is the measure of humility. Nothing humbles the soul so deeply as love: It casts out all 'high conceits, engendering pride;' all arrogance and overweening; makes us little, and poor, and base, and vile in our own eyes. It abases us both before God and man; makes us willing to be the least of all, and the servants of all . . ."[13] It might seem from this quote that humility is concerned with self-deprecation, but in the context of Wesley's theology that would be a misreading. His model for humility is the same as his model for love: Jesus Christ. It was, after all, the divine Son of God who (as Wesley comments on Philippians 2:7–10) took the form of a servant, became a "common man, without any peculiar excellence or comeliness," and humbled himself, even to death on a cross.[14] Such humility is engendered by our encountering the love of God in Christ; it is shaped by our then following Christ by loving as he loved.

John Fletcher makes the same point in his address to "perfect Christian Pharisees," those extreme perfectionists we have discussed earlier. Although "ye are most ready to profess Christian perfection," says Fletcher, "alas! Ye stand at the greatest distance from perfect humility, the grace which is most essential to the perfect Christian's character . . ."[15] "One of the greatest ends of Christ's coming into the world," he admonishes, "was to empty us of ourselves, and to fill us with humble love; . . . ye are still full of yourselves and void of Christ, that is, void of humility incarnate."[16]

"Humility incarnate." That gets to the heart of the matter. Jesus Christ images the love of God in which we were created, and embodies what it would mean for God's will to be done on earth as it is in heaven

---

12. See, for example, Wesley's sermons "The Way to the Kingdom" II.1; "The Circumcision of the Heart" I; "The Sermon on the Mount I" I.7; "The Repentance of Believers."

13. John Wesley, "On Charity" I.4, *Wesley's Works* 3:296. See also "On Zeal" II.1, in ibid., 312.

14. John Wesley, Phil 2:7–8, *Explanatory Notes*, 730–31.

15. Fletcher, "The Last Check to Antinomianism" XVII, in *Works* 2:611.

16. Ibid., 612; see also ibid., XX, 662–63.

in this present age. Whatever is said about love, sanctification, or "heaven below" must be governed by the life and death of Christ. Thus love *is* humble, *is* self-sacrificial, *is* directed even to stranger as well as neighbor, and especially to "the least of these." That is the love in which God seeks to renew us, and that is the love in which God will renew all creation.

The Power of the Spirit

Humble love—the way of the cross—is the antidote for a perfectionist enthusiasm that in effect replaces Christ with seeking and experiencing spiritual power. But Wesleyan theology is also designed to counter a second set of spiritual dangers: complacency in the Christian life, or the despair that nothing significant can change until Christ returns (or until we die and leave this world for another). Wesleyanism engenders expectant hope in the present, and does so through a strong emphasis on the work of the Holy Spirit.

It is in this sense that Albert Outler is correct to call Wesley's a "pneumatocentric soteriology."[17] As we have seen, the Holy Spirit is at work throughout the entire process of salvation, enabling and inviting human response, and transforming hearts and lives. New birth, gradual sanctification, and Christian perfection are all seen as the work of the Spirit in us. The promised kingdom of heaven and the present work of the Spirit combine to produce an expectant yearning for further growth in love, for more of God's grace.

Although drawing on pietist and puritan predecessors, both Wesleys were, as Outler noted, "working with a distinctive pneumatology that has no exact equivalent" in previous Christian theology.[18] D. Lyle Dabney has with great insight shown why this is the case.

Dabney argues that Western theology "has been dominated by two fundamentally conflicting trajectories or tendencies of thought."[19] The first, typified by medieval theology, begins with "the capacities of created human nature" as their starting point, "and interpret salvation accordingly as the ascent of the soul to knowledge of God the creator through the assistance of grace." Rather than contrasting nature and grace, it posits "a

17. Outler, in *Wesley's Works* 1:81.
18. Outler, cited in Whaling, *John and Charles Wesley*, xv.
19. Dabney, "Pneumatology in the Methodist Tradition," 574.

continuum between nature and grace, the creator and the created, creation and redemption, for it is a theology of nature fulfilled by grace."[20]

The second trajectory is rooted in the Reformation, which protests against the governing assumption of the first "that human nature by virtue of being God's good creation possesses an innate capacity for God and is thus intrinsically open to and in search of its creator." Instead it begins with "not the goodness but the sin and consequent incapacity of the creature for the creator, not the yearning for but the flight from God . . ."[21] Christ as redeemer thus confronts us as sinners and calls us to faith; salvation comes through trusting in Christ, who graciously "imputes his righteousness to us." Finding "its point of departure not in creaturely good, but in creaturely sin," Reformation theology "takes the form not of creation's ascent to its God and Father, but of God's descent to creation in Jesus Christ the Son."[22]

As an Anglican, Wesley was faced with proponents of both trajectories, with the first elevating human freedom at the expense of divine activity and the other emphasizing God's electing grace at the expense of human works. Although, as Dabney points out, the Wesley of the Holy Club was captivated by the first trajectory with its emphasis on holiness, and after Aldersgate gravitated strongly to the second with its emphasis on salvation through faith alone, the mature Wesley combines and transcends them both through a theology of the Holy Spirit.[23] For Wesley, "the point of departure . . . became neither created human capacity nor sinful human incapacity, but rather the faithful presence and activity of God through the Spirit in the midst of creation . . ."[24]

As this all too brief sketch of Dabney's analysis shows, Wesley's contribution was to see the work of the Spirit as fundamentally transformative. He took with Protestant seriousness the dire reality of sin, but was unwilling to abandon the vision of holiness found in the first trajectory. It is because the work of the Spirit is to *transform* human hearts—to make us new creatures—that God can enable a totally corrupted human nature to attain the holiness and happiness of Christian perfection in this life.

20. Ibid., 575.

21. Ibid., 576.

22. Ibid.

23. Ibid., 577.

24. Ibid., 578.

Thus the work of the Spirit is at its heart eschatological—the present beginning of the new creation.

Theological innovation with regard to the Holy Spirit also marked the hymns of Charles Wesley. John Tyson argues that while Charles drew upon Henry Scougal's *The Life of God in the Soul of Man* for his understanding of Christian perfection as being filled with the life of God, he went beyond Scougal by describing that indwelling "as the presence of the Holy Spirit." This "robust pneumatology" was evident as early as 1740[25] and found bountiful expression in *Hymns of Petition and Thanksgiving for the Promise of the Father* (1746, jointly published with John) and *Hymns on the Trinity* (1768, published by Charles alone).

Tyson cites an early example from *Hymns and Sacred Poems* (1740):

> Come, Holy Ghost, my heart inspire,
> > Attest that I am born again!
> Come, and baptize me now with fire,
> > Or all Thy former gifts are vain.
> I cannot rest in sin forgiven;
> Where is the earnest of *my* heaven?
>
> Where the Indubitable Seal
> > That ascertains the kingdom mine?
> The powerful stamp I long to feel,
> > The signature of Love Divine:
> O, shed it in my heart abroad,
> Fulness of love, of heaven, of God![26]

Here we see the Spirit as the agent of new birth and Christian perfection, and the linkage between the Spirit and the love of God and life of heaven.

A second example can be found in the 1780 hymnal published by John Wesley:

> O come, and dwell in me,
> > Spirit of power within,
> And bring the glorious liberty
> > From sorrow, fear, and sin.
> The seed of sin's disease,
> Spirit of health, remove,

25. Tyson, *Charles Wesley on Sanctification*, 192.
26. Ibid., 193.

Spirit of finished holiness,
   Spirit of perfect love.

Hasten the joyful day
   Which shall my sins consume,
When old things shall be passed away,
   And all things new become.
   Th' original offence
   Out of my soul erase;
Enter thyself, and drive it hence,
   And take up all the place.[27]

In this hymn the connection between the indwelling of the Spirit and Christian perfection is explicit.

But even though there is distinctive and abundant reference to the sanctifying work of the Spirit in hymns both early and late, Tyson nonetheless insists that the "key to Charles's conception of Christian perfection was its christocentricity."[28] Even in *Hymns of Petition and Thanksgiving for the Promise of the Father,* which Charles called "Hymns for Whitsunday," there are actually no references to the day of Pentecost. All of the hymns are based on John 14–16, and the Spirit is frequently called "the Comforter." For Charles Wesley, "Christ was the foundation upon which" his "Pentecostal imagery stood"; the Spirit was inextricably linked to Christ, as was sanctification.[29]

This reinforces my earlier point: the *content* of the Christian life is for both Wesleys understood christologically, in terms of the life, teaching, and cross of Christ. We receive and grow in this new life through the *power* of the Spirit which indwells the believer. In this sense not only is the Spirit linked to Christ, but Christ is likewise inextricably linked to the Spirit. Through this dynamic Trinitarianism the Wesleys are able to maintain a consistently christocentric vision of sanctification while proclaiming a distinctive and even uniquely powerful pneumatology, one eminently suited to bring "heaven below."

27. Hymn 356:1–2, *Wesley's Works* 7:525.

28. Tyson, *Charles Wesley on Sanctification,* 190. This point should not be overemphasized. In hymns on the Holy Spirit not included in this collection Charles Wesley frequently uses the imagery of "fire" or "burning," certainly allusive of both John the Baptist's language and Pentecost.

29. Ibid., 196.

The Age of the Spirit

In 1985 Melvin Dieter argued that "the adoption of Pentecostal and Baptism of the Holy Ghost paradigms" by the nineteenth-century Holiness movement was not "unnatural or unWesleyan" but "a natural outgrowth of a weighted factor in Wesley's own teaching on Christian perfection and the work and witness of the Holy Spirit," one that could not be supported by "the traditional structures of Reformed theology."[30] Dieter sees the emergence of this Pentecostal paradigm in the theology of John Fletcher.

Fletcher's distinctive contribution to Wesleyan theology was his Trinitarian theology of dispensations. While not the first to develop such an understanding of history—the Cappadocians and Joachim of Fiore had similar schemes—Fletcher's was especially designed to explicate and clarify the way of salvation of John Wesley, and especially his teaching on Christian perfection.

Each of Fletcher's dispensations contained within it a promise whose fulfillment would usher in the next dispensation. For the dispensation of the Father there was the promise of the coming Messiah; for that of the Son the promise of the Spirit; and for the age of the Spirit the promise of Christ's second coming.[31] But the dispensations were not simply eras of salvation history; they also represented stages in the Christian life: "Converted sinners, or believers, are either under the dispensation of the Father, under that of the Son, or under that of the Holy Ghost, according to the different progress they have made in spiritual things."[32] Those under the dispensation of the Father have the faith of a servant, are "ordinarily surrounded with . . . uncertainty and doubt," and experience the fear of God. Those under the dispensation of the Son have the faith of a child of God, their "doubts . . . are dissipated," and they begin to love more than fear God. Those under the dispensation of the Spirit have become heirs of God, are anointed and led by the Spirit, and have been filled with full assurance and perfected in love.[33]

As Patrick Strieiff summarizes the relation of the dispensations historically: ". . . the dispensation of the Father is given to everyone. The dispensation of the Son was promised to God's people in the Old Testament, and found fulfillment in the death and resurrection of Jesus Christ.

---

30. Dieter, "Development of Holiness Theology," 67.

31. Fletcher, "The Portrait of St. Paul—Part Second," *Works* 3:166–68.

32. Ibid., 170.

33. Ibid., 170–71.

The dispensation of the Spirit was promised to the disciples of Jesus, and found fulfillment after Pentecost."[34] With regard to individuals, "The Father can draw people who believe in him as Creator to the Son as their redeemer, Christ can fill those who believe in him as redeemer with the fullness of the Holy Spirit."[35] In connecting Christian perfection with the Age of the Spirit and Pentecost, Fletcher also links it with receiving the Baptism of the Holy Spirit.

Whether and to what extent John Wesley endorsed Fletcher's theology of dispensations with its Pentecostal emphasis has been the subject of a major debate. Dieter certainly believed it had Wesley's general endorsement, and more recently Laurence Wood has made an extensive defense of both Wesley's endorsement and (somewhat less controversial) its adoption among early Methodists.[36] On the other hand, Donald Dayton and Randy Maddox have vigorously insisted that Wesley and Fletcher not only were not in full agreement, but their differences have significant theological implications.[37]

Much of the historical argument revolves around the interpretation of letters, essays, and sermons, as well as their respective usage of terms such as "Pentecost" and "Baptism of the Spirit." It is not my intention here to try to sort out the historical questions. I do however want to address the theological issues insofar as they relate to my argument. At the heart of the theological controversy is this: does Fletcher's theological contribution enhance and strengthen Wesley's theology, or does it veer away from Wesley and is it in need of correction?

Dieter clearly believes the former. He argues that the Protestant reformers had their own way of dividing history into the kingdom of nature (or kingdom of the Father), the kingdom of grace (or kingdom of the Son), and the (coming) kingdom of glory. What is lacking is a kingdom of the Spirit. Thus "the activity of the Spirit . . . is either subsumed in the age of grace and of the Son or in the final kingdom and consummation of all things in the age to come."[38] What Fletcher pioneered was a "new pneu-

---

34. Streiff, *Relunctant Saint,* 202.

35. Ibid.

36. Wood, *Meaning of Pentecost.*

37. See Wood, "Pentecostal Sanctification"; Maddox, "Wesley's Understanding"; and Wood, "Historiographical Criticisms" See also Dayton's review essay, "John Fletcher"; Wood, "An Appreciative Response"; Dayton, "Rejoinder"; Wood, "Can Pentecostals Be Wesleyans?"; and Dayton, "A Final Round."

38. Dieter, "Development of Holiness Theology," 71–72.

matology . . . based on a different concept of history than that accepted by the traditional Protestantism."[39] This not only gave new emphasis to the Holy Spirit as such, it directly linked the Spirit to the promised coming kingdom of heaven.

Maddox (here responding to Laurence Wood) does not dispute that John Wesley spoke of "dispensations of grace," but argues that Wesley understood Pentecost to be an event in church history in which the sanctifying Spirit became available to all persons, enabling new birth and sanctification. This is in contrast to Fletcher, who argued that regeneration, in Maddox's words, "provides only a small degree of divine life" and should be followed by a subsequent Pentecostal baptism of the Spirit which fully sanctifies. "In other words," concludes Maddox, "while the 'dispensations of grace' model can allow that individual Christians may appropriate in progressive degrees the full sanctifying grace that is *continually available* to them," Fletcher's dispensational "model maintains that God actually makes this grace available to believers in a standard pattern of *progressive stages,* just as God did in history."[40]

To put it in other words, Maddox argues that for Wesley the *day* of Pentecost made the sanctifying Spirit universally available to all believers in a way it was not beforehand as a means of their ongoing growth in sanctification, while Fletcher is insisting believers each need to have something like *their own* personal Pentecost event in their lives.

Dayton agrees with this assessment. He has also argued that the "thrust of the dispensational patterns in Fletcher pushes Methodism further out of a Christocentric pattern of thought and closer to a Pneumatocentric one."[41] He fears that Fletcher has laid the foundation for an unWesleyan separation of the work of the Spirit from that of Christ (a separation he believes occurred in the nineteenth-century Holiness movement), and with it the loss of Wesley's christological understanding of sanctification. As Dayton says, "I have always appreciated the way in which Wesley defines the content of Christian Perfection in christological terms. . . . The point for me is precisely the unity of Christ and the Spirit and the role of the Spirit to mediate the presence of Christ—as defined by the concretion of Christ found in the historical Jesus of the New

---

39. Ibid., 73.

40. Maddox, "Wesley's Understanding," 79–81.

41. Dayton, *Theological Roots,* 52.

Testament and his teachings."[42] Dayton finds in both Karl Barth and John Wesley "profound allies in attempting to keep these together in unity."[43]

Laurence Wood, who both Maddox and Dayton critique, has a different set of theological concerns. Drawing especially on Wesley's later writings in the *Arminian Magazine* and elsewhere, Wood argues that Wesley endorses and adopts Fletcher's Trinitarian dispensationalism with its emphasis on a subsequent sanctifying baptism of the Spirit and its linkage of Pentecost to Christian perfection. He sees a parallel to conversion and Spirit baptism in the relation of Easter to Pentecost, and of baptism to confirmation. As to whether understanding Pentecost as a paradigm for entire sanctification would make it "static and absolute," Wood insists, "Fletcher did not see it that way, nor did Wesley. If Pentecost is seen as a static and once-for-all event that is unrepeatable, this is surely a misconception of Pentecost. . . . The problem with the Wesleyan-Holiness tradition has not been the connection between entire sanctification and Pentecost, but the tendency to hold to a static view of Pentecost."[44]

There are, then, two related theological issues at the heart of this debate. Is the baptism of the Holy Spirit a one-time event for Fletcher in which the believer receives something like what the disciples did on the day of Pentecost, and is this consistent with Wesley's theology? The second is whether Fletcher's dispensational theology opens the way for subsequent generations to separate the work of the Spirit from that of Christ, and redescribe sanctification in pneumatological rather than christological terms.

With regard to the first issue, Fletcher's language can certainly imply a single "Pentecost" in a person's life, as he does in the quote with which this chapter opened. He believed that the early chapters of the book of Acts show "that a peculiar power of the Spirit is bestowed upon believers under the Gospel of Christ," and we through faith can today receive that power and "fully embrace the promise of full sanctification."[45] Yet he goes on to say "Should you ask, how many baptisms, or effusions of the sanctifying Spirit are necessary to cleanse a believer from all sin, and to kindle his soul into perfect love; I reply, that the effect of a sanctifying

42. Dayton, "Revisiting," 169.

43. Ibid.

44. Wood, "Appreciative Response," 169–70.

45. Fletcher, "The Last Check to Antinomianism" XIX, *Works* II:632.

truth depending upon the ardour of the faith with which that truth is embraced, and upon the power of the Spirit with which it is applied, I would
betray a want of modesty if I brought the operations of the Holy Ghost,
and the energy of faith, under a rule which is not expressly laid down
in the Scriptures."[46] Comparing it to the number of doses of medicine
needed to heal a stomach disorder, Fletcher concludes that "if one powerful baptism of the Spirit" is all that is needed, "so much the better," but
should "two or more be necessary, the Lord can repeat them . . ."[47] Then
Fletcher goes on to affirm with Wesley that the process of sanctification is
both instantaneous and gradual.

Fletcher does not, then, insist that the baptism of the Spirit is necessarily a one-time event in a believer's life, nor does he deny gradual, day-
by-day growth in sanctification. Even so, the emphasis of his language is
on the instantaneous and episodic, a partial replication of what occurred
to believers at Pentecost. While it is arguable that John Wesley in his later
ministry came to emphasize instantaneous Christian perfection more
(and Charles to emphasize it less), there nonetheless seems to be a difference in the way Wesley and Fletcher characteristically speak about it.
Fletcher's language does have a significant impact on the Holiness movement, which we shall return to in later chapters.

It is the issue of the relation of Christology to pneumatology that is
most relevant to our theme of "heaven below." There is, as Dayton warned,
a real danger of in effect separating the work of the Spirit from the person
and work of Christ when you distinguish the dispensation of the Spirit
from that of the Son. But as Dieter pointed out, there is also a danger of
understating the work of the Spirit by subsuming it under Christ, as he
believed the Reformers had done. To put this in biblical terms, how do
you relate the common Johannine and Pauline understanding of Christ
and the Spirit with that of Luke-Acts?

I agree with Amos Yong's assessment of this debate when he argues
that "Wesley could have endorsed in the main Fletcher's dispensational
and Pentecostal pneumatology without relinquishing his own christological commitments."[48] In his own theological work Yong has come
to insist that "Christian Trinitarian theology requires a fully developed
pneumatology, but . . . this in turn assumes not only a 'high' Christology

46. Ibid.

47. Ibid., 632–33.

48. Yong, "Wesley and Fletcher," 189.

of some sort but also an inseparable relationship between pneumatology and Christology."[49] Thus "pneumatology fills out Trinitarian theology not by discarding or neglecting christology, but by filling out, expanding, and even deepening the ongoing reception of the Christian confession of Jesus Christ as Lord."[50] This is what I see the Wesleys and Fletcher trying to do in their theologies.

I see no reason to revise my own earlier assessment of the arguments of Dayton and Dieter: "Dayton accents the need for christological identity and humble love; Dieter stresses pneumatological presence and expectant hope."[51] Thus, "To speak of an age of the Spirit can be a helpful way of designating the transforming presence of God between the past and future Christ events, provided that it is understood as intrinsically connected to the life, death and resurrection of Christ, and to the coming kingdom. The work of the Spirit, then, is to transform present lives in accordance with and in response to their christological norm, and to realize in the present the eschatological life to come."[52] In the redemptive work of the triune God, it is the Holy Spirit who brings "heaven below"; it is Jesus Christ who reveals to us the content of heaven, both now and yet to come.

49. Ibid., 188.

50. Ibid., 189.

51. Knight, *Presence of God*, 194.

52. Ibid.

PART TWO

Heaven in the Heart

CHAPTER 5

The Way of Holiness

God usually gives a considerable time for men to
receive light, to grow in grace, to do and suffer
his will before they are either justified or
sanctified. But he does not invariably adhere
to this. Sometimes he "cuts short his work" . . .

—JOHN WESLEY[1]

I cannot believe there is any lingering on the part
of God in fulfilling promises to the seeking soul.

—PHOEBE PALMER[2]

HOLINESS IS HEAVEN BELOW in its purest form. Whether termed holiness, Christian perfection, entire sanctification, or full salvation, it is the element of salvation that most reflects the kingdom of heaven, because it enables humans in this age to have hearts and lives that image the love of God. It is, as we have seen, the theology of the Wesleys and Fletcher.

Methodism found fertile soil in America, and brought with it the promise of Christian perfection. Francis Asbury and his preachers promoted it; the Methodistic German-speaking Evangelical Association, with its "Pentecostal meetings," was if anything even more committed to

---

1. Wesley, "A Plain Account of Christian Perfection," *Wesley's Works* (Jackson) 11:423.

2. Palmer, *Faith and Its Effects*, 30.

proclaiming it. Yet as Methodism rapidly grew in numbers, many during the 1830s perceived a decline in the emphasis on holiness. Out of that discontent would emerge a movement focused on the promotion of holiness. Its leading theologian was Phoebe Palmer.

Context makes a difference in theology. The antebellum America of Phoebe Palmer had a different set of cultural and philosophical assumptions than John Wesley's eighteenth-century England. While she identified her theology with that of the Wesleys and Fletcher, Palmer's optimism of grace took a distinctively different form than that of John Wesley, especially with regard to the *way* of holiness. Moreover, her altering the way of holiness had implications for its content.

Instantaneous and Gradual

Wesley insisted, especially in his later writings, that Christian perfection is both instantaneous and gradual. In 1767 he wrote "As to the manner, I believe this perfection is always wrought in the soul by a simple act of faith; consequently in an instant. But I believe a gradual work, both preceding and following that instant."[3] Wesley is here integrating two critically important emphases; in Kenneth Collins words, "the conjunction of co-operant and free grace."[4] The first is a gradual, day-by-day growth in grace as we continue to respond to the Holy Spirit's work in our lives, normally in and through means of grace. The second is an instantaneous transformative work of the Spirit, which we seek—indeed, yearn for— and are hence open to receive.

Because the instantaneous work is a free gift of God, Collins notes, "divine freedom, and yes sovereignty, determines the timetable for crucial receptions of grace."[5] In Wesley's words, "As to the time. I believe this instant generally is the instant of death, the moment before the soul leaves the body. But I believe it may be ten, twenty, or forty years before."[6] Because it *can* and at times *does* come decades before death, Wesley can exhort believers to "look for it in every moment." Since it is received by

3. John Wesley, "Brief Thoughts on Christian Perfection," *Wesley's Works* (Jackson) 11:446.

4. Collins, *Theology of John Wesley*, 293.

5. Ibid., 290.

6. Wesley, "Brief Thoughts on Christian Perfection," *Wesley's Works* (Jackson) 11:446.

faith, there is nothing one must "first *be* or *do*" to receive it. "If you seek it by faith," he says, you may expect it *as you are*; and if as you are, then expect it *now*.[7] Randy Maddox describes the theological import of Wesley's exhortation this way: "On the one hand he continued to insist here that Christian perfection is a present possibility because it is God's gift, not our accomplishment. On the other hand he emphasized the way to 'wait' for this gift is by repentance and growth through the means of grace, so there is no danger of antinomianism or enthusiasm should the gift not come immediately."[8] There is nothing lost in expectantly seeking the instantaneous work, for if it does not come immediately our very seeking of it furthers the gradual growth.

Having before us this framework of thinking about how grace works, we can now look more closely at the nature of sanctification itself. To do this I will need to recall and elaborate on some of the discussion in chapter 2.

For Wesley sanctification begins with the new birth, or regeneration, and continues as a process whose goal is Christian perfection, or entire sanctification. Should Christian perfection be attained prior to the moment of death, one grows in perfection. Wesley understands both new birth and Christian perfection to be transformative moments in the Christian life which lay new foundations for further growth. That is, they are not simply points on a line of continued growth, but crucial turning points on the way of salvation that make subsequent gradual growth possible.

New birth belongs to a complex of transformative events that can collectively be called "conversion" (a term Wesley uses infrequently). Each element is essential for there to be growth in sanctification. The gift of the faith of a child of God is an epistemological transformation giving us a spiritual sense that enables us to know God more fully and deeply. Justification transforms our relationship with God through knowing our sins are forgiven. New birth transforms the heart itself through the emergence of fruit of the Spirit or "holy tempers."[9] Enabled by faith and reconciliation with God, sanctification is the process by which the Spirit enables those holy tempers to grow in the heart and increasingly govern the life.

7. .John Wesley, "The Scripture Way of Salvation" III.18, *Wesley's Works* 2:169.

8. Maddox, *Responsible Grace*, 186.

9. I develop this in some detail in Knight, "The Transformation of the Human Heart."

For Wesley "tempers" are a more precise way of referring to our will. They are fundamentally dispositions of the heart, the fount of our motivations and desires. Tempers shape our character: what we desire and value in large measure makes us the kind of persons we are. As a consequence they decisively influence how we "see" the world and live out our lives. True Christians are the kind of persons who love, trust, and hope in God, and who love their neighbor; it is these dispositions (holiness of heart) that motivate and direct our thoughts and actions (holiness of life).

While the will indicates a capacity to choose, its choices are normally determined by the motivations and desires of the heart. The will is not "free" if by freedom is meant a neutral capacity for choice. Rather the exercise of the will expresses the dispositions of the person who is willing. A sinful heart inclines the will differently than holy tempers. Wesley does believe that prevenient grace gives us both a generalized conscience to judge our will and the liberty to act contrary to our sinful inclinations. But it is new birth which provides a new set of inclinations in the heart in the form of holy tempers.

Christian perfection is a second instantaneous work of grace in which the holy tempers, with love at their center, fully govern the heart and restore us to the image of God, which is love. Like the new birth, Christian perfection brings a qualitative change in our relationship with God, a deeper communion that now enables growth in perfection.

If sanctification is at its heart growth in holy tempers (and a consequent diminishing of the presence of intentional sin in the heart), how does this growth occur? The short answer is of course by grace through faith, that is, our trusting in Jesus Christ and receptivity to the work of the Holy Spirit in our lives. More specifically, it is our participation in those spiritual disciplines and means of grace through which the Spirit works.

This brings us to a second important characteristic of tempers: in addition to being dispositions they are also necessarily relational. That is, we do not simply "love", we love someone or something, and what we love (or hope for, or have faith in) determines the nature of the heart and life. To love wealth produces a very different heart and life than loving God. Moreover, how we understand and describe the God we love also decisively shapes the heart and life.

For Wesley, the spiritual disciplines of daily devotion, weekly worship, and service to the neighbor enabled Methodists to stay in relationship with God, aided by regular accountability to and conversation about those disciplines in weekly class meetings (for all Methodists) and band meetings (an option for those growing in sanctification). This weekly accountability counteracted the tendency of the things of life to draw persons away from God and neighbor; the weekly conversation nurtured their faith and enabled them to keep their relationship with God alive. It helped Methodists avoid the danger of formalism, a minimalist understanding of the Christian life in which persons go to church and engage in its practices as an end in itself rather than a means of relationship with God. In other words, through nurturing faith the spiritual disciplines and class meetings enabled persons to know God as a living reality in their lives.[10]

As noted in chapter 1, it was the Methodist discipline that enforced regular participation in the means of grace, both works of piety and works of mercy. This countered a danger to the Christian life found in religious awakenings which Wesley, using language common in his day, called "enthusiasm." He defines the term with much more theological precision than either many of his contemporaries or later historians. Enthusiasm occurs, says Wesley, when persons "imagine themselves to be so influenced by the Spirit of God, as, in fact, they are not" or "who imagine they have such gifts from God as they have not."[11] They "think to attain the end without using the means, by the immediate power of God."[12] Enthusiasm is thus centered on having certain kinds of feelings or impulses that are taken to come directly from God.

Works of piety such as searching the Scriptures, the Lord's Supper, and prayer counter the danger of enthusiasm through providing descriptive access to the character, actions, and promises of God—that is, to God as revealed rather than God as a projection of our thought or feelings. When Wesley speaks of love for God as a holy temper, he is presupposing that it is the works of piety that provide meaning for the word "God" and are thereby used by the Holy Spirit to shape our hearts and lives over time, enabling genuine growth in the knowledge and love of God.

There is a parallel to this with works of mercy. The question here is not only *who* is our neighbor but do we actually *know* our neighbor? Works of mercy, especially visiting the poor, are used by the Holy Spirit to overcome our ignorance and stereotypes, and thereby to enable us to genuinely know our neighbor, provided—as Wesley continually

10. My extended argument for this and the paragraphs that follow is found in Knight, *Presence of God.*

11. John Wesley, "The Nature of Enthusiasm" 19, *Wesley's Works* 2:53.

12. Ibid., 27, 2:56.

insists—they actually entail genuine relationship with the neighbor, in which we come to see the world they experience through their eyes. God uses the relationships through which we care for others as a means of our own continued transformation in love. Indeed relationship is central to both works of piety and mercy as the means through which transforming relationships with God and neighbor actually occur.

We can now step back and visualize how a relationship with God is facilitated by means of grace. Faith is nurtured in the class meetings, where the conversation and discipline encourages persons to maintain a focus on and trust in God in the midst of everyday life. Growing in faith, they find prayer to be a communication with God, encounter the presence of God in the Lord's Supper, and hear God speak to them in Scripture. But the God they encounter and hear is none other than the God revealed in prayer, sacrament, and Scripture, whose nature elicits praise, gifts of creation and redemption are celebrated with thanksgiving, and promises received in hope. Much as we come to know another person over time, ongoing relationship with God through means of grace enables one to grow in the knowledge and love for God. It fuels gradual sanctification and elicits a hunger for the fullness of Christian perfection.

The Shorter Way

Phoebe Palmer was immersed in early nineteenth-century American Methodism. She grew up in a Methodist home, and makes references to class meetings, love feasts, means of grace, and other Wesleyan beliefs and practices throughout her writings. She understood herself as a faithful recipient and proponent of the teachings of the Wesleys and Fletcher, and her ideas show the impact of not only this trio of thinkers but of other widely read British Methodists including Hester Ann Rogers, Mary Bosanquet Fletcher, William Carvasso, and Adam Clarke.[13]

Consequently her theology and life reflected Wesleyan norms and values, from the primacy of Scripture to the centrality of sanctification. Her descriptions of Christian perfection or holiness were likewise Wesleyan: "the image of God re-enstamped upon the soul";[14] being "filled

13. As Harold Raser has shown, most of those British Methodists who strongly influenced Palmer's theology were themselves deeply shaped by that of Fletcher. Thus her reading of Wesley's theology was often through the lens of Fletcher's. See Raser, "Holding Tightly to 'the Promise of the Father.'"

14. Palmer, *Way of Holiness*, 61.

with the fullness of God" and "made a partaker of the divine nature";[15] "the rest of perfect love";[16] "a perfect sympathy with the heart of Christ," "that mind which was in your Saviour," "conformity to the divine image."[17] Like Wesley, she insists that Christian perfection "does not imply perfection in knowledge or light, but a state of supreme love to God, where all the powers of body and mind are perfectly subject to love's control, and ceaselessly offered up to God *through* Christ."[18] Such a state of perfection "*requires* progression," and cannot be retained unless it is growing.[19] Christ is the standard of holiness, and its content is that same love which was in Christ.[20]

It is important to emphasize just how Wesleyan she was, especially in her understanding of holiness. Her distinctive theological insights were not designed to alter this goal of holiness but to enable Christians to more readily attain it.

But as much as she was immersed in the culture of Methodism, she was also very much a person of American evangelical culture in the second quarter of the nineteenth century, marked as it was by individualism, egalitarianism, and revivalism. Palmer would be surprised and perhaps dismayed to be called a theologian; as Charles Edward White notes, she understood theology to be a humanly constructed "substitute for God's simple truth,"[21] a focus on (in her words) "theological hair-splittings and technicalities" rather than "the simple, naked word of God."[22] As Nathan Hatch has shown, this disdain for "the wrangling of theologians" and insistence on the ability of each person to understand the Bible on their own was characteristic of the popular evangelicalism that emerged early in the century, in which groups like the Methodists, Baptists, and Disciples challenged the theological monopoly of the educated, upper-class elites centered in Puritan New England.[23] This belief in the accessibility of scriptural understanding for all was undergirded by the "common sense" philosophy of the Scottish Enlightenment that by Palmer's day

15. Ibid., 118.

16. Ibid., 147.

17. Palmer, *Faith and Its Effects*, 57.

18. Ibid., 52.

19. Ibid.

20. Palmer, *Way of Holiness*, 58

21. White, *Beauty of Holiness*, 105.

22. Palmer, *Incidental Illustrations*, 308, cited in White, *Beauty of Holiness*, 105.

23. Hatch, *Democratization of American Christianity*, 22.

had become popularized and deeply rooted in American culture (and to which we will return later in the chapter). Yet in her negative assessment of theology, Palmer was not simply echoing the culture. Primarily she was reflecting her own experience with (in Diane Leclerc's words) "theologians and sophisticated preachers" who had made "holiness so elusive to her" in her own search for sanctification.[24]

Palmer's commitment to understanding and teaching the simple message of Scripture, the influence of her Methodist predecessors, and the assumptions embedded in American evangelical culture together enabled her to develop a new theology of the way to holiness, clearly Wesleyan yet distinctively her own. Her motivation was that the inherited way of salvation, with its insistence on a convicting struggle with sin prior to both justification and entire sanctification, and their confirmation through a witness of the Spirit, was not working for her. What she desired—and what she expected others did as well—was a shorter way to holiness. And in examining the Scripture, that is what she found: "O! I am sure this long waiting and struggling with the powers of darkness is not necessary. There is a shorter way."[25]

Critical to her discovery of the shorter way was her reading the command "Be ye holy." If "God requires that I should *now* be holy," she reasoned, then, whether she felt convicted, her duty was plain. She then "apprehended a simple truth before unthought of, i.e., *Knowledge is conviction.*"[26] It is enough to know God commands holiness to turn to God and ask it be given. In good Wesleyan fashion, she believed that what God commanded, God also enables: "Hath he given the command 'Be ye holy' and not given the ability with the command, for the performance of it?"[27] What is especially distinctive is her further assumption that when God commands holiness in Scripture, God commands it *now*, and hence enables persons to receive it *now*.

Palmer's shorter way consists of three elements. The first is *entire consecration.* Her premise here is two-fold: the altar sanctifies the gift (Matt 23:19), and Christ is the altar (Heb 13:10). If we place our lives on the altar through surrendering them entirely to God, we *are* at that moment entirely sanctified. "The act" of presenting the sacrifice, she

24. My thanks to Diane Leclerc for this important insight.

25. Palmer, *Way of Holiness,* 17–18.

26. Ibid., 19.

27. Ibid., 34–35; see also *Faith and Its Effects,* 93.

says, "must necessarily induce the promised result on the part of God."[28] Such an act of consecration involves giving up everything we might place ahead of God—not only sins but life-style, family and friends, occupation, reputation—as well as placing our time and talents in the service of God. While Wesley might see persons gradually overcoming these impediments to holiness over time—much of this he would term "self-denial"—Palmer believes persons can make a commitment to consecrate their lives at once, analogous to entering a covenant.

The second element is *faith*, which appropriates the gift of entire sanctification through believing the promise of Scripture. She interprets Scripture to say in 2 Cor 6:17 that if we fully consecrate our lives to Christ God will receive us; "In view of this declaration of my heavenly Father," she continues, "had I any reason to doubt that it was his will, even my sanctification?"[29]

Faith consists in believing the promises of Scripture; to doubt those promises is to doubt God. Again and again Palmer challenges those who seek experiential evidence that they have been entirely sanctified, in the form of a witness of the Spirit. "But *is not the entire voice of the Scriptures the voice of the Holy Spirit*?" she asks;[30] doesn't our assurance rest in God's faithfulness to the promises therein? Thus, "Faith is taking God at his word, relying unwaveringly upon his truth."[31] It is, borrowing language from Fletcher and Hester Ann Rogers, reliance "with naked faith, upon a naked promise."[32]

Having met the conditions, to doubt that one is entirely sanctified is to doubt God's own work, and thereby to lose the blessing. "We cannot honor God more than by trusting him," Palmer argues, "neither can we dishonor him more than by doubting his word." She compares the promises of Scripture to a promissory note from a reputable bank: to have "a promise fully credited does in itself convey the thing promised."[33]

It is important to note in countering those who seek experiential assurance, she is not (in Elaine Heath's words) "denying the validity or even desirability of emotional experience as part of sanctification."[34] She

28. Palmer, *Faith and Its Effects*, 104.

29. Ibid., 343; see also 99.

30. Ibid., 152. Palmer's italics.

31. Palmer, *Way of Holiness*, 37.

32. Ibid., 99; see also 133.

33. Palmer, *Faith and Its Effects*, 185.

34. Heath, *Naked Faith*, 105.

herself had such emotional experiences, which she reports with joy and thanksgiving. Her concern is "to make clear the contingency of emotional experience," to caution others not to "base their testimony of God's sanctifying grace on emotional experiences."[35] In other words, like Wesley, she wanted to avoid the danger of enthusiasm where intensity of emotion could lead to a false claim for entire sanctification, or absence of feeling could cause someone to fear they had lost it.

The third element in the shorter way is *testimony*. Citing the experience of John Fletcher, who said he lost entire sanctification five times due to failure to testify, Palmer considered this a binding requirement. It is both an encouragement to others, entailed in our conversation, and a public expression of our faith.[36] Palmer tells one correspondent that he lost entire sanctification "by degrees, in precisely the ratio you became cautious in professing it." She then notes, "God does not impart his blessings to us for our own exclusive enjoyment. It is his design that we should be vessels sanctified to his use. . . . It was his purpose that you should have been used as a channel, through which should flow out to the greatest possible number a knowledge of full redemption . . ."[37]

That testimony is absolutely necessary to retain entire sanctification points to a further feature of Palmer's theology: "one act of faith" is "not sufficient to insure a continuance in the 'way of holiness,' but . . . a *continuous* act" is required.[38] The three elements are all to be continued on an ongoing basis. This is especially the theme of her book *Entire Devotion to God*,[39] in which she argues, "It is only by an entire and continual reliance on Christ, that a state of entire sanctification can be retained."[40] Our sacrifice must ceaselessly remain on the altar, for it is the altar that sanctifies the gift; our faith must likewise continuously rest only in the promise of God.

35. Ibid.

36. See the discussions in White, *Beauty of Holiness,* 139–40; Heath, *Naked Faith,* 106–7; and Raser, *Phoebe Palmer,* 175–76.

37. Palmer, *Faith and Its Effects,* 329.

38. Palmer, *Way of Holiness,* 69.

39. Raser, *Phoebe Palmer,* 179–80.

40. Palmer, *Entire Devotion to God,* section XVI, cited in Heath, *Naked Faith,* 23.

Encouraging an Expectant Faith

The most obvious difference between Palmer and the Wesleys is not whether sanctification is instantaneous or gradual; clearly they all held it was both. The difference lies in the timing, or to put it differently, *what to expect when*. The distance between Palmer and Charles Wesley is the greatest. His strong reaction against the claims of the perfectionists in the 1760s was aimed at their claim of perfection as attainable now; their very act of claiming it demonstrated their distance from the humble, patient love manifested in Christ:

> "Go on? but how? from step to step?
> No, let *us* to perfection *leap!*"
> 'Tis thus our hasty nature cries,
> Leap o'er the cross, to snatch the prize . . .[41]

He specifically challenged the teaching that Christian perfection was immediately attainable by faith:

> Which of the *old* apostles taught
> Perfection is an instant caught,
> Show'd *our* compendious manner how,
> "Believe, and ye are perfect *now*;
> This moment wake, and seize the prize;
> Reeds, into sudden pillars rise";
> Believe delusion's ranting sons,
> And all the work is done at once![42]

For Charles Wesley, lifelong, gradual growth in sanctification is essential for Christian perfection, in the end, to be authentic:

> Shall we mistake the morning-ray
> Of grace for the full blaze of day?
> Or humbly walk in Jesus' sight.
> Glad to receive the gradual light
> More of his grace and more to know,
> In faith and in experience grow,

41. Charles Wesley, No. 187, "Short Hymn on Heb. 6:1," in Tyson, *Charles Wesley: A Reader*, 390.

42. Ibid.

> Till all the life of God we prove,
> And *lose ourselves* in perfect love![43]

John Wesley's dissent from his brother is shown by his writing in the margins beside "the gradual light" the words "And the sudden."

Palmer could rightly object that Charles had not taken into account entire consecration as a precondition for Christian perfection; she was not, after all, identical to the "ranting sons" Maxfield and Bell. For her entire consecration was not leaping over the cross but the way of the cross. But if pressed on this point, both Wesleys would likely argue that consecration itself requires growth over time if it is not to become self-deception. Charles Wesley writes, "Must we not then with patience wait / False to distinguish from sincere?"[44]

This was the central issue for Charles Wesley: distinguishing the false from the authentic. How do we anticipate holiness as heaven below without presuming to have received what we in fact have not? How can we avoid encouraging a testimony in words that is contradicted by the testimony of the life lived, and with it the resultant undermining of the faith of others in the promise of Christian perfection? His solution was to depict both the way to holiness and its content in such a way as to discredit false claims for Christian perfection based solely on experience or faith. Indeed, to claim full salvation at all was almost certainly evidence that one had not received it.

For Phoebe Palmer, the central issue was not presumption but despair. She had sought Christian perfection in the prescribed way to no avail. Were the Wesleys and Fletcher wrong in their insistence on the promise of holiness? Or is the promise only for some rather than all? No, says Palmer, God is ready at this moment to fulfill the promise of entire sanctification. There is no need for months or years of waiting in disappointment and frustration. "God is love," she insists, "and it is my desire to encourage you in the assurance, that there will be no delay on his part in meeting you on the ground of the promises."[45] "He has assured you of his willingness to save you *this* moment," she affirms, "and it is sinful to doubt either his ability or his willingness to save you *now*."[46] For Palmer the barrier to Christian perfection cannot be in God so therefore must be

---

43. Charles Wesley, No. 170, "Short Hymn on Prov. 4:18," in ibid., 380.
44. Charles Wesley, No. 171, "Short Hymn on Matt. 7:10," in ibid.
45. Palmer, *Faith and Its Effects*, 31.
46. Ibid., 337.

in us, in our own unwillingness to consecrate our lives and believe. The answer to despair is an expectant faith that acts to meet those conditions, and hope that doesn't dream of holiness sometime in an indefinite future but decisively claims the promise in the moment.

Like Palmer, John Wesley wants to encourage expectant faith; like his brother he also desired to avoid presumption. His approach was to emphasize Christian perfection as a promise of God that should be sought and expected, but also awaited in confident hope. Thus, having "tasted of the powers of the world to come," you should not complain that God has not given you the full salvation for which you yearn. No, "Instead of repining at your not being wholly delivered, you will praise God for thus delivering you. You will magnify God for what he hath done, and take it as an earnest of what he will do. . . . Instead of uselessly tormenting yourself because the time is not fully come, you will calmly and quietly wait for it, knowing that it 'will come, and will not tarry.'"[47] For John Wesley, an expectant faith is joined to a patient hope, a spirituality of attainment and expectation that holds on in gratitude for what has already been given while yearning for that which is yet to come.

So unlike Charles, John Wesley believes God can and at times does cut the work short. Yet on this issue he is still perhaps a bit closer to Charles than he is to Phoebe Palmer. For John Wesley, since we receive it at God's timing, it can be now (and we should be by faith willing to receive it at any moment), but most likely will occur later in life. For Palmer, God's time *is* now, and God is waiting on us to fulfill the unchangeable scriptural conditions of entire consecration and faith. For all of Wesley's insistence that Christian perfection can be received sooner rather than later, the primary focus of his teaching was on the gradual sanctification that aims for Christian perfection rather than the growth that follows; Palmer's focus is on retaining and growing in entire sanctification already received. For Wesley the emphasis is on an expectant faith waiting on God; for Palmer it is on a faithful God waiting on us. And found within this contrast are further theological issues critical to the promise of holiness as heaven below which we examine in chapter 6.

---

47. John Wesley, "Satan's Devices" II.5, *Wesley's Works* 2:150.

CHAPTER 6

The Promise of Holiness

... true religion, in the very essence of it, is
nothing short of holy tempers.

—JOHN WESLEY[1]

Holiness and sanctification most expressly signify
the state intended. You cannot consistently expect it,
until you make up your mind to live in the
continuous act of unreserved consecration.

—PHOEBE PALMER[2]

BOTH JOHN WESLEY AND Phoebe Palmer insisted salvation, from prevenient grace to Christian perfection and beyond, is by grace alone. They
rejected the Calvinist claim that grace is irresistible, and argued for the
necessity of grace-enabled human response. For them grace provides not
only forgiveness of sins but a full transformation of the heart.

Yet within this Wesleyan consensus lies a crucial theological difference. A statement by Lorna Khoo nicely captures what is at stake: "The
intentionality and intensity of commitment to a focused, achievable (albeit grace-bestowed) goal has to preserve the delicate balance between
the understanding of the freedom of human beings to cooperate with

1. Wesley, "On Charity" III.12, *Wesley's Works* 2:306.
2. Palmer, *Faith and Its Effects,* 351.

God and the freedom of God to do as he wills in the process of salvation."[3] While Khoo is here thinking of the Wesleys and the Calvinists, this is also an apt description of the primary difference between Wesley and Palmer.

We can frame this difference around the terms "faithfulness" and "freedom." With regard to God, I use "faithfulness" to describe what is entailed in God's being faithful to divine promises, and "freedom" to refer to the manner and timing of how God fulfills those promises. From the human side, "faithfulness" has to do with the manner in which persons appropriate those promises, and "freedom" with their capacity to do so. Examining the differences provides significant insight not only in how grace works but also in the nature of the change it effects.

Working Out Our Own Salvation

Let's begin with the human side of the question. In chapter 5 we made reference to the impact of the common sense philosophy of the Scottish enlightenment in America. By the second quarter of the nineteenth century, this philosophy was not only dominant in intellectual circles but in a popularized form had permeated American culture. With its egalitarian premise that all persons have a natural "moral sense" and a common rational capacity to know and understand reality, common sense philosophy was especially suited to the republicanism of the new American nation.[4] By the time of Phoebe Palmer it was the unconscious assumption of almost everyone, whether orthodox or unitarian, Calvinist or Arminian, revivalist or anti-revivalist.

For our purposes here the important feature of common sense philosophy was its moral psychology. Put simply, it depicts the will as a neutral capacity to choose and to act; reason and emotion are two often conflicting faculties that seek to control the will. Only a consciously intentional act, guided by reason, can be considered genuinely moral; motivations and inclinations rooted in emotion or feeling are amoral at best.

As Randy Maddox argues, this is a highly decisionistic and rationalist type of moral psychology. An earlier parallel tendency toward rationalism and decisionism could already be seen in British Methodists like Fletcher, Adam Clarke, and Richard Watson. The confluence of the seeds of this way of thinking among those influential Methodist thinkers with

3. Khoo, *Wesleyan Eucharistic Spirituality*, 177–78.

4. Mark Noll tells the story of how theistic common sense philosophy came to dominate American life in *America's God*, 93–113.

the rapid cultural dominance of common sense philosophy led American Methodists to come "to view the 'will' as our autonomous ability to assert rational control over our various motivating dynamics, thereby freeing ourselves to make moral choices."[5]

In reacting against the insistence that new birth and Christian perfection must be accompanied by a witness of the Spirit, Palmer creatively revisions the way of holiness in terms appropriate to this moral psychology. Thus we can rationally apprehend the promises in Scripture and the conditions necessary to receive them. We can then decide to act on those conditions, to consciously and intentionally consecrate our lives to God and through "naked faith" believe the sacrifice is acceptable, based on Scripture alone. The rationalist and decisionistic elements are evident throughout.

Methodists as a whole were by Palmer's day thinking in these terms. Most were redescribing sanctification as gradual, "*habituated rational control* over our lower (affectional) nature that is developed by repeated practice," made possible by the regenerating grace of the new birth.[6] What made Palmer's approach distinctive, Maddox argues, was that she conceived of an instantaneous way to remove the barriers to entire sanctification through consecration, thereby permitting "an enduring *spontaneous* rational control over the passions and affection," provided that the decision to place our lives on the altar is maintained "by renewing our consecration moment-by-moment."[7]

This is strikingly different from Wesley's moral psychology. As we have seen, for Wesley affections and tempers *are* the will; they constitute morally significant motivations and desires. While prevenient grace restores (through conscience and liberty) a capacity to deny our will, it takes regenerating grace to change our will through changing the tempers of the heart. Because these tempers shape our understanding as well as our inclinations, reason by itself cannot control and direct the will. Thus prior to new birth reason operates within one framework of understanding shaped by unholy tempers; and within a new and different framework through the gift of faith and emergence of holy tempers with the new birth. Sanctification is growth in those holy tempers, such that they increasingly govern the desires of the heart. This occurs through

5. Maddox, "Reconnecting the Means to the End," 45. See also Raser, *Phoebe Palmer*, 238–46, 274–77.

6. Maddox, "Reconnecting the Means to the End," 47.

7. Ibid., 48.

means of grace, which are the normal environment, so to speak, through which the Holy Spirit sanctifies the heart.

It is this understanding of the means of grace as central to reception and growth in holy tempers that becomes lost in the shorter way.[8] It is not that Palmer did not have a theology of grace. The issue is rather the manner in which grace works. For Palmer and her contemporaries the will in itself is essentially free; the question is whether it will be motivated by reason or passions. Palmer's shorter way envisions grace enabling the rational control of the will, directing it to attain the scriptural promise of entire sanctification through a ceaseless act of consecration and an abiding faith, putting a decisive end to sinful inclinations and desires. Later proponents of the shorter way (who often taught it in a more formulaic manner that lacked the nuance of Palmer's original) would emphasize only those means of grace that inform the intellect[9] rather than Wesley's more holistic approach that had its focus on the formation of holy tempers, that is, on the heart as well as the mind.

We can elaborate on this by looking at how Wesley understood self-denial, a spiritual practice whose content is similar to that of consecration in Palmer's theology. The larger framework for self-denial is Wesley's advice for persons to "work out their own salvation," in which he grounds their ability to do so on grace: "God works; therefore you *can* work," and "God works; therefore you *must* work."[10] The work he advises persons to undertake is to "cease to do evil" by avoiding known sin and to "learn to do well" through works of piety and mercy. If one does this, he adds, "It only remains that ye deny yourselves and take up your cross daily."[11] Self-denial and its companion practice, taking up a cross, are so essential to Christian growth that Wesley holds them out for special emphasis. The reason is ". . . in every stage of the spiritual life, although there is a variety of particular hindrances of our attaining grace or growing therein, yet are all resolvable into these general ones,—either we do not deny ourselves, or we do not take up our cross."[12] Wesley defines self-denial as "the denying or refusing to follow our own will, from a conviction that the will of

8. This is at the heart of Maddox's argument in "Reconnecting the Means to the End."

9. Ibid., 59.

10. John Wesley, "On Working Out Our Own Salvation" III.2, *Wesley's Works* 3:206.

11. Ibid., II.4, 206. See my discussion of self-denial as one of the general means of grace in Knight, *Presence of God*, 122–26.

12. John Wesley, "Self-Denial" 4, *Wesley's Works* 2:240.

God is the only rule of action to us,"[13] and taking up a cross as "anything contrary to our will, anything displeasing to our nature"[14] which we must nonetheless do if we are to follow Christ.

While the content of self-denial and taking up a cross is quite similar to Palmer's consecration, the purpose is quite different. We can begin to see this difference in how Wesley illustrates the need for self-denial: "The will of God is a path leading straight to God. The will of man, which once ran parallel to it, is now another path, not only different from it, but, in our present state, directly contrary to it: It leads from God. If, therefore, we walk in the one, we must necessary quit the other."[15] Wesley here is not calling on persons to exercise their will but to deny it. As long as we are sinners, our motivations and desires will put us on a path leading away from God. We see again how different the anthropology of Wesley is from that of common sense philosophy.

Thus for Wesley, self-denial cannot be accomplished in a single decision and then maintained thereafter, for it is the will through which that decision would be made that is itself compromised by sin. *Entire* consecration as an act of will could only be conceivable as a result of Christian perfection, not as a condition for receiving it, for it is only then that the will is fully governed by holy tempers.

Wesley also grounds our need for self-denial in our creaturely finitude, which necessarily limits the exercise of our will in relation to God's.[16] Thus Wesley understands the practice of self-denial as necessary for the entirety of the Christian life, for the awakened sinner as much as for the entirely sanctified believer. Self-denial by its very nature is a means to continued growth, enabling persons to remain on the way of salvation. Therefore he advises everyone to "practice it daily, without intermission, from the hour you first set your hand to the plough, and enduring therein to the end, till your spirit returns to God."[17]

Self-denial is not only advocated by Wesley as a personal spiritual practice, it is an intrinsic element in more communal means of grace as well, most notably the covenant service and the Lord's Supper. With regard to the latter, Wesley (drawing on the terminology of Daniel Brevint)

13. Ibid., I.2, 242.

14. Ibid., I.7, 243.

15. Ibid., I.4, 242.

16. Ibid., I.2, 242.

17. Ibid., III.4, 250.

understood the Lord's Supper to be both a sacrament through which God graciously works, and our sacrifice in response, made acceptable through Christ. The pattern of our sacrifice consists of three interconnected elements: grief at the death of Christ caused by our sins; self-denial, in which our sins are put to death; and taking up our cross in service to God.[18] As Lorna Khoo describes it, "In response to the grace and love of God in Christ, the Christian becomes a living sacrifice (cf. Romans 12:1), living a crucified life (Galatians 2:20) in union with Christ, sharing in the fellowship of his sufferings. . . . One's sins, one's property, one's body parts and one's life itself, in the *now*, have been offered up to God."[19] This self-offering is repeated at each celebration of the Lord's Supper, which Wesley urged should be at least weekly, if possible—indeed, as often as one can.[20]

The Lord's Supper is therefore an occasion for continued growth in our ability for self-denial, enabled and led by the Holy Spirit. Khoo describes the work of this "intimate God" in this way: "Eucharistic spirituality of the Wesleys placed the Spirit alongside the struggling believer, initiating, inspiring, encouraging, correcting and leading the person into deeper consecration of heart and life."[21]

Thus for Wesley, self-denial *is* moment by moment and day by day, but its purpose is to enable our growth in grace throughout the way of salvation by denying "ourselves any pleasure that does not spring from, and lead to, God."[22] Likewise, taking up a cross is to part "with a foolish desire, with an inordinate affection; or a separation from the object of it, without which it can never be extinguished."[23] In other words, the goal of self-denial is, through grace, both to uproot unholy tempers and reject that which would draw us away from God, thus allowing holy tempers to take root and grow. Self-denial, over time, increasingly redirects the heart to God, enabling continued growth in grace while maintaining the gains that have been made.

---

18. See my discussion of our sacrifice in the Lord's Supper in *Presence of God*, 144–47.

19. Khoo, *Wesleyan Eucharistic Spirituality*, 194.

20. See John Wesley, "The Duty of Constant Communion," *Wesley's Works* 3:427–39.

21. Khoo, *Wesleyan Eucharistic Spirituality*, 196.

22. John Wesley, "Self-Denial" I.6, *Wesley's Works* 2:243.

23. Ibid., I.9, 243.

God's Faithfulness and Freedom

How we understand human faith and freedom is necessarily correlated with how God's freedom and faithfulness is conceived. Phoebe Palmer strongly emphasizes the faithfulness of God to divine promises in Scripture. As we have seen, she regularly describes the Bible as the very words of God, and to not believe its promises is therefore to doubt God's word. As Harold Raser observes, she understands these promises as moral or spiritual laws, in a manner analogous to nineteenth-century understanding of physical laws such as gravity in terms of cause and effect.[24] Therefore, regarding both justification and entire sanctification, "Such effects must of necessity follow such acts of obedience and faith. I say must of *necessity* follow, because the principles by which the kingdom of grace is governed are unchangeable."[25] This is an exceptionally strong view of God's faithfulness, one in which (through grace) our meeting the conditions *immediately* brings the promised divine response.

It was this claim for God's faithfulness that lay behind the controversy that emerged over the witness of the Spirit. For Palmer, given that the Bible *is* the words of the Holy Spirit, assurance of entire sanctification as a witness of the Spirit can be deduced from our having met the scriptural conditions of receiving it.[26] The challenge to her argument came in 1858 from Palmer's friend and ally Nathan Bangs, a leading figure and theologian in the Methodist Episcopal Church. Bangs' concern, expressed at Palmer's Tuesday meeting for the Promotion of Holiness (although in Palmer's absence), was that to claim entire sanctification (in Charles White's words) "on the evidence of Scripture alone, without any inward witness, change in disposition, or emotion" opens the door to self-deception.[27] So while Palmer clearly saw the danger of self-deception in claiming entire sanctification simply on the basis of having an experience, Bangs argued that there is also a danger to claiming it based on Scripture alone. We can be certain of God's faithfulness to promises in Scripture, he said, but those promises "are not in themselves any evidence to *me* that I am . . . sanctified; they simply declare who [is] sanctified, and give marks of evidence of that work." This claim, he warned, "strikes at

---

24. Raser, *Phoebe Palmer*, 185.

25. Palmer, *Faith and Its Effects*, 40.

26. Raser, *Phoebe Palmer*, 187.

27. White, *Beauty of Holiness*, 142.

the root of experimental religion," and is directly contrary to the teaching of Wesley, Fletcher, and Scripture itself.[28]

The words were strong, but the issue was critical. Had Palmer, in her quest for a shorter way, compromised the freedom of God in her desire to proclaim God's faithfulness? Palmer never directly responded to Bangs' critique, but in Harold Raser's view may have indirectly addressed the issue through "her very marked turn to the baptism of the Holy Ghost" in the second half of the 1850s.[29]

Language of "Pentecost" and "Spirit baptism" was only infrequently mentioned in her early writings in the 1840s. Yet beginning with *Incidental Illustration on the Economy of Salvation* (1855) the language of the Spirit becomes more pervasive, and by *The Promise of the Father* (1859) "Pentecostal" and "Spirit baptism" terminology becomes the dominant way she describes entire sanctification. As Raser notes, the baptism of the Spirit is something *God* does, shifting the balance back toward divine activity.[30] In these two books she also makes the theological linkage of holiness with power, arguing that it is the full baptism of the Spirit that enables and emboldens disciples to witness for Christ. Likewise, she begins to describe this present age as the dispensation of the Spirit, drawing on the theology of Fletcher.[31]

As we have seen, the seeds for the identification of Christian perfection with a Pentecostal baptism of the Spirit are found in Fletcher, as well as those influenced by him such as Mary Bosanquet Fletcher and Hester Ann Rogers. And while the terminology is infrequent, the linkage between Pentecost and entire sanctification can be found as early as *The Way of Holiness* (1843). Whether the decision in the 1850s to make this her predominate language for Christian perfection was in response to criticism or for other reasons, it was the emphasis and not the idea itself that was new. Yet while the use of Spirit baptism language does place more emphasis on divine *agency*, it nonetheless does not provide a greater role for divine *freedom*. The basic theological structure of the shorter way remains unchanged.

28. Stevens, *Life and Times of Nathan Bangs*, 396–402, cited in White, *Beauty of Holiness*, 142.

29. Raser, *Phoebe Palmer*, 273.

30. Ibid.

31. Ibid., 198. White suggests several other reasons Palmer may have adopted Pentecostal and Spirit baptism language in *Beauty of Holiness*, 126–28.

How, then, does Palmer's understanding of God's faithfulness shape our relationship with God? One way to look at this is in terms of the object of our faith. A clue can be found in contrasting the role of Scripture for Wesley and Palmer.

Wesley's desire was to *know* God, not just know about God, and then to grow in the knowledge and love of God. Faith was *how* we know God, and that occurred most especially in and through means of grace. A formalist might believe the contents of Scripture and yet have only a dead orthodoxy; it is faith that enables us to be receptive to the voice of the Spirit as it speaks through the Scripture. The Bible is indeed "the oracles of God" for Wesley, but without the Spirit as divine interpreter (as Charles Wesley would put it) it remains a dead letter.

For Palmer, Scripture as the word of God meant the written words *are* the voice of the Spirit, so to read and understand them is in effect to hear God speak. Thus the promises of Scripture are the promises of God and have the absolute authority and constancy of the One who made them. This is a subtle but significant shift from Wesley: by equating Scripture with God's word in this way, Palmer identifies them so closely that it is the promises in the Bible that become the object of our faith. She, of course, could well protest that her constant admonition to trust the promises is presupposing a relationship with God that was entered with the new birth. That is fair enough. But it remains the case that her language is predominantly transactional or contractual rather than personal or relational.

Perhaps the overall lesson in this section for proponents of holiness as heaven below is to reinforce the insight of Lyle Dabney discussed in chapter 4. There he described the two Western traditions Wesley was navigating between as the medieval emphasis on the human capacity for ascending to the knowledge of God through grace, and the Reformation focus on human incapacity due to sin and the resulting need for grace and forgiveness. Wesley's optimism of grace, centered on the transforming power of the Holy Spirit, enabled him to combine and transcend these two traditions.

Phoebe Palmer, as a conscious heir of Wesley, found herself facing that same tension in a new form shaped by her American context. As she sought to use Scripture to make sense of her own spiritual struggles, she found herself leaning more to the human capacity side of the tension than did Wesley. Yet she too endeavored to combine and transcend the tension, embracing not only God's promises but also the transforming power of the Spirit,

For those who believe with Wesley and Palmer that God indeed promises fullness of sanctification in this life, there will always be a need for a corresponding emphasis on the power of the Holy Spirit as the agent of that transformation. What is essential in proclaiming the way to holiness is to maintain the dynamic balance between God's faithfulness to divine promises, and God's freedom in the fulfillment of those promises.

And therein lies the most significant difference between Palmer and Wesley. Palmer places her emphasis on what *we* do to elicit the promised response from a waiting God. Wesley speaks more of our actively waiting on *God* with open and expectant faith. For Wesley, God's faithfulness to divine promises does not circumscribe God's freedom as to the timing or circumstances of their fulfillment. Wesley describes the divine/human relationship in terms of mutual freedom, shaped and enabled by divine initiative, but involving responsive interaction on both sides. This does not mean that God arbitrarily withholds Christian perfection from some earnest seekers; rather it assumes that God knows our hearts more deeply than we do, and the timing of the gift is determined by a divine wisdom motivated by infinite love.

The Lens of Mysticism

Elaine Heath has recently offered an alternative way of reading Palmer that radically reframes many of the issues raised thus far. She argues that Palmer rediscovers a type of apophatic mysticism, and in so doing reintroduces a needed element to the way of holiness that John Wesley had minimized in his own theology. Rather than emphasizing human freedom at the expense of the divine, she provides instead a needed balance to Wesley's strong emphasis on the divine.

For apophatic mysticism the path of spiritual growth is through a *via negativa*, involving "renunciation of the ego and a detachment from all religious images, forms, created things and experiences in order to enter a deeper union with the ultimately unknowable God." It is grounded in the theological insight that although truly revealed in creation, Scripture, and most fully in Christ, God nonetheless transcends human concepts and understanding. Heath wisely insists that the apophatic way does not supplant the kataphatic, but both are mutually necessary for a holistic and biblically faithful mysticism.[32]

Central to Heath's argument is that, unlike some later oversimplifications of Palmer's theology, her way of holiness is most centrally characterized by continual consecration and faith. The initial act of consecration and faith is therefore an entering into a new relationship with God. Keeping this in mind, let us briefly look at how Heath describes the shorter way.

According to Heath, consecration is "a profound emptying of oneself onto the altar of Christ":[33] "the one who is on the altar is there utterly for God."[34] In making her own initial consecration, "Palmer experienced the necessary detachment of the *via negativa*: the letting go of people, created things, religious feelings, and her own will in order to embrace the God who is wholly other. She entered into quietness of soul by means of the *via negativa*, rather than through kataphatic experiences of having her heart 'strangely warmed' as John Wesley did, or some other affective experience."[35] Likewise, Heath argues, Palmer's call for "naked faith in the naked word" was not (as it became for later holiness proponents) "a statement for a simple, uncritical hermeneutic of Scripture" but "a description of the profound angst of 'the cloud of unknowing' that Palmer experienced."[36] It called for a de-emphasis of experience rather than its disavowal, for, as Heath notes, Palmer does have and deeply values kataphatic experiences such as dreams and visions.[37] Rather, Palmer had "learned over the course of many years" to accept such experiences as "part of the journey" while not allowing them "to determine her level of commitment to God." If anything, Heath adds, "the more desolate she feels emotionally, the more firmly she clings to the word of God."[38]

Perhaps this citation can serve as an apt summary of this all-too-brief presentation of Heath's argument, as it captures so well this aspect of the spirituality of Palmer's way of holiness: "In the ensuing interaction with God, Palmer surrendered herself unconditionally to mystical union

---

32. Heath, *Naked Faith*, 43.

33. Ibid., 99.

34. Ibid., 102.

35. Ibid., 72.

36. Ibid., 29.

37. Ibid., 49–59.

38. Ibid., 104–5.

on God's terms, acknowledging the probability that union would involve seasons of walking by sheer faith, trusting in the 'naked word of God' in the perceived absence of spiritual passion and emotion."[39]

Thus, Heath argues, Palmer's shorter way is in effect a recasting of Wesleyan categories in terms of a certain kind of mysticism. This mysticism was not a form of quietism, which Palmer opposed just as strongly as did Wesley. Her mysticism is more biblically centered in focus and activist in result. In some ways, it looks very much like a return to the sort of mysticism of the will that so captivated John and Charles Wesley in the days of the Holy Club, prior to their conversions in 1738. If this is so, it shows a similarity with how Palmer understood growth in entire sanctification with how Charles Wesley, who never quite abandoned that early mysticism, understood growth in sanctification prior to it being entire. It also would have some commonality with Fletcher, who had pronounced mystical leanings.

Heath's analysis is especially valuable in shedding new light on Palmer's insistence that a witness of the Spirit is not necessary to entire sanctification. Rather than an invitation to self-deception, as Nathan Bangs feared, it can be seen as just the opposite: letting God set the terms for deepening the relationship rather than us. Palmer is not simply dispensing with an accompaniment to entire sanctification she believed unnecessary, but inviting persons into a more profound trust in God.

That said, I'm not convinced Palmer was any more a mystic than was Charles Wesley or Fletcher. While looking at Palmer through a mystical lens illumines certain features of her theology and enables fresh appreciation of some of her insights, she is, after all, intentionally rooted in Scripture, and consistently wary of going beyond or outside it. She is, to borrow a well-known phrase of John Wesley, a woman of one book. This is a kataphatic sensibility she shares with the Wesleys, though perhaps with a literalism that exceeds their own.

Moreover, she embraces much of the spirituality she inherits from the Wesleys. That spirituality was predominantly kataphatic, especially in the prominence of the means of grace where words, signs, and actions mediate the presence of God. While they did not diminish the traditional Protestant emphasis on Scripture and the preached word, Lorna Khoo highlights their "appreciation for the physical, the material and the sensory as instruments of grace." Because sight, taste and touch are used as

39. Ibid., 78.

frequent metaphors for sacramental encounter with God, Khoo argues that the Wesleys expect a "surprising level of familiarity or intimacy" with God at the eucharist." We love, as 1 John says, because God first loved us; for the Wesleys we encounter that love again and again as we meet God in the means of Grace.

Thus the focus of the Wesleys' spirituality is on our knowing God as love, through God's revelation in Christ. We encounter this God through means of grace that are the central and necessary means for our hearts and lives to be transformed. Both Palmer and the Wesleys were concerned to detach themselves from anything or anyone that would supplant God as the center of their devotion. But Palmer was also determined if necessary to let go of experience itself, placing her trust not in religious feelings but in God alone.

What we have then is the Wesleys' emphasis on knowing the depth and fullness of *God's* love for us in Christ, coupled with Palmer's emphasis on *our* unreserved devotion to God. Both are essential to holiness, provided that we always remember that it is only God's prior love that makes our own possible. And in light of the promise that one day those in Christ will see God face to face, in the intense light of divine love, and worship with our own now unconstrained love, holiness understood in this way is indeed an anticipation of heaven below.

CHAPTER 7

Christ Our Sanctifier

Christ is no more freely offered in the faith
of his atonement, than in the assurance of
his personal presence and sanctifying power!
...He is a full Saviour. And to all who trust
Him he gives a full salvation.

—WILLIAM BOARDMAN[1]

In conversion we come into Christ, our Sanctifier,
and are made holy, as well as righteous. When
one really comes into Christ he is as much in
Christ as he will ever be. He is in a state of holiness
and righteousness....If he keeps there he will continue
to be holy and righteous.

—WILLIAM H. DURHAM[2]

THE WESLEYAN VISION OF holiness proved attractive to many outside
Methodism who were discontented with the lukewarm Christianity they
found in the churches, as well as the persistence of sin in their lives. The
promise of a happy, sinless afterlife did not satisfy their hunger for a more
vibrant Christianity in the present. The availability of a fuller sanctifica-

---

1. Boardman, *Higher Christian Life*, 76.
2. Durham, "Sanctification," cited in Jacobsen, *Reader in Pentecostal Theology*, 84.

tion of the sort proclaimed by Wesley would be just the cure for sin-sick souls and complacent churches.

But as Presbyterians, Congregationalists, Baptists, Anglicans and others began to adopt holiness teaching, they also transformed it. Phoebe Palmer revisioned Wesleyan sanctification in light of her own American context. These non-Methodists would take things a step further and reframe it within a more distinctively Reformed theology. For many of them, while retaining a strong emphasis on the power of the Spirit, this meant giving Christ more of a role as the agent of sanctification as well as making it possible and defining its content. In addition, their differing understandings of sin and grace produced distinctive portrayals of sanctification and an optimism of grace.

Permanent Sanctification

Charles G. Finney, along with his colleague Asa Mahon, were the central figures in shaping what became known as the Oberlin theology.[3] Finney began his ministry in the 1820s, becoming the most prominent evangelist in early nineteenth-century America. But it was as a pastor of a Presbyterian Church in the early 1830s that Finney became aware of the need for something beyond conversion that would enable persons to lead more authentically Christian lives. It was after becoming a professor at Oberlin College in Ohio that Finney was able to develop his mature theology of sanctification.

Like Palmer and most other early nineteenth-century Americans, Finney assumed common sense philosophy's moral psychology with its three faculties of reason, sensibility, and the will. But Finney, originally a lawyer steeped in the legal philosophy of William Blackstone, linked this moral psychology to Blackstone's argument that humans bear legal responsibility because through reason they can understand the requirements of the law, and with their will they can obey it. In like manner, Finney would argue that persons can understand and obey God's moral law as well. Finney therefore understood sin as, in the words of James Reeve, "a free and voluntary transgression of God's moral law";[4] humans bear guilt for sin because it is in their power to obey God's law.

---

3. For a fine recent biography of Finney, see Hambrick-Stowe, *Charles G. Finney*. For Asa Mahon, see Madden and Hamilton, *Freedom and Grace*.

4. Reeve, "Holiness and the Holy Spirit," 36. Reeve's excellent summary of the

This strong belief in human free will placed a fundamental barrier between Finney and Calvinist orthodoxy. Traditional concepts of divine sovereignty and indwelling sin contradicted both Finney's reason and his reading of Scripture. As Reeve notes, the problem for Finney was that "God, if he were to be just, could not require of human beings, if they were to be free, what they were unable to do."[5]

The comparison of Finney's view with that of Wesley is instructive. Wesley had insisted that whatever God commands is at the same time a promise that, through grace, God will enable us to do. Because Finney, unlike Wesley, rejected indwelling sin as a disposition of the heart, he had no need for prevenient grace to restore us to a freedom he believed we never lost. Finney, facing claims for irresistible grace from orthodox Calvinists and Universalists alike, argued that the fact God commands us to obey moral law was in itself conclusive evidence we by nature are capable of doing so.

Given these basic commitments, it was no wonder Finney would gladly embrace the Arminianized Calvinism of the New Divinity theology, especially that of Nathaniel William Taylor. Like Finney, Taylor understood God as moral governor and humanity as possessing freedom of the will. While the desires of the sensibility influence the will, Taylor insisted they cannot compel it. Nevertheless, Taylor argued, while persons were completely free to obey God, they were so strongly disposed to do otherwise that, apart from divine grace, they would not do so.[6] Thus Taylor provided a convincing explanation for why persons with free will nonetheless continued in sin and were still in need of grace.

Following Taylor, Finney argued that universal well-being was the moral obligation of humanity, and the only conditions necessary for persons to meet that obligation was free moral agency and the light of knowledge.[7] While the appetites and desires of the sensibility are not in themselves sinful, when their gratification becomes the primary concern of our lives we, through intentional decisions of the will, reject universal well-being for our own selfish ends. Because we regularly indulge our desires long before we develop any concept of moral obligation, sin becomes habitual. What is needed to remedy this situation is

---

influences on Finney's thought (see 18ff.) are the major source for my own discussion.

5. Ibid., 39. See also Gresham, *Charles G. Finney's Doctrine*, 28.

6. Reeve, "Holiness and the Holy Spirit," 50–52.

7. Ibid., 96–104.

the light of knowledge, with which the reason can guide the will toward disinterested benevolence rather than selfishness, holiness rather than sin.[8] Such knowledge occurs through the proclamation of the gospel, through which the Holy Spirit uses the power of the cross to inform the reason and persuade the will.[9] It is this theology of conversion that informs Finney's revivalism, and it is the necessity of the Holy Spirit to persuasively impart the knowledge of the cross that in the end saves Finney from the semi-Pelagianism with which he is so often charged.

It was as a pastor that Finney first turned his attention to sanctification. There he read Wesley's "A Plain Account of Christian Perfection," and his earliest writings on the subject were marked by Wesleyan concepts and terminology. He equated the Edwardsean term "disinterested benevolence" with Wesley's "perfect love," seeing them as both denoting the heart of Christian perfection.[10]

What initially separated Finney from Wesley was his belief in human free will, an optimism of nature in contrast to Wesley's pessimism of nature. But in 1841 Finney and his Oberlin colleagues adopted another doctrine that would lead to a thoroughgoing rethinking of conversion and sanctification, and would give Oberlin perfectionism its own distinctive shape. This was the doctrine of "the simplicity of moral action" or "unity of moral action," which held that it was impossible for the will to be simultaneously divided between good and evil.[11] Thus Finney now argued that "the mind cannot choose one ultimate end, and choose at the same time another ultimate end. . . . In other words, it cannot be selfish and benevolent at the same time."[12] "The only sense in which obedience to moral law can be partial," Finney concluded, "is, that obedience may be intermittent"; holy and sinful choices "may succeed each other an indefinite number of times, but coexist they plainly cannot."[13]

This reframes how sanctification is understood. No longer can it be a gradual growing in love while at the same time a gradual decrease in sin. Rather, when the will is benevolent, it cannot be any more entirely sanctified than it is at that moment, and when it is selfish it cannot be any

---

8. Ibid., 111–21; see also Gresham, *Charles G. Finney's Doctrine*, 29.

9. Reeve, "Holiness and the Holy Spirit," 160–67.

10. Ibid., 69.

11. Ibid., 77–78; see also Gresham, *Charles G. Finney's Doctrine*, 29–30.

12. Finney, *Systematic Theology*, 105.

13. Ibid., 120.

more or less selfish than it is at that time. Entire sanctification is now a consequence of conversion.

Given this new understanding, Finney now says, "Sanctification may be entire in two senses: (1.) In the sense of present, full obedience, or entire consecration to God; and (2.) In the sense of continued, abiding consecration or obedience to God."[14] Entire sanctification in the latter sense, what he will elsewhere call "permanent sanctification," "consists in being established, confirmed, preserved, continued in a state of sanctification or of entire consecration to God."[15] It provides *constancy* to sanctification by putting an end to the inconsistent exercise of the will.

This does not mean for Finney that there is no growth in sanctification. Progress is always possible because "all creatures must increase in knowledge; and increase of knowledge implies increase of holiness in a holy being."[16] Much as Wesley argued for an increase of knowledge as a remedy for involuntary transgressions, Finney argued that the more completely we come to understand God's moral law the more fully we can obey it. But the critical issue is how we can attain a permanent sanctification wherein we consistently obey God's law.

The answer was for Christians to receive a subsequent baptism of the Holy Spirit. Drawing on a distinction he made in the 1830s between Christians who were and were not "filled" or "indwelt" by the Spirit,[17] Finney in 1841 began more precisely to link the baptism of the Spirit with holiness. This baptism of the Holy Spirit is received by faith, which is "a yielding up of our voluntary powers to the guidance, instruction, influences, and government of the Holy Spirit," a yielding "up the whole being to His influence and control."[18]

If at conversion the Spirit uses the cross to inform the reason and persuade the will, in the baptism of the Spirit the focus is on the sensibility. As Finney says, "One great thing that needs to be done, to confirm and settle the will in the attitude of entire consecration to God, is to bring about a counter development of the sensibility, so that it will not draw the will away from God. It needs to be mortified or crucified to the world. . . . This can easily be done through and by the Holy Spirit, who takes the

---

14. Ibid., 380.

15. Ibid.

16. Ibid., 381; see also Reeve, "Holiness and the Holy Spirit," 213.

17. Finney, *Systematic Theology*, 235.

18. Finney, *Promise of the Spirit,* 188.

things of Christ and shows them to us."[19] Thus, Finney argues, "The Baptism or sealing of the Holy Spirit subdues the power of the desires, and strengthens and confirms the will in resisting the impulse of desire, and in abiding permanently in a state of making the whole being an offering to God."[20]

In fact, for Finney, a number of fresh baptisms of the Spirit are necessary and desirable. John L. Gresham describes the process this way: "A time of intense desire and hunger and thirst for righteousness leads to a time of the soul being filled to overflowing with the Spirit." Gaining "a greater vision of God" and experiencing "deeper union with Christ," the believer is brought "into a higher level of Christian living." But after a time, the Christian will again "desire an even higher experience with God," leading to another baptism of the Spirit. For Finney, this process of "impulsive progression" will likely continue in heaven.[21]

The baptism of the Spirit is so closely connected to Christ that Gresham insists, "Finney's view of sanctification is decidedly christocentric";[22] Reeve argues that for Finney "the term baptism of the Holy Spirit did not draw one away from the role of the cross, rather towards it," because "the baptism of the Holy Spirit was the very thing which truly made the cross efficacious."[23] Indeed, Finney insists, "It is Christ . . . who secures our sanctification";[24] it is the Spirit that shows us our need for Christ and reveals Christ powerfully to the soul.

The concern for permanent sanctification and the turn to the power of the Holy Spirit as the means to subdue the sensible appetites creates, in Reeve's words, "an implicit tension between a growing awareness of a necessary work of divine power and cleansing in sanctification and the power of the human will."[25] At the root of that tension was Finney's growing recognition that only persuading the will, even when done by the Holy Spirit, was not enough for persons to become what God calls them to be. That takes divine power—the power of the cross and the power of the Spirit. As Finney came to qualify his optimism of nature, he began to

19. Finney, *Systematic Theology*, 413.

20. Finney, *Power from on High*, cited in Reeve, "Holiness and the Holy Spirit," 256.

21. Gresham, *Charles G. Finney's Doctrine*, 20; see also Reeve, "Holiness and the Holy Spirit," 253.

22. Gresham, *Charles G. Finney's Doctrine*, 36.

23. Reeve, "Holiness and the Holy Spirit," 249.

24. Finney, *Systematic Theology*, 411.

25. Reeve, "Holiness and the Holy Spirit," 319.

emphasize a more robust optimism of grace, bringing increased balance as well as tension to his theology.

The Higher Life

A second stream of holiness theology outside of Methodism was launched by Presbyterian William E. Boardman, whose widely read *The Christian Higher Life* (1858) put holiness teaching into non-Wesleyan categories. Boardman had read Finney and Mahon, been influenced by Methodist teachings, and attended Palmer's Tuesday meetings.[26] His irenic account of the promise of a fuller salvation was designed to transcend the differences between Oberlin and Wesleyan theologies, in the words of Bernie Van De Walle, by switching "the focus from the extent of sanctification to the content or means of sanctification."[27]

Boardman argued "that the sinner's necessities are two-fold and distinct":[28] they must be justified before God, and they "must also be holy in heart and life."[29] There is a need for a "second experience" distinct from the first, a "second conversion."[30] He did not insist this second conversion necessarily had to be subsequent from the first, nor that either the first or second had to be proceeded by a struggle with sin.[31] Like Phoebe Palmer, Boardman was not insisting on having a certain kind of experience but on its outcome. And for him that outcome was highly christocentric, nothing less than union with Christ. What is attained through this second conversion, he says, is "Christ. Christ in all his fullness. Christ as all in all. Christ objectively and subjectively received and trusted in. That is all. And that is enough."[32]

Through giving up our struggle to be holy and instead depending absolutely on Christ, along with believing Christ can and will act as promised, we place our souls in the hands of Christ, have a deeper union with Christ, and are shaped by Christ's power.[33] Then "By the power of

26. Dieter, *Holiness Revival*, 25.

27. Van De Walle, *Heart of the Gospel*, 74.

28. Boardman, *Higher Christian Life*, 51.

29. Ibid., 52.

30. Ibid., 47.

31. Ibid., 53.

32. Ibid., 58.

33. Ibid., 59.

God . . . a new starting point has been gained. A new and higher level has been reached, and from the new starting point the race becomes swifter and yet easier."[34]

That this "second conversion" is a starting point is absolutely central to Boardman's higher life theology. As was true for Palmer, it is more a beginning of a journey than its destination. But Boardman's description of the "second conversion" is quite different from Palmer's entire sanctification. This difference is made clear in the way Boardman compares justification and sanctification:

> Pardon is instantaneous, but cleansing from sin is a process of indefinite length. . . . In the second, as in the first, the apprehension of Christ as the way, is instantaneous, the difference being simply that in the first, the work of Christ is done the instant the soul believes, while in the second, the work of Christ remains yet to be done in the future after the soul believes. In the one the atonement has been made, and the moment it is accepted, the pardon is complete; in the other, although the righteousness of Christ is perfect in which the soul is to be clothed yet the work of . . . the unfolding of Christ to the heart . . . is a work of time and progress.[35]

Here, in this important passage, are the seeds that will make the higher life and Keswick tradition of holiness a distinct alternative to both the Wesleyan and Oberlin varieties.

Two points should be noted in Boardman's comparison. First, he most typically speaks of the first work of justification as pardon from sin, and only occasionally mentions regeneration or new birth. This is especially the case where he describes at length two classes of Christians, the first whose sins have been forgiven through the atonement, and who know Jesus as a far off Savior, and the second who know Jesus "as a present Saviour from the present power of sin."[36] In Wesley's terminology what Boardman describes as the "first conversion" is justification without a new birth; what he describes as the second sounds more like Wesley's new birth, which frees us from the power of sin and enables growth in sanctification, rather than Christian perfection.

This leads to the second point. While Boardman clearly intends the "second conversion" to be equivalent to Christian perfection and entire

34. Ibid., 60.

35. Ibid., 116–17.

36. Ibid., 269.

sanctification as understood by Wesleyans and Oberlin, his description is significantly different from both. What occurs in this second work is the clothing of the believer with the righteousness of Christ, followed by the gradual conforming of the believer's heart to that righteousness. We might say that sanctification is entire in Christ, but beginning in the heart and life of the believer.

Boardman links the work of Christ with the work of the Holy Spirit; "Strictly and literally," he says, "Jesus is our justification, sanctification and glorification; and the Holy Spirit is our justifier, sanctifier, and glorifier."[37] The Spirit is the actual power that works in us to prepare the heart, produce faith, and effect salvation; Jesus is the object of faith and the giver of the Spirit.[38]

Boardman calls this second work the baptism of the Holy Ghost, and links it to Pentecost.[39] Before the day of Pentecost, he says, the disciples "knew something of Jesus." But after "the apostle's second conversion" through the power of the Holy Spirit they now for the first time began "to know the love of Christ which passeth knowledge," and "to be filled with all the fullness of God." They also received power enabling them to be effective witnesses for Christ.[40]

Boardman's theology, along with that of the husband and wife team of Robert Pearsall and Hannah Whitall Smith, brought higher life teaching to England. There it gave birth to the Keswick movement, named for the location of the initial Convention for the Promotion of Holiness held in 1875. While there is no single Keswick theology of holiness, there are certain common emphases that make it distinct from both the Wesleyan and Oberlin traditions. Chief among these is their understanding of sin. Like Wesley and in contrast to Finney, they believe sin is an indwelling tendency or disposition of the heart. But in contrast to Wesley, they understand sanctification not as the elimination of indwelling sin but as victory over its influence in our lives. Their Reformed pessimism of nature qualifies their optimism of grace.

Thus for the Keswick movement, sanctification does not involve replacement of unholy tempers with holy tempers, as in Wesley, nor is it a conversion of the sensibility, as in Finney. "Sin," as Van De Walle puts

37. Ibid., 48–49.
38. Ibid., 98.
39. Ibid., 110, 237, 278.
40. Ibid., 111.

it, "is a resident, though still alien disposition. . . . Sanctification does not consist in a final state of separation—as either a present experience or a future aspiration—from this tendency to sin. The proclivity would always remain."[41]

The promise of holiness then does not entail cleansing from sin but victory over sin; in Wesleyan terms less a holiness of heart than a holiness of life. There is a fullness of the Holy Spirit through which, in the words of Evan Hopkins, "the flesh is . . . effectively countered by . . . the Holy Ghost within us, so that we can walk in the paths of continuous deliverance from it."[42]

Grace is not as transformative as it is for Wesley. From their more Reformed perspective, if indwelling sin no longer remains, then there would no longer be a need for grace, or to put it more starkly, for Christ. Wesley, of course, insists otherwise; holy tempers only remain within a relationship with Christ. But in the Keswick understanding, counteracting grace enables victory over sin while the persistence of sin insures the continued need for Christ.

As with Boardman, Keswick theology distinguishes sharply between justification and sanctification, and although both are received through faith, the first is through faith in Christ as our Savior, the second through Christ as our Holiness. Sanctification need not occur long after conversion, but it is ushered in through a crisis involving the surrender of self-will and consecration to God, moving from reliance on ourselves to dependence on Christ. And again as with Boardman, this crisis is a beginning; in Handley C. G. Moule's words, "Crisis with a view to a process."[43]

Keswick continues and perhaps deepens the christological emphasis found in Boardman. Thus Evan Hopkins can define sanctification as "*counter-action* in which the soul is delivered, and kept, and led from strength to strength only through the grace and mightiness of One who dwells within it, a sin-restraining and sin-conquering Saviour."[44] It is

---

41. Van De Walle, *Heart of the Gospel*, 78.

42. Hopkins, *Hidden Yet Possessed*, 63, cited in Bebbington, *Holiness in Nineteenth-Century England*, 83.

43. Quoted in Lees, "Effect on Individual Ministry," 180, cited in Bebbington, *Holiness in Nineteenth-Century England*, 81.

44. Quoted in Pollock, *Keswick Story*, 76, cited in Van De Walle, *Heart of the Gospel*, 79.

Christ, who through the Spirit dwells within us, that gives us the victory over our own sinful disposition.

John Gresham notes that, in addition to union with the risen Christ, Keswick also emphasized a union with the cross of Christ. According to Steven Barabas, whom Gresham cites, "Calvary, Keswick tells us, is God's answer to the whole problem of sin. . . . In the whole manner of man's salvation everything begins at the cross. . . . Man cannot become holy without the cross. The ground of the believer's sanctification is his identification with Christ in his death to sin."[45] Thus for Barabas, deliverance from sin has already taken place in the cross. The "cross is the ground" while "the Holy Spirit is the agent of our sanctification."[46]

Gresham finds this Keswick teaching theologically preferable to that of Finney, who only emphasized "the believer's present union with the resurrected Christ."[47] A Wesleyan perspective would assess it differently. Rather than seeing our sanctification as already accomplished on the cross and then gradually appropriated, a Wesleyan approach would understand Christ's death and resurrection as the triune God beginning a process of redemption that will only be fully accomplished with the advent of the coming new creation itself. That is, Reformed thinking tends to look back to the cross and see everything essentially completed in it; Wesleyan theology looks to the cross and resurrection as the hinge that both enables a new future and directs us to expectantly anticipate it both in the present and at the end.

It is the other christological strand, that of the indwelling Christ, that is at the heart of the distinctive sanctification theology of A. B. Simpson. A Presbyterian who ultimately founded the Christian and Missionary Alliance, Simpson operates within a Keswick framework while also drawing upon Wesleyan ideas.

Like Wesley, Simpson described sin as in the motive or intent of the heart, most especially lack of love for God and neighbor. While he agrees with Keswick that we can't ever be freed from this sinful nature in this life, he insisted, as Van De Walle puts it, "the power of the resurrected Christ would more than enable the believer to consider the sin nature a

45. Barabas, *So Great Salvation*, 94, cited in Gresham, *Charles G. Finney's Doctrine*, 72.

46. Barabas, *So Great Salvation*, 94, cited in Gresham, *Charles G. Finney's Doctrine*, 73.

47. Gresham, *Charles G. Finney's Doctrine*, 72.

vanquished foe and to behave as though it were."[48] Here is how Simpson describes this "Christ Life":

> . . . the resurrection of Christ is the power that sanctifies us. It enables us to count our old life, our former self, annihilated, so that we are no longer the same person in the eyes of God, or of ourselves; and we may with confidence repudiate ourselves and refuse either to obey or fear our former evil nature. Indeed, it is the risen Christ Himself who comes to dwell within us, and becomes in us the power of this new life and victorious obedience. It is not merely the fact of the resurrection, but the fellowship of the Risen One that brings us our victory and our power.[49]

This union with the risen Christ occurred through the work of the Holy Spirit, and was subsequent to justification.

In terms quite similar to Phoebe Palmer, Simpson held that the condition for receiving sanctification following awareness of our need and faith in Christ as Sanctifier, was consecration and faith: our fully yielding our lives to Christ and then believing or reckoning that Christ receives our consecration. We then begin to act in accordance with our faith. As with Boardman and the Keswick tradition, this is not an arrival but a starting point. Simpson insists, "We do not grow into sanctification. Christian progress really grows out of sanctification. There must be a definite and divine beginning before there can be wholesome growth."[50]

While Simpson's description of sanctification still falls short of the more thoroughgoing optimism of grace of a Wesley or Palmer, it remains an especially powerful vision of holiness. The indwelling of the risen Christ has intimations of heaven below, much as the presence of the Holy Spirit has for Wesley and Fletcher. It is a fitting culmination of the christological trajectory begun by Boardman four decades earlier.

The Finished Work

As children of the Holiness movement, Pentecostals were strongly committed to the promise of holiness. Where they differed was in not

---

48. Van De Walle, *Heart of the Gospel*, 97.

49. Simpson, *Self Life and the Christ Life*, cited in Van De Walle, *Heart of the Gospel*, 97.

50. Simpson, *Earnests of the Coming Age*, 20–21, cited in Van De Walle, *Heart of the Gospel*, 98–99.

identifying the baptism of the Holy Spirit with entire sanctification. Following the lead of fire-baptized holiness adherents, early Pentecostals understood Spirit baptism as a distinct third work of God, subsequent to sanctification, which endued the recipient with power for ministry and mission. We shall have more to say on power and its relationship with holiness in chapter 8.

For the first decade after the emergence of Pentecostalism, founding theologians like Charles Parham and William Seymour had considered themselves faithful Wesleyans with regard to sanctification, understanding it out of the tradition begun by Phoebe Palmer. But in 1910 a new teaching on sanctification would rock the young movement, dividing it theologically and ultimately bringing over half of American Pentecostals into its ranks. That new teaching—the finished work of Calvary—was developed and vigorously proclaimed by William H. Durham.

Durham was deeply concerned about the spiritual state of the church. Mainline churches, under the influence of liberal theology, were failing to proclaim the gospel of salvation. Conservatives (soon to be termed fundamentalists) preached salvation but joined with liberals in denying the miraculous work of God in the present day. Thus people seeking the power of God turned to movements like New Thought, Christian Science, and Theosophy.[51]

This spiritual vacuum could have been filled by the Holiness movement, Durham argues, but they were prevented from doing so by their two-stage understanding of salvation that separated justification from sanctification. This theology created doubts in believers about whether or not they were actually sanctified, and inevitably led to a kind of external legalism to gain divine approval and assurance.[52] Pentecostalism was raised up by God to be a witness to the present power of God; however it too was compromised by the two-stage theory of salvation it had inherited from the Holiness movement. It was Durham's mission to purge from Pentecostalism this theological error and the spiritual anxiety it produced, freeing the movement to accomplish its God-ordained mission.[53]

Durham's theology of salvation, succinctly put, is this: "Identification with Jesus Christ saves and sanctifies, no second work of grace [is]

---

51. Jacobsen, *Thinking in the Spirit*, 142–44.

52. Ibid., 144–45.

53. Ibid., 151–53.

taught [by Scripture] or necessary."[54] Specifically, that identification is with the cross of Christ. When we trust in Christ and his cross, we are not partly saved but fully, not just outwardly but inwardly; we are both justified and fully sanctified. This shifts attention away from whether or not one has had a genuine sanctifying experience and toward the cross of Christ itself. By placing our faith there, in what Christ has done, we are freed from spiritual anxiety.

While rejecting the two-stage theology of the Holiness movement, Durham continued to maintain a distinctively Wesleyan understanding of the content of sanctification. Thus he argues, "In conversion we come into Christ, our Sanctifier, and are made holy, as well as righteous. When one comes into Christ he is as much in Christ as he will ever be. He is in a state of holiness and righteousness. . . . If he keeps there he will continue to be holy and righteous."[55] This sounds much like Phoebe Palmer's understanding of ongoing faith and consecration, except that for Durham it begins with conversion. As for Wesley himself, Durham says he cannot "find where Wesley ever taught dogmatically that sanctification is and must be a second instantaneous work," and argues that in "A Plain Account of Christian Perfection" Wesley "admits one can come into a state of sanctification in the first work of grace, and also that it may be entered by a gradual process."[56] While this is a clear misreading of Wesley, it is notable that Durham offers no objection to Wesley's actual description of sanctification.

Indeed, Thomas Farkas and William Faupel both agree that Durham's finished work theology is a "radicalized Wesleyanism," a "single work perfectionism" in the words of Farkas.[57] What Durham means by sanctification is much like what Wesley and Palmer mean.

Yet there are echoes of Keswick theology here as well. Durham understands conversion and the subsequent Baptism of the Holy Spirit in the lives of believers as corresponding to Calvary and Pentecost in salvation

54. Durham, "Finished Work of Calvary," 1, cited in Faupel, *Everlasting Gospel*, 237.

55. Durham, "Sanctification," in Jacobsen, *Reader in Pentecostal Theology*, 84.

56. Ibid., 83.

57. Faupel, "William H. Durham," 242. This aspect of Durham's theology had echoes of the teaching of Count Ludwig von Zinzendorf, which Wesley had so strongly rejected. This similarity was not missed by Pentecostal critics such as J. H. King: "We hear the cry of 'finished work' throughout the world. . . . It is Antinomianism, Darbyism dressed up in a Zinzindorfian garb . . . doing its old destructive work among believers" (*From Passover to Pentecost*, 85).

history. His focus on the cross and our identification with Christ is much like the account of Keswick theology by Steven Barabas cited earlier. In addition, like Keswick, Durham rejected the Holiness teaching that sin is eradicated in entire sanctification; for him, as for Keswick, that would imply the believer no longer needs Christ. "It is a sad mistake," he warned, "to believe that any one, or even two experiences . . . can ever remove the necessity of maintaining a helpless continual dependence on Jesus Christ, and bearing our daily cross, and living the overcoming life."[58] Neither Wesley nor Palmer, of course, taught that it did, but Durham is dealing here with what he understands to be the implications of the teachings of their descendents. Instead Durham held that, in the words of Faupel, "like an alcoholic, forever addicted, the Christian could live an overcoming life by surrendering to the higher power now dwelling within."[59]

It is the idea of sanctification as a "finished work" that sets Durham most at odds with Wesley. Durham intended for his theology to counter the spiritual anxiety and legalism he believed the two-stage understanding produced. But claiming sanctification as a finished work would in Wesley's mind raise the specter of an antinomianism wherein we do not need to be actually sanctified ourselves since we are identified with Christ's sanctification. This was not what Durham intended, but it was a central concern of his Pentecostal critics who continued to hold to entire sanctification as a second work of grace.

In the end, those who followed Durham abandoned his radicalized Wesleyanism for a more standard variant of Keswick teaching, and with it a diminishing of his optimism of grace. There is in Durham's theology a robust anticipation of heaven below, expressed in explicitly eschatological terms. "A believer," he says, "is in the Kingdom of Jesus Christ. . . . It is in conversion that a man receives Jesus Christ, the glorious Son of God, and is made a new creature in Him, and old things pass away and all things become new."[60] It is this expectation of a present new creation in the hearts and lives of believers that for all their differences links Durham to the Wesleyan vision.

John Wesley typically spoke of salvation in Trinitarian terms: justification is what God has done for us in Christ, and sanctification is what God does in us through the Spirit. While not losing the agency of the

58. Durham, "Sanctification," in Jacobsen, *Reader in Pentecostal Theology*, 84.

59. Faupel, "William H. Durham," 241.

60. Durham, "The Finished Work of Calvary—It Makes Plain the Great Work of Redemption," cited in Jacobsen, *Reader in Pentecostal Theology*, 89.

Spirit, the non-Methodists clearly had a more christocentric approach to holiness. For Wesley sanctification had to do with our response to God's love in Christ through death on a cross, having the mind that was in Christ and walking as Christ walked, and having a continual communion with God. In the non-Methodist's expanded christology, Christ is understood as the agent as well as norm of sanctification. They did this in a variety of ways, from speaking of our identification with the crucified Christ and his cross to the indwelling of the risen Christ. The work of the Spirit in sanctification was to point to Christ, present Christ, or be the means for Christ to indwell hearts and lives.

Sometimes, as in the case of Boardman and the Keswick movement, their vision of the result of sanctification was less than Wesley's Christian perfection, and more about the life than the heart; others such as Finney and Durham came closer to Wesley's own vision of holiness. But in all of these we see the same kind of expectant faith and hope in God's promises for this present age that drove Wesley's own optimism of grace and eager anticipation of heaven below.

CHAPTER 8

Holiness and Power

Holiness is power.

—PHOEBE PALMER[1]

The baptism with the Holy Ghost is a gift
of power upon the sanctified life . . .

—WILLIAM J. SEYMOUR[2]

WHEN JOHN FLETCHER LINKED Christian perfection with Pentecost, he made it inevitable that the relation of holiness to power would become a central theological concern of the Holiness movement. Jesus had, after all, promised his disciples that they would receive *power* to be his witnesses, and that this enduement of power would occur when the *Holy Spirit* would come upon them (Acts 1:8). If this Pentecostal baptism of the Spirit is understood not as simply a one-time historical event but something to be sought and expected in every Christian life, and its effect is entire sanctification, then how holiness and power are connected would necessarily force itself onto the theological agenda.

But within this concern is a second theological issue that would have radical implications for church and mission: *who* are the proper recipients of this Pentecostal blessing? The obvious answer is everyone who

1. Palmer, *Promise of the Father*, 206.

2. William J. Seymour, *The Apostolic Faith* 1:11 (October-January 1908), 2. The article is unsigned, but the doctrine and likely the words are Seymour's.

has faith in Jesus Christ. All are meant to be entirely sanctified, and all are meant to be witnesses. All, then, would receive power.

This expectation was dramatically different from the practice of the medieval church. There the body of Christians was divided into the "religious" and the laity. It was the former—those in religious orders or the priesthood—who, by being withdrawn from the everyday life of family and occupation, were able to live undistracted from God, and were thereby capable of holiness and empowered by God to fulfill their calling. The Protestant reformers strongly challenged this distinction, arguing that *all* Christians are called to follow Christ in and through their occupations and everyday lives. Pietism carried this further: with its emphasis on small, lay-led "colleges of piety," a host of social ministries, and sometimes on irregular lay preaching, the Pietist movement insisted that ordinary persons are also called by God into avenues of distinctively Christian ministry. It was this Pietist vision of widespread lay leadership and activity that in turn decisively shaped the Wesleyan movement.

Ordinary Christianity and Extraordinary Callings

John Wesley did not use "power" in the same way as it would be used by his Holiness and Pentecostal heirs. He quite often spoke of "the power of God" or "the power of the Holy Spirit," but this was largely his way of speaking about divine grace. He could also speak of "the power of sin" or "the power of the devil," formidable adversaries from a human perspective who should never be taken lightly, yet unable to stand before the power of God. Wesley comes closer to the later usage when he speaks of persons having the form of godliness but not the power. Here, however, his focus is more on the new birth as the beginning of sanctification than its culmination in Christian perfection, and it lacks the Pentecostal emphasis on power to witness.

That said, it's quite clear that the early Wesleyan movement on both sides of the Atlantic largely consisted of highly active and committed laity involved in a wide range of ministries of witnessing, nurturing, and meeting human needs. God calling laity into these ministries was God's way of renewing the church.

Much of this lay activity, considered unusual by the larger society, was for Wesley simply a recovery of primitive Christianity. In his 1744 Oxford sermon "Scriptural Christianity" Wesley took as his text Acts

4:31, "And they were all filled with the Holy Ghost," which he notes also describes what happened on the day of Pentecost in Acts 2.[3] The purpose of being filled with the Spirit in these chapters, Wesley argues, was not to impart gifts but fruits of the Spirit: "To fill them with 'love, joy, peace, long-suffering, gentleness, goodness' . . . to enable them to 'crucify the flesh with its affections and lusts', its passions and desires; and in consequence of that *inward change*, to fulfill all *outward* righteousness, 'to walk as Christ also walked', in the 'work of faith, the patience of hope, the labour of love.'"[4] Then follows a description of early Christianity, focused on love for God that necessarily leads to love of neighbor, a love that not only abstains "from doing evil" but is "athirst to do good."[5] "Such was Christianity in its rise," Wesley concludes. "Such was a Christian in ancient days."[6] This Christianity then spread, through word and deed. But soon tares appeared among the wheat, corrupting the church and leading God to raise up in each generation witnesses to true Christianity.[7]

As Wesley makes clear in his concluding application, what is considered normal Christianity in England is by apostolic standards hardly Christianity at all. He asks "Where does the Christianity now exist? Where, I pray, do the Christians live? Which is the country, the inhabitants whereof are 'all (thus) filled with the Holy Ghost'? . . . who one and all have the love of God filling their hearts, and constraining them to love their neighbor as themselves? . . . why then, let us confess we have never yet seen a Christian country upon earth."[8] In exhorting the faculty in particular concerning their formation of students, he makes clear that he is not calling for something extraordinary: "Let it not be said that I speak here as if all under your care were intended to be clergymen. Not so; I only speak as if they were all intended to be Christians."[9]

At the heart of Wesley's vision of a renewed church are Christians whose hearts have been renewed in love by the Holy Spirit, who have a new disposition, new motivations and desires, and new vision, and who therefore actively seek to live out that love through sharing the gospel and

---

3. John Wesley, "Scriptural Christianity" 1, *Wesley's Works* 1:159.

4. Ibid., 4, 1:160–61.

5. Ibid., I.9, 1:164.

6. Ibid., I.10, 1:165.

7. Ibid., II.9, 1:169.

8. Ibid., IV.1, 1:173.

9. Ibid., IV.7, 1:176.

caring for human need. This was also the core of the Methodist discipline of doing no harm, doing good to the bodies and souls of others, and attending the ordinances of God. As we have seen, these rules of discipline are ways to keep both awakened sinners and Christians growing in sanctification focused on God and neighbor, and open and receptive to the work of the Spirit in their lives. As they love, God at the same time enables their growth in love. The result is a movement in which Methodists take initiative to reach out to their neighbors, even as they daily seek God in prayer, not as something "extra" but as part of an ordinary, joyful Christian life.

Thomas Fildes was one of those ordinary Christians among Wesley's Methodists. Fildes was a grocer in Manchester and a member of the Methodist Society there. By the late 1700s Manchester had grown from a market town of two thousand residents at the beginning of the century to a hundred thousand as persons flocked to the city to work in the cotton industry. There they lived in hastily built dwellings, many below ground with raw sewage running in ditches outside their only open window. Poverty and disease were widespread.[10]

Fildes helped organize the Strangers' Friends Society in 1791 to locate and care for these working poor. In recounting the work of the Society, Steve Rankin notes that they "raised money to provide clean bedding, food, medicine and sometimes larger items like furniture for people suffering these afflictions. They also shared the Gospel with the people they visited, combining attempts to tend to both material and spiritual needs."[11]

Rankin argues that the story of Methodists like Fildes provides at least implicit evidence for the "link Wesley makes between the change that the Holy Spirit works in the hearts of believers and the love they demonstrate in practical ways toward their neighbors."[12] In other words, there is in Wesleyanism an intrinsic link between doctrine and life: the doctrine of Christian perfection "promises and describes the life of God in the human soul," and the "evidence of the reality of God's love in the believer's heart was the practical and tangible expression of love for the neighbor (and even the enemy)."[13] It is this love that motivates and directs

10. Rankin, "People Called Methodists," 40–41

11. Ibid., 41.

12. Ibid., 38.

13. Ibid., 40.

persons like Fildes, a love in response to and shaped by God's love in Christ, enabling him and others to seek out persons he might otherwise never meet in order to share good news and alleviate suffering.

The initiative shown by Methodists like Fildes was often a challenge to the larger society with its hierarchy of social ranks and roles. In fulfilling their beliefs about what Christ commands and the motivations of their hearts, Methodists would take on public roles at odds with societal norms. One notable example is his encouraging and enabling ordinary men and women to keep spiritual journals, write spiritual correspondence, give public testimony, and even preach. As Vicki Tolar Burton argues, Wesley did so "because he understood the powerful role of language in spiritual formation." Thus Wesley became "a powerful and successful sponsor of literacy and rhetoric for the laboring classes and for women. By encouraging marginalized people to read, write, and speak publicly about the life of the spirit, Wesley transformed the nature of public discourse in England."[14] This means of witnessing and spiritual nurture became embedded in early Methodism on both sides of the Atlantic, and would be continued and expanded by both the Holiness and Pentecostal movements.

But in addition to what we might today term a calling of all Christians to active discipleship, Wesley also insisted that God issued extraordinary callings, especially at pivotal points in the history of the church. Such was his own calling to lead the Methodist movement, and such was the calling of the lay preachers in his connection.

Wesley could cite biblical precedent for such a distinction. First, he argued that originally, in the Old Testament, the offices of priest and prophet (or preacher) were separate, as were the offices of pastor and evangelist in the New Testament. It was not until "that evil hour" when Emperor Constantine became a Christian that the two offices were combined.[15] Thus, in having unordained preachers without sacramental authority, Wesley's movement is in part a recovery of the primitive model.

But a second distinction is just as crucial. Wesley argues that while ordinary prophets "were those who were educated in the 'schools of the prophets,'" extraordinary prophets such as Nathan, Isaiah, and Jeremiah were those "on whom the Holy Ghost came in an extraordinary manner."[16]

---

14. Burton, *Spiritual Literacy*, 1.

15. John Wesley, "Prophets and Priests" 8, *Wesley's Works* 4:77.

16. Ibid., 6, 4:76–77.

In like manner his preachers were "extraordinary messengers," directly called and empowered by God to proclaim the gospel of salvation.

Yet while drawing on precedent, Wesley nonetheless believed there was also something unprecedented about his Methodists: "Ye are a new phenomenon in the earth,—a body of people who, being of no sect or party, are friends to all parties, and endeavor to forward all in heart-religion, in the knowledge and love of God and man."[17] Their accountability was to God and to the Methodist connection God had raised up; their obligation was to preach the doctrine and enforce the discipline of Methodism.

Wesley's preachers came from among the common people rather than the educated classes. As Adrian Burdon describes them, they were usually "uncomplicated artisans who had been enlivened and empowered by a sense of the presence of the living God acting in their lives."[18] The irregularity of such persons preaching led to ridicule and often hostility, especially from those higher in the social order.

This same pattern characterized the early Methodist preachers in America. They were, says John Wigger, "cut from the same fabric as their predominantly middling and artisan audiences," giving them "the advantage of a natural social affinity with their listeners."[19] Francis Asbury, their Bishop, was himself a former blacksmith. The leaders of the German speaking Methodistic groups were similar: while William Otterbein was ordained, Martin Boehm was a farmer-preacher and Jacob Albright had been a farmer and tilemaker.

It was in 1741 that Wesley, at his mother's urging, changed his mind and came to acknowledge the extraordinary call of Thomas Maxfield to preach. But overcoming this initial reticence concerning male lay preachers was relatively easy compared to his accepting that God might also be calling women to preach. Wesley had always recognized the gifts of women as spiritual leaders, appointing them to lead classes and encouraging their public testimony and prayer. But in 1761, Sarah Crosby, who had expected to lead a society meeting of some thirty people, found herself facing two hundred. As Crosby recorded it, "I was not sure whether it was right for me to exhort in so public a manner, and yet I saw it impracticable to meet all these people by way of speaking to each individual. I,

17. Ibid., 18, 4:82.

18. Burdon, *Authority and Order*, 28.

19. Wigger, *Taking Heaven by Storm*, 49.

therefore, gave out a hymn, and prayed, and told them part of what the Lord had done for myself, persuading them to flee from all sin."[20] This was very close to preaching, and she immediately reported it to Wesley. "I think you have not gone too far," he responded, and "you could not well do less." He advised her to tell the people, "You lay me under a great difficulty. The Methodists do not allow of women preachers; neither do I take upon me any such character. But I will just nakedly tell you what is in my heart."[21]

It was a decade later that Mary Bosanquet wrote Wesley with a defense of women's preaching as an extraordinary call. Noting that many acknowledge that a woman can speak publicly on occasion, "if under a peculiar impulse, but never else," Bonsanquet asks, "But how often is she to feel this impulse? Perhaps you will say, two or three times in her life; perhaps *God* will say, two or three times in a week, or day—and where shall we find the Rule for this?"[22]

Wesley's response was a full-scale endorsement of women as lay preachers in Methodism: "I think the strength of the cause rests there, on your having an *Extraordinary Call*. So, I am persuaded, has every one of our Lay Preachers. . . . It is plain to me that the whole Work of God termed Methodism is an extraordinary dispensation of His Providence. Therefore I do not wonder if several things occur therein which do not fall under ordinary rules of discipline."[23] While far from endorsing women as ordained priests, Wesley opens the way for women to peach under the auspices of Methodism. Wesley did not appoint women to circuits, but did develop the practice of providing some with letters of endorsement that would open Methodist doors and pulpits to their ministry. The result was the remarkable preaching ministries of Crosby, Bosanquet Fletcher,

20. *Arminian Magazine* 29:518, cited in Chilcote, *Wesley and the Women Preachers*, 121.

21. John Wesley, *Letters*, 4:133, cited in Chilcote, *Wesley and the Women Preachers*, 122. Is Wesley telling Sarah Crosby to preach? Earl Kent Brown interprets Wesley's advice to mean she could give testimony and exhortation but not preach in the technical sense of taking a passage of Scripture, dividing it into parts, and speaking on each part (*Women of Mr. Wesley's Methodism*, 26). Chilcote does not believe Wesley is here prohibiting her preaching "in a more formal sense" (*Wesley and the Women Preachers*, 136 n. 22).

22. "Appendix D: Mary Bonsanquet Letter to John Wesley, June, 1771," in Chilcote, *Wesley and the Women Preachers*, 301.

23. *Methodist Archives*, cited in Chilcote, *Wesley and the Women Preachers*, 143.

and dozens more, until an increasingly middle-class British Methodism revoked its approval in 1803.

Holiness Is Power

Methodism after Wesley became increasingly unwelcome to women preachers. Certainly the first generation of women continued their ministries, regardless of official approval, with Mary Fletcher continuing to preach until her death in 1815. In America, Methodism was initially a dynamic, decentralized movement, where women served as class leaders, exhorters (most often unlicensed), and even as unlicensed preachers. But by the second and third decades of the nineteenth century, Methodism became more institutionalized, more middle class, and less hospitable to women as evangelists and even class leaders.[24] This did not mean women were less active, but that they were increasingly marginalized from formal and even informal leadership roles.

Yet the seeds had already been planted for a more theologically robust defense of women's preaching, one that would have implications not only for male preaching as well, but for the broader theme of holiness and power. As we have seen, Wesley made reference to the early chapters in Acts to defend the extraordinary calling of his lay preachers. John Fletcher, responding to a 1776 letter from Joseph Benson concerning the exposition of Scripture by women in the societies, said he would neither encourage nor dissuade women from doing it. He argued that God is not bound by gender, and in Acts 2:18 "handmaidens" were mentioned as receiving the gift of prophesying along with men.[25] A year or two later, in a letter to Mary Bosanquet, Fletcher referred to "the glory of the promise made to the daughters and handmaids, as well as to the sons and servants of the Lord."[26] By the time Fletcher married Mary Bosanquet in 1781, he fully supported her preaching ministry. Mary Fletcher herself referred to Acts 1–2 as a scriptural basis for her preaching.[27]

The full development of this Pentecostal argument for women preaching was Phoebe Palmer's *Promise of the Father* (1859). There she asks, "Has not a gift of power, delegated to the church on the day of

24. Wigger, *Taking Heaven by Storm*, 164, 171–72.
25. Streiff, *Reluctant Saint*, 234.
26. Chilcote, *Wesley and the Women Preachers*, 170.
27. Stanley, *Holy Boldness*, 57.

Pentecost, been neglected?"[28] On that day *all*—male and female—were filled with the Holy Spirit and spoke as the Spirit gave utterance. Yet now the church restricts this endowment of power to men. "Who can tell," she asks, "how wonderful the achievements of the cross might have been, if this gift of prophecy, in woman, had continued in use as in apostolic days?"[29] Would it not "have hastened the latter-day glory?"[30]

Furthermore, this gift of prophecy was not for the apostles alone: "No," she says, "they had a laity for the times." "Impelled by the indwelling power within" and dispersed by persecution, "these Spirit-baptized men and women . . . made all their scatterings the occasion of preaching the gospel everywhere . . ."[31] This "theology of the laity," as Harold Raser calls it, insisted God would empower all Christians to carry out the mission of the church as God did in the apostolic church, enabling the gospel to be spread throughout the world.[32]

Throughout the book Palmer described the "full baptism of the Spirit" as both entirely sanctifying and empowering. Indeed, "Holiness is power,"[33] she argued, such that the recipients of entire sanctification often find themselves compelled to speak in praise and testimony. Some, especially women, refrain out of fear, and as a result lose their full sanctification. But many others obey the urging of the Spirit and give public testimony to what God has done, and this often in turn propels them into public ministry.

The reason Palmer and so many others found holiness empowering was because it was at its heart a gift of love. Holiness of heart, Wesley insisted, is made manifest in holiness of life. To receive the gift of entire sanctification intrinsically calls for both praise to the Giver, and testimony to what God has done. Love for one's neighbor necessarily entails the motivation and desire to share this good news with others, as well as minister to their bodily needs. This might lead a farmer, or cobbler, or blacksmith to cross social boundaries. For a woman, or an African American, it almost certainly required acting contrary to societal norms.

28. Palmer, *Promise of the Father*, 14.

29. Ibid., 23.

30. Ibid., 69.

31. Ibid., 23–24.

32. Raser, *Phoebe Palmer*, 92–93.

33. Palmer, *Promise of the Father*, 206.

Public testimony could not only be the result of entire sanctification, it could also be a precondition for receiving it. Consider the case of Osie M. Fitzgerald, a Presbyterian woman who sought entire sanctification at a Methodist Episcopal Church in 1856. The Spirit led her to consecrate her children, husband, and property to the Lord. But then "the Spirit said, 'If I give you a clean heart, and sanctify you wholly will you speak before this people and tell them what I have done for you?'" As one brought up Presbyterian, Fitzgerald said, "I was very much opposed to women speaking in the church. I thought no one but a bold Methodist woman would speak in church." She resisted the Spirit, until finally she reluctantly agreed: "Yes, Lord, though it be before a thousand people." Immediately she received entire sanctification.[34]

For both men and women in the Holiness movement, as Susie Stanley argues, the sanctified self *is* the empowered self. Sanctification entails the death of the old self and the rising of a new self, being freed from sin and becoming governed by love. The result for women was dramatic. As Stanley notes, for holiness women preachers "What died was the sinful or carnal self, which was replaced by the sanctified self, a self empowered to contest cultural expectations based on sex and race. Sanctification resulted in a new construction of the self, a self no longer plagued by self-doubt or fear."[35] Or, as Estrelda Alexander put it, for African American women preachers "sanctification gave them the courage to pursue their perceived calling without the need to be accepted by those who could not see beyond their dark skin and their female-gendered bodies."[36]

Phoebe Palmer and her Holiness colleagues had ample evidence for the empowering effects of entire sanctification. But by the end of the century, others would raise questions about this way of linking holiness and power. On both exegetical and experiential grounds they will argue that holiness and power are distinct, and at the same time conceive of the baptism of the Spirit as a more radical form of empowerment for mission than had been envisioned.

34. Hardesty, *Your Daughters Shall Prophesy*, 91–92.

35. Stanley, *Holy Boldness*, 85.

36. Alexander, "Conversion and Sanctification," 86–87.

Power Rests on the Sanctified Life

As Donald Dayton has shown, as early as 1856 a letter writer identified as "J. D." asked in the *Guide to Holiness* if one might be entirely sanctified yet still lack a "fullness of the Spirit."[37] In 1879 Methodist Asbury Lowrey made a stronger argument for making a distinction between them, describing sanctification as "renovating" and the baptism of the Spirit as "qualifying"; the "first purges and refines, the second empowers." If Christ was holy his entire life, he asked, why then did he seek and receive "the baptism of the Spirit"?[38]

This exegetical concern spoke to those in the late nineteenth-century Holiness movement for whom entire sanctification did not seem especially empowering, or at least not empowering enough. It also occurred when large segments of the movement had shifted eschatologically from postmillennialism to premillennialism, imbuing them with a missional urgency to proclaim the gospel to all nations. Accompanying this new urgency was heightened expectancy: God would endow this last-days mission with supernatural power and manifestations as in apostolic times; some even thought that gifts of the Spirit would be fully restored.

While this missional urgency and last days expectancy impacted the Holiness mainstream, it was determinative for the spirituality of the radical wing of the movement. Two key figures in that wing—Benjamin H. Irwin and R. C. Horner—promoted a "three-blessing" theology in which the baptism of the Holy Spirit was distinct from and subsequent to entire sanctification.

Irwin was a Baptist pastor who, after experiencing entire sanctification in 1891, read deeply in the writings of Wesley and Fletcher and became an evangelist for the Wesleyan Methodist Church. Reading Fletcher's language about many baptisms or effusions of the Spirit, as well as references by some more contemporary holiness writers to a "fire baptism," led Irwin to believe there was a third blessing subsequent to entire sanctification. In 1895 he experienced what he called a "baptism of fire," and began to actively promote a three-blessing theology.[39]

37. Dayton, *Theological Roots*, 95.

38. Lowrey, "Is the Baptism of the Holy Ghost a Third Blessing?" 47, cited in Dayton, *Theological Roots*, 96.

39. See the accounts in Synan, *Holiness-Pentecostal Tradition*, 51–54, and Stephens, *Fire Spreads*, 179–81.

While Irwin left few writings, more is known of Horner's theology. The substance of Horner's teaching was anticipated by that of Methodist Simon P. Jacobs. Arguing that purity of heart was found in believers in both Old and New Testaments, and that Jesus was certainly pure in heart prior to his own baptism of the Spirit, Pentecost could not have been an event of entire sanctification. "Therefore," Jacobs concluded, ". . . the baptism of the Holy Ghost and perfect heart-purity are neither identical nor inseparably connected. It follows then that one being cleansed from all sin (I John 1:7) is not thereby necessarily baptized with the Holy Ghost."[40]

Horner, a Canadian Holiness evangelist deeply schooled in Wesley's theology, came to conclusions quite similar to Jacobs', conclusions which also strongly resonated with his own experience. For Horner, entire sanctification was not empowering so much as it made him hunger for more power; "perfect love," he said, "made me groan for power to reach the perishing masses and lead them to Jesus." This distinct baptism of the Spirit "brought all the dormant powers of my soul into activity and energized all my faculties for efficiency in the vineyard of the Lord."[41]

Pentecostalism in North America was born out of this radical holiness ethos, and its earliest theological expression was the work of Charles F. Parham. Briefly a Methodist pastor, Parham became an independent evangelist with a healing ministry. He was deeply impressed by Irwin's three-blessing theology and by the premillinnial urgency of world evangelism in these last days. He also shared the expectancy that God would do some further dramatic work that would enable the gospel to be preached to the nations before the return of Christ.

In the summer of 1900 Parham decided to visit three prominent ministries that emphasized healing and other manifestations of the Spirit: the mainstream Holiness ministry of A. B. Simpson in Nyack, New York, and the more eccentric ministries of Alexander Dowie in Chicago and Frank Sandford in Shiloh, Maine. It was Sandford's ministry that had the greatest impact on Parham's emerging theology. At the beginning of 1900, Sandford reported "a real Pentecost" at Shiloh,[42] in which gifts of the Spirit, including the gift of speaking in tongues, were manifested. At

40. S. P. Jacobs, "Receiving the Holy Ghost," *Canadian Methodist and Holiness Era* 2 (September 13, 1893), 146, cited in Dayton, *Theological Roots*, 98.

41. Horner, *Ralph C. Horner, Evangelist*, 13–14, cited in Dayton, *Theological Roots*, 99.

42. Sandford, "Morning Lessons in the Classroom at the Bible School," 38, cited in McGee, *Miracles*, 73.

the time Sandford saw this, in Gary McGee's words, as "a momentous happening in the end times," although later Sandford would come to de-emphasize tongues.[43]

But Parham would not. Parham was also aware of the highly controversial testimony of Jenny Glassey, which Sandford had publicized, of receiving the ability to speak several African languages as a gift of God at a revival in Missouri.[44] For Parham these disparate events and theological currents formed a single, coherent picture of divine activity in these last days: Through the baptism of the Holy Spirit, received subsequent to entire sanctification, God would empower persons to carry the gospel to the ends of the earth, most especially by giving them the ability to speak in foreign tongues. The ability to speak in tongues would also be the evidence one had been baptized by the Spirit. (Later Pentecostals would, in contrast to Parham, consider the gift of foreign languages rare and heavenly languages the norm for speaking in tongues, but would continue his emphasis on tongues as the evidence of Spirit baptism.)

As a theologian, Parham was part of a long line of popular evangelicals who read the Bible straight, without mediation of creed or denominational tradition. While not abandoning what Wesley would have considered the essentials of Christian and Protestant orthodoxy, Parham did develop novel and eccentric ideas concerning history and eschatology, positions he advanced with absolute certainly but which had almost no impact on subsequent Pentecostal theology.[45] But his major theological contribution, his understanding of the baptism of the Spirit, has decisively shaped the movement from then to the present day. Even here, however, some of his specific ideas remained particular to his own theology.

For example, while Parham accepted the common Holiness understanding of sanctification, he expanded its definition in two distinct ways. First, he insisted it had an impact on bodily as well as spiritual health: "Sanctification is cleansing to make holy, and is an act of God's free grace. Sanctification begins in the inner man and reaches out until the soul is sanctified entirely; then comes sanctification of the body from

43. McGee, *Miracles*, 73. See also Stephens, *Fire Spreads*, 189. For a detailed account of Sandford's ministry, see Faupel, *Everlasting Gospel*, 136–58.

44. McGee, *Miracles*, 74.

45. See the account in Jacobsen, *Thinking in the Spirit*, 28ff. Leslie Callahan carefully examines these ideas, including their racialist dimensions, in "Redeemed or Destroyed."

all inbred disease, and from the inbred principle of disease."[46] Secondly, Parham believed that sanctified persons have a kind of psychic influence on others, their families, and even neighborhoods, such that persons "with whom we come in contact will feel a benign, a beneficial influence flowing out from us to them."[47] For Parham, sanctification has its own distinctive power impacting the lives of others.

While sanctification is the completion of the work of salvation, Parham considered it insufficient for ministry. Something more was needed. Thus Christians through the centuries have received "occasional anointing" to enable them to accomplish specific tasks. These anointings illumine the Scriptures and enable the recipient to be in "communication with the mind and will of God . . ."[48] Others, like John Wesley, enjoyed a more enduring "mighty anointing that abideth,"[49] which gave special power to their ministry and could for some include gifts of healing and casting out demons.[50]

These are not, however, the baptism of the Holy Spirit, with which they are often confused. Douglas Jacobsen notes two critical distinctions made by Parham. The first has to do with the "purpose and effect" of the baptism of the Spirit. It was not especially to give one additional power— many already had anointing by the Spirit enabling them to heal or cast out demons. The purpose of the baptism of the Spirit is, said Parham, "to take that life of yours and pour it out in service to your fellowman."[51] Thus it is a decisive, even radical redirection of life from self to sacrificial ministry for others.

The second thing that distinguishes the baptism of the Spirit from prior anointings was the evidence of speaking in other tongues. The central characteristic of the baptism of the Spirit was prophesying, whether in one's own tongue or another; "Pentecost," said Parham, "is power to witness."[52] But it was speaking in other tongues—which Parham un-

46. Parham, *The Everlasting Gospel*, cited in Jacobsen, *Reader in Pentecostal Theology*, 40.

47. Ibid., 39. See the discussion in Jacobsen, *Thinking in the Spirit*, 42.

48. Parham, *Everlasting Gospel*, cited in Jacobsen, *Reader in Pentecostal Theology*, 41–42.

49. Parham, *Kol Kare Bomidbar*, cited in Jacobsen, *Reader in Pentecostal Theology*, 37.

50. See discussion in Jacobsen, *Thinking in the Spirit*, 47.

51. Parham, *Everlasting Gospel*, cited in Jacobsen, *Thinking in the Spirit*, 47.

52. Parham, *Everlasting Gospel*, cited in Jacobsen, *Thinking in the Spirit*, 49.

derstood to be foreign languages—that connected Spirit baptism with proclaiming the gospel to all nations in the last days. While everyone baptized in the Spirit would speak in another tongue at that moment, for those called by God into mission that initial gift of tongues would develop into a full language. Thus, as Jacobsen succinctly puts it, "For Parham, the gift of tongues was an eschatological empowerment for mission."[53]

As was true for many Wesleyans, Parham's theology was forged by the interplay of exegesis and experience. His early thought on the baptism of the Spirit evidenced by missionary tongues was confirmed for him at his Bethel Bible School in Topeka, Kansas, when on January 1, 1901, Agnes Ozmond spoke in tongues, soon to be followed by the others. For the next several years Parham extended his Apostolic Faith movement from Kansas southward into Texas, forming churches and opening a new Bible school in Houston in 1905. At this point Parham's group was just one more small segment of the radical fringe of the Holiness movement. But that was soon to change, and the catalyst would be the other central figure in the emergence of Pentecostalism, William J. Seymour.

The son of former slaves, Seymour grew up in Louisiana, and then migrated north to Indianapolis where he was converted through Methodism. He experienced entire sanctification through D. S. Warner's Evening Light Saints, an interracial Holiness body that was precursor to the Church of God, Anderson, Indiana. A convinced premillennialist, Seymour then left this amillennial body, probably to attend Martin Wells Knapp's God's Bible School in Cincinnati, Ohio, before returning south as a Holiness evangelist.[54]

By 1905 he was in Houston, Texas, where he attended a small African American Holiness church pastored by Lucy Farrow. In 1905 she agreed to serve as governess for Charles Parham's family, and when she traveled with the Parhams on an evangelistic tour she left Seymour in charge of the church. When she returned she had experienced the baptism of the Spirit, and encouraged Seymour to attend the new Bible school Parham was starting in Houston. Although Seymour as an African American had to sit outside the door rather than be in the classroom with the white students, he was persuaded by Parham's argument that the baptism of the

53. Jacobsen, *Thinking in the Spirit,* 49.

54. The story of William J. Seymour's life before coming to Texas is sketchy at best. See the accounts in Robeck, *Azusa Street,* chapter 1; Sanders, *William Seymour;* Synan and Fox, *William J. Seymour;* and Faupel, *Everlasting Gospel,* 194–97.

Spirit is distinct from sanctification, is evidenced by tongues, and missional in purpose.

Seymour accepted the invitation to pastor an African American Holiness church in Los Angeles founded by Julia Hutchins, who was going on to the mission field. But his new message was not welcomed and, barred from that pulpit, began ministering to some of the church members in a Bible study at one of their homes. It was there in April, 1906, they experienced the baptism of the Spirit evidenced by speaking in tongues, and as crowds grew they moved their meeting to a deserted AME church at 312 Azusa Street. What followed was a massive three year revival that more than anything launched the Pentecostal movement.

Seymour's early theology was conveyed in the pages of *The Apostolic Faith*, published in Los Angeles from 1906 to 1908. Most of the articles are unsigned, and some were likely written by editor Clara Lum and others. But it is a fair supposition that what appeared in this periodical reflects Seymour's own beliefs at the time, and certainly the teaching of the Azusa Street mission.

Parham and Seymour fundamentally understood the baptism of the Spirit in the same way. Most importantly, both understood it as a gift of power upon the sanctified life, a statement found both in Parham's published work and repeatedly on the pages of Azusa's *The Apostolic Faith*.[55] On the most obvious level, Parham and Seymour are simply saying one must first be entirely sanctified before one can be baptized in the Spirit. But Seymour expands and deepens this theological claim in ways that Parham does not. While sharing Parham's eschatological urgency, Seymour gives attention to what the baptism of the Spirit means for the Christian life, and especially to how it enables both persons and churches not only to give a witness but to *be* a witness of God's love to the world. Seymour linked the Pentecostal baptism to Paul's discussion of gifts of the Spirit, of which speaking in tongues is one. These gifts are for building up the church as well as proclamation to the world.

More central to Seymour's concern is love. To say the baptism of the Spirit rests on the sanctified life is for him to say it is love that motivates and directs the exercise of power. But Spirit baptism is not only grounded in love, it also brings more love. "The Pentecostal Power," says *The*

55. See, for example, Parham, *Everlasting Gospel*, in Jacobsen, *Reader in Pentecostal Theology*, 41, and in *The Apostolic Faith* (Los Angeles): untitled article, I:6, 6; "Is it necessary to have hands laid on in order to receive the Holy Ghost?" I:11, 2; and in issues I:10, I:12, II:13 (all on p. 2).

Apostolic Faith, "when you sum it up, is just more of God's love. If it does not bring more love, it is simply a counterfeit."[56] Some have thought that this emphasis on love is in response to the harsh and bitter conflicts Seymour and his colleagues experienced first from Parham (who objected to Azusa's exuberant style of worship, tongues that seemed to him only gibberish, and failure to maintain racial separation), and then William Durham (who aggressively promoted his two-blessing theology). Seymour was not opposed to theological conflict, but much like the Pietists and Wesley believed differences should be debated in a loving spirit.

These conflicts, then, may be the reason Seymour began to deemphasize tongues as the evidence of Spirit baptism in favor of love. As *The Apostolic Faith* insisted, "Tongues are one of the signs that go with every baptized person, but it is not the real evidence of the baptism in everyday life. Your life must measure up with the fruits of the Spirit. If you get angry, or speak evil, or backbite, I care not how many tongues you may have, you have not the baptism with the Holy Spirit. You have lost your salvation."[57] Speaking in tongues is not evidence at all if empowerment is neither grounded in love nor has brought more love.

Love is not only a personal evidence, it also marks the community. "Pentecost," says *The Apostolic Faith,* "makes us love Jesus more and love our brothers more. It brings us all into one common family."[58] This vision of community was concretely modeled in the leadership at Azusa Street, in which the Credentials Committee that ordained ministers and commissioned missionaries was interracial and included both men and women. The baptism of the Spirit, Seymour believed, knits diverse people together as it did on the day of Pentecost, overcoming divisions of race, nationality, class and gender. The Azusa Street mission was a present-day manifestation of the kingdom of God, a taste of heaven below.

This understanding of Spirit baptism as an infilling of divine love was not limited to Azusa Street. Tony G. Moon has shown how in 1907 J. H. King of the Fire-Baptized Holiness Church described it as putting "more love in us for God and His people, and for the lost, than anything that has ever come to the world. . . . It fills us with unspeakable love for God and one another." In 1926 King, now leading the Pentecostal Holiness Church, argued against those who understood Spirit baptism as only

56. *The Apostolic Faith* (Los Angeles) II:13, 3.

57. Ibid., I:9, 2.

58. Ibid., II:13, 3.

about power, insisting it is also "the love of Jesus in us that He [has] for us."[59] Frank Macchia has found similar language in E. N. Bell, Stanley Frodsham, and Frank Ewart, among others, all with roots in the Assemblies of God tradition.[60]

In insisting the baptism of the Spirit is both grounded in and a deepening of love, Seymour is addressing an issue faced not only by Pentecostals and Charismatics, but by Pietist movements and religious awakenings more broadly. Contemporary Anglican Charismatic Tom Smail has helpfully posed the question as "The Love of Power or the Power of Love."[61] Smail's own critique is aimed at Third Wave Charismatics who have a two-blessing schema that identifies conversion with the cross and pardon, and the baptism of the Spirit with Pentecost and power. This way of thinking forgets that "the only power with which Jesus works is the power of that utterly self-giving love that was itself weak and helpless on Calvary."[62] "What heals," he argues, "is not esoteric techniques, or even special supernatural endowments as such; what heals is Calvary love."[63] If "some of us who have been charismatic leaders had been set on being filled with the love of God as we have on being filled with the power of God, the charismatic renewal would be a more unambiguous wholesome affair than it has sometimes been . . ." Smail argues that a two-stage Pentecostal model separates the cross from the Spirit, whereas his proposed Paschal model does not segregate "cross and Spirit, love and power" into "separate compartments," but holds them "together in the closest possible identity with each other."[64]

Certainly the Wesleys and Fletcher would join Smail in opposing the separation of cross and Spirit, even if their approach is more Trinitarian than Smail's strong christocentrism. What they would find missing in this Third Wave conversion/power schema is holiness, or love. The problem, using Parham's and Seymour's phrase, is that power is not resting on the sanctified life. Seymour would agree, avoiding separating love and power through strongly identifying Jesus and Calvary not only with

---

59. Moon, "J. H. King's, 'Expansive' Theology," 337–38.

60. Macchia, *Baptized in the Spirit*, 81–82.

61. Smail et al., *Love of Power or the Power of Love*, 26.

62. Ibid., 27.

63. Ibid., 28.

64. Ibid., 29.

sanctification but with the love he associates with the baptism of the Spirit.

Contemporary Pentecostal theologians have followed in the tradition of Wesley and Seymour. Steven J. Land reenvisions Pentecostal theology in explicitly Trinitarian terms, centering it on the God who is love. He argues that the "three dimensions of salvation"—justification, sanctification, and Spirit baptism—are "interrelated in a way analogous to the perichoretic Trinitarian relations," and "correspond to the resurrection, the cross and Pentecost."[65] Thus cross and Pentecost are not separate but necessarily integrated. Indeed for Land, love *is* the integrating center of the Christian life, a participation in the divine life. "To speak of power without the integrating center of love," Land warns, "is to run the risk of becoming a 'sounding brass and a tinkling cymbal' or worse to pursue justice to the letter while excluding mercy and humility born of whole-heartedness toward God."[66]

Pentecostal identity, then, is not a matter of power but of an apocalyptic spirituality that both yearns for and embodies the age to come, what Land terms "a passion for the kingdom." Drawing on Wesley, he conceives of this spirituality as consisting of "apocalyptic affections" such as gratitude, compassion, and courage, anticipating the kingdom even as they provide eschatological vision and impetus for mission.[67]

Amos Yong proposes a Pentecostal theology oriented around pneumatology but finding its thematic focus in christology. The metaphor of baptism of the Spirit is broadened in Yong's theology to include not only power to witness but also "to capture the dynamic and full experience of Christian salvation not only in dying with Christ but also in terms of being raised with him to do the things that he did. In this way the baptism of the Holy Spirit denotes Christian salvation, broadly considered, as nothing less than the gift of Jesus Christ himself to us in the totality of his Spirit-anointed life, death, and resurrection."[68] This "christologically directed and pneumatically driven soteriology" has both personal and cosmic aspects, including "the transformation of human beings into the

---

65. Land, *Pentecostal Spirituality*, 205.

66. Ibid., 203.

67. Ibid., 139–61.

68. Yong, *Spirit Poured Out on All Flesh*, 101. Yong further develops this line of argument in *Spirit of Love*.

image of God by the power of the Holy Spirit and the transformation of all creation into the new heaven and new earth by the triune God."[69]

Congruent with my own approach in this book, Yong emphasizes both the "already" and "not yet" aspects of salvation, and its redemptive promise for persons, families, ecclesial communities, materiality (including healing), society, and the cosmos.[70] The baptism of the Spirit is the first fruits of this eschatologically oriented salvation in persons' lives, both linking and encompassing Christian initiation, forgiveness, sanctification, and empowerment for mission.[71] In this way power cannot be conceived apart from Christ, holiness, or love.

A similarly broad interpretation of the baptism of the Spirit has been proposed by Frank Macchia. His concern is how to reconcile two biblical understandings of Spirit baptism: a more Pauline focus on soteriology, and a more Lukan charismatic emphasis on empowerment. He suggests that "a broader eschatological framework for Spirit baptism as a Trinitarian act" provides a way to do so. Correlating Pentecost with the kingdom of God, Macchia argues that "as a pneumatological concept, the kingdom is inaugurated and fulfilled as a 'Spirit baptism.' God's kingdom is not an oppressive rule but the reign of divine love. . . . [T]he highest description possible of the substance of Spirit baptism as an eschatological gift is that it functions as an outpouring of divine love. This is the final integration of the soteriological and the charismatic."[72]

In Land, Yong, and Macchia we see in different ways a strong desire to show the intrinsic interrelation of Christ and Spirit, cross and Pentecost, and love and power. Their theologies are contemporary, but their concerns are faithfully rooted in those of William Seymour and Azusa Street.

Strong and persuasive arguments can be and were made in support of holiness as power and power as resting on the sanctified life. While much can be said for these two historic ways of relating holiness and power both exegetically and experientially, what is critical is that both insisted holiness and power cannot be separated. Love must be the motivation, desire, direction, and purpose of empowerment if it is to be a means

69. Yong, *Spirit Poured Out on All Flesh*, 91.

70. Ibid., 91–98.

71. Ibid., 102.

72. Macchia, *Baptized in the Spirit*, 17.

of proclaiming and manifesting the kingdom of God in this age. This is a crucial Wesleyan insight that cannot be ignored without spiritual peril.

Although it is clear that holiness centered in love is a manifestation of heaven below, it is not so obvious that power is. After all, as Paul reminds us, gifts of the Spirit will cease in the age to come, while it is faith, hope, and love that are eternal (1 Cor 13). One could well argue that empowerment of the Spirit is a means to an end, the proclamation of the promise of heaven below rather than an instance of it. But this is to say too little. To receive power is to be touched and gifted by the power of God, to encounter in this age the life-giving presence of God. To be empowered is, in terms of this life, a foretaste of the power of the life to come, in which love is mutually and actively manifested in the redeemed community as it stands in the presence of God.

PART THREE

On Earth as It Is in Heaven

CHAPTER 9

The Presence of Transcendence

About three in the morning, as we were continuing
instant in prayer, the power of God came mightily
upon us, insomuch that many cried out for exceeding
joy, and many fell to the ground. As soon as we
recovered a little from that awe and amazement
at the presence of his Majesty, we broke out with one
voice, "We praise thee, O God; we acknowledge
thee to be the Lord."

—JOHN WESLEY[1]

Three days of fasting and prayer were set apart at
the Mission for more power in the meetings. The Lord
answered and souls were slain all about the altar the
second night. We have felt an increase of power every night.

—*THE APOSTOLIC FAITH* (LOS ANGELES)[2]

AMONG THE PROMISES OF the new heaven and the new earth is that we
shall be in the presence of God. Yet though one day we will see God face
to face, Paul reminds us, in this age we see God dimly, as through a mirror (1 Cor 13). This does not mean that God is not present, only that God
is present in less direct ways.

1. John Wesley, *Journal,* January 1, 1739, *Wesley's Works* 19:29.
2. *The Apostolic Faith* (Los Angeles) I:8, 2.

It is generally acknowledged by all Christians that God is omnipresent, real though unseen, and providentially involved in creation and history. But Scripture also points to distinctive and intense modes of God's presence as well: in a burning bush, a cloud, a pillar of fire, in the Holy of Holies, and in a still, small voice among others. Less direct yet still particular is God's presence in dreams and visions, or through angelic intermediaries. These are all modes of presence which can to some degree be sensed, even as they retain their mystery and transcendence.

The most direct presence of God is incarnational, in Jesus Christ, God with us. Yet even here, God is veiled in order to be unveiled; God's glory is revealed in a particular human life and in a human death, occurring with a particular culture and time. The Pentecostal presence of God in the Holy Spirit is unseen and universal, available in all times and places; sometimes sensible in terms of manifest presence and more often evident in terms of its effects.

Early Methodists, along with their Holiness and Pentecostal descendents, had a strong sense of God's presence in worship and in everyday life. It was sometimes mediated, sometimes manifested in their midst, and sometimes intensely personal, but always an anticipation of that day in which God is seen face to face.

Mediated Presence

According to Scripture, John Wesley insisted, "all who desire the grace of God are to wait for it in the means he hath ordained,"[3] that is, in the means of grace. He succinctly defines means of grace as "outward signs, words, or actions, ordained of God, and appointed for this end, to be the ordinary channels whereby they might convey to men, preventing, justifying, or sanctifying grace."[4] Means of grace included those instituted by Christ (prayer, searching the Scriptures, the Lord's Supper, fasting, and Christian perfection) as well as other prudential means which God chooses to use. These, as we noted in chapter 1, are works of piety that are directed to God. Also included by Wesley as means of grace are works of mercy, directed toward the neighbor. For Wesley, the use of means of grace was absolutely essential for growth in the Christian life.

---

3. John Wesley, "The Means of Grace" III.1, *Wesley's Works* 1:384.

4. Ibid., II.1, 381.

The reason for their indispensability is that they are where we encounter the presence of God. It is not that God is tied only to means of
grace, for God is free to act through any means or "by none at all."[5] We
use the means of grace because this is where God has promised to meet
us. Thus, Wesley advises, "the sure and general rule for all who groan for
the salvation of God is this,—whenever opportunity serves, use all the
means which God has ordained; for who knows in which God will meet
us with the grace that bringeth salvation?"[6] Grace as understood by Wesley is not something apart from God, given, so to speak, from a distance.
For Wesley grace most centrally refers to the presence and power of the
Holy Spirit.

It is no wonder, then, that Wesley was dissatisfied with debates
over whether grace is mediated through means or immediate apart from
means. He rejects the views of both Anglican critics who denied that
God works through immediate inspiration in the present as God did in
the apostolic age, and Moravian advocates of "stillness" who sought an
unmediated presence of God. In speaking particularly to his Anglican
opponents, Wesley insists that

> all inspiration, though by means, is immediate. Suppose, for
> instance, you are employed in private prayer, and God pours his
> love into your heart. God then acts *immediately* on your soul;
> and the love of him which you then experience is immediately
> breathed into you by the Holy Ghost as if you had lived seven-
> teen hundred years ago. Change the term: say, God then *assists*
> you to love him? Well, and is not this immediate assistance? Say,
> his Spirit *concurs* with yours. You gain no ground. It is immedi-
> ate concurrence, or none at all. God, a Spirit, acts upon your
> spirit.[7]

Wesley rejects a sort of practical deism in which it is acknowledged that
one day we will stand directly in the presence of God, but for now receive
the benefits of God at a distance. When you participate in means of grace
you are in the presence of God, no less real for its being mediated. It is a
genuine and immediate anticipation of the glory to come.

This understanding of mediated immediacy is most evident in the
Lord's Supper. The focus of the Eucharist for the Wesleys, says Lorna

5. Ibid., II.3, 382.

6. Ibid., V.3, 395.

7. John Wesley, *A Farther Appeal to Men of Reason and Religion* I.V/28, *Wesley's Works* 11:71–72.

Khoo, "is on the reality of a dynamic encounter with the presence of Christ."[8] Moreover, this "encounter can be experienced," touching not only "the five senses" but radically affecting "the lives of those who have experienced it."[9]

Who is encountered is Jesus Christ. John Calvin had argued that in the Lord's Supper the Holy Spirit so unites us with Christ that we are raised to heaven to partake of Christ's life. But for John Wesley, as Theodore Runyon observes, "*the direction is reversed.* Rather than our thoughts rising to heaven, *the Spirit brings Christ to us . . .*"[10] The emphasis for the Wesleys is on heaven below.

The agent through whom Christ is present in the sacrament is the Holy Spirit. Indeed, as Khoo says, "the Wesleys placed the Holy Spirit at the heart of the happening. Consecration is understood to take place by the direct, immediate action of the free Spirit of God descending upon the offerings of the elements and of the people. The dynamism of the event cannot be missed."[11] The Wesleys did not describe the presence of Christ in a way that located it purely in the bread and wine, but more in terms of an interaction between the Spirit and the communicants in which the latter are transformed by the former. As I have argued elsewhere, this encounter with Christ is facilitated by the nature of the Lord's Supper itself, which both depicts and enacts the identity of Christ. Thus the spiritual encounter is both immediate and mediated through signs, words, and actions that convey who Christ is.[12]

The work of the Holy Spirit in the Lord's Supper is multi-faceted, encompassing the enabling of remembrance (understood not as simply recalling to mind but through participation experiencing anew what God has both done and promised in Jesus Christ), and the giving of faith, sanctification, and assurance. Khoo describes all of this as a "divine intimacy," in which the Holy Spirit comes "alongside the struggling believer to inspire, encourage, correct, and lead,"[13] and I would add, transform. This intimate God also at times "breaks in" to the Lord's Supper in surprising ways. Khoo notes "there were phenomena involving sound and

8. Khoo, *Wesleyan Eucharistic Spirituality*, 56.

9. Ibid., 55.

10. Runyon, *New Creation*, 130; see also Khoo, *Wesleyan Eucharistic Spirituality*, 61.

11. Khoo, *Wesleyan Eucharistic Spirituality*, 98.

12. Knight, *Presence of God*.

13. Khoo, *Wesleyan Eucharistic Spirituality*, 196.

sight, physical healings that took place, lives were changed and people felt intensely the presence of Christ as they communicated." There was, then, an "openness and expectancy" among the Methodists as they came to the sacrament.[14]

This powerful sense of God's presence in the Lord's Supper was found among early Methodists on both sides of the Atlantic. Lester Ruth quotes American Methodists who spoke of the presence of the Lord in communion as being "powerfully felt" such that "almost every heart was melted into love," or of the Lord meeting "with us in Maraculous Manner, a time of refreshment from his presence." At times, Ruth adds, "the intense sensibility of God's presence led Methodists to experience what they called 'raptures' or 'ecstasies' of joy in the sacrament."[15] This was an especially striking confirmation of the sacramental presence of God.

A recent study by Chris E. W. Green has shown that the same sense of God's presence found in early Methodism marks the sacramental spirituality of early Pentecostals. The evidence for this from testimonies and accounts in a wide range of early Pentecostal publications is overwhelming. Participants in the Lord's Supper would at times shout, weep, dance, and speak in tongues, and healings commonly occurred. A participant in a Pentecostal Holiness communion service recalled that "during this time it seemed that I was about as near heaven as I have ever been. The real power of God was present."[16] William Durham, after presiding over a 1912 communion service in which the "power of the Holy Spirit" rested "so mightily upon them that they are speaking in tongues and singing in the Spirit much of the time, with the most blessed unity existing," marveled that "if we can have such fellowship and blessing here, what must Heaven be like?"[17]

Along with these intense experiences of God's presence, many early Pentecostals saw the Lord's Supper as an eschatological meal. Green notes that Alice Reynolds Flower echoes many in insisting, in Green's words, "that the Lord's Supper directs believers' attention to the *future*, as well as

14. Ibid., 197; see also 56–57.

15. Ruth, *Little Heaven Below*, 138.

16. *The Pentecostal Holiness Advocate* 1:45 (March 7, 1948), 6, cited in Green, *Pentecostal Theology of the Lord's Supper*, 125.

17. *Pentecostal Testimony* 2:1 (January 9, 1912), 13, cited in Green, *Pentecostal Theology of the Lord's Supper*, 138.

the past, bringing into the present-day experience of believers a 'taste' of the future messianic banquet."[18]

Green argues that, despite their memorialist language, in early Pentecostal "theology the Lord of the Supper is risen and through the Spirit makes himself present to the church, not least in the church's celebration of the Sacrament."[19] "The evidence indicates," he concludes, that "first generation Wesleyan-Holiness and Finished Work Pentecostals experienced these rites as 'sacred occasions', unique opportunities for the Spirit to work in the community. For them, they were moments in which heaven met earth and believers found themselves overwhelmed by God's real, active presence."[20]

For both early Methodists and early Pentecostals, what the Holy Spirit did in the lives of those at the Lord's Table, as well as the intensity of God's presence, is determined by the will of God. But the promise *that* God will meet us there was certain. If we come to the Lord's Supper with any degree of faith, they believed, however slight, we will encounter Christ through the Spirit. To participate in the Lord's Supper was a foretaste of heaven.

Manifest Presence

The mediated presence of God in the Lord's Supper and other means of grace was a central characteristic of both Wesley's Methodists and those in early America. But in America this sacramental sensibility waned after the Civil War in both mainline Methodism and in the rapidly growing Holiness movement. In the mainline a growing liberal theology pushed sacramental understanding in a Zwinglian direction, which was more compatible with modern post-enlightenment thought. Many in the Holiness movement began to emphasize unmediated immediacy, and greatly lessen the expectation of meeting God in means of grace such as the Lord's Supper. Sometimes this latter shift has been described as losing the balance between ecclesiology (and means of grace) and pneumatology. I would describe it as moving from one pneumatology to another, or more precisely, a narrowing of pneumatology, in which the expectancy to meet

18. *The Christian Evangel* 61 (October 3, 1914), 2, cited in Green, *Pentecostal Theology of the Lord's Supper*, 154.

19. Green, *Pentecostal Theology of the Lord's Supper*, 161.

20. Ibid., 178.

God in and through means of grace had been largely lost. What came to be emphasized was God's manifest presence.

This is not to say that the experience of the manifest presence of God is not Wesleyan. It has deep roots in the eighteenth-century awakening and in pietism. The "Moravian Pentecost" of 1727 (which occurred in the context of a communion service) and the revivals at Jonathan Edwards' church in Northampton in 1734 were marked by this more directly felt presence of God, as would be Wesley's own ministry throughout his life. What is common in all these accounts is a communal sense of the presence of God in an unusually intense manner, often accompanied by persons crying out, praising God, and most dramatically falling to the ground.

Wesley provides numerous accounts of this in his *Journal*. For example, here is one from 1739, early in his ministry while he was preaching at Newgate: "Immediately one, and another, and another sunk to the earth: They dropped on every side as thunderstruck. One of them cried aloud. We besought God on her behalf, and he turned her heaviness into joy. A second being in the same agony, we called upon God for her also: and he spoke peace unto her soul . . ."[21]

George Whitefield raised objections to what he saw as Wesley's encouraging these manifestations. Talking with Whitefield, Wesley "found his objections were chiefly grounded on gross misrepresentation of fact. But the next day he had an opportunity of informing himself better: For no sooner had he begun . . . to invite all sinners to believe in Christ, then four persons sunk down close to him, almost in the same moment. One of them lay without sense or motion. A second trembled exceedingly. The third had strong convulsions all over his body, but made no noise, unless by groans. The fourth, equally convulsed, called upon God, with strong cries and tears."[22] Wesley concludes: "From this time, I trust, we shall all suffer God to carry on his own work in the way that pleaseth him."[23]

While perhaps less frequent, the same phenomena was not uncommon in Wesley's later ministry. In 1784 he records that "after preaching to an earnest congregation at Coleford, I met the Society. They contained themselves pretty well during the exhortation, but when I began to pray the flame broke out; many cried aloud; many sunk to the ground; many

---

21. John Wesley, *Journal*, April 26, 1739, *Wesley's Works* 19:51.

22. Ibid., July 7, 1739, 19:78–79.

23. Ibid., 19:79.

trembled exceedingly; but all seemed to be quite athirst for God and penetrated by the presence of his power."[24]

Although field preaching was one occasion of this intense presence of God, the locus was often in classes, bands, and love feasts, referred to by some as "experience meetings." As Ann Taves notes, this set Methodists apart from the Reformed tradition, for which "Hymns were sung in church and piety was practiced in private." In these meetings, Methodists united the personal and the public; God was experienced communally and testimonies were shared. Taves concludes that in so doing they "created a quasi-public space in which they expected they might physically experience the power of God" as well as "democratized the process whereby such experiences were authenticated."[25] This innovation would have a dramatic impact on the movements to come, from camp meetings to the revivals held at and inspired by Azusa Street.

The felt presence of God and its effects was certainly a feature of early American Methodism. The preacher Benjamin Abbott's ministry, for example, was marked by "people fainting during his sermons." Indeed, Abbott found that "some feared to sit too near to him, 'having been informed that the people on the circuit fell like dead men when he preached.'"[26] While Abbot's ministry might be different in degree from that of his fellow preachers, it was not different in kind.

As Lester Ruth has shown, the early quarterly meetings were also characterized by a similar spirituality. At the preaching services of the quarterly meetings "They prayed for God to be present; they longed for God to be present; they hungered and thirsted for God to be present. In their estimation God was often present, since they could feel the gracious presence in their hearts. They could see the effects of that presence in the variety of reactions in the worshippers: from the first awakenings to God to the joyful, clapping testimonies of those entirely sanctified."[27] This was expectancy without presumption: there "Methodists were willing to live with the unpredictability of grace," open to God pouring "out grace in whatever manner God might chose."[28] As A. Gregory Schneider has observed, this experience of spiritual community for early Methodists "was

24. John Wesley, *Journal*, September 8, 1784, *Wesley's Works* 23:331.

25. Taves, *Fits, Trances, and Visions*, 75.

26. Wigger, *Taking Heaven by Storm*, 108; see also Taves, *Fits, Trances, and Visions*, 92f.

27. Ruth, *Little Heaven Below*, 81.

28. Ibid., 23.

earth's closest approach to the joys of heaven." Methodist preacher James Finley, Schneider notes, "spoke and felt as if heaven had come down to earth in some of his class meetings and love feasts."[29]

The spirituality of the quarterly meetings was transferred to the camp meetings, wherein it found fertile soil. The antecedents of the camp meetings are many. Besides the worship at Methodist quarterly meetings precursors included Baptist revivals, the "Big Meetings" of pietistic German speaking groups, and especially the Presbyterian Holy Fairs, which were sacramental meetings preceded by days of preaching that originated in Scotland and were transplanted to America.[30]

It was at a series of sacramental meetings in Kentucky in 1788 that a religious awakening began that would lead to the development and spread of camp meetings. James McGready's three Presbyterian congregations had already begun to experience revival by way of these gatherings. In June 1800, members from all three churches came together at the Red River meetinghouse for a sacramental meeting led by McGready and two colleagues, William Hodge and John Rankin. They were soon joined by two brothers known for their awakening preaching, Presbyterian William McGee and Methodist John McGee.[31]

On the fourth night of the gathering Hodge preached an exceptionally powerful sermon, leading one congregant to shout and sing as a witness to the sense of assurance she had received. The sermon concluded, Hodge, McGready, and Rankin began to leave, but not the McGee brothers nor the congregation. As John B. Boles relates the story, William McGee was so overcome he simply sat and wept. His brother John stood and said that "it was his turn to preach, but 'there was a greater than I preaching,'" and he exhorted the congregation to open their hearts to God. Many then began to cry and shout, and the three Presbyterian preachers "returned and stood amazed at what was happening." They were themselves awakening preachers, "but this was beyond their experience."[32]

John McGee was warned by someone that this was a Presbyterian meeting, and such emotionalism would not be condoned by the congregation. As the Methodist preacher recounted, "I turned to go back, and was near falling; the power of God was strong upon me, I turned again,

29. Schneider, *Way of the Cross*, 97.
30. See Schmidt, *Holy Fairs*.
31. Boles, *Great Revival*, 53.
32. Ibid., 54

and losing sight of the fear of man, I went through the house shouting, and the floor was soon covered with the slain."[33] This phenomenon of falling under the power of God was a hallmark of the early camp meetings, along with cries, shouts of praise, and other responses to encountering the manifest presence of God. Indeed, as Ann Taves has noted, "The defining feature of the Methodist camp-meeting tradition was its insistence on the presence of God in the camp and in the individual."[34]

While the falling phenomenon was a mark of that presence, its absence did not mean God was not present. Even the more regularized and relatively less exuberant camp meetings still carried the expectation of an encounter with God, resulting in expressive praise and changed hearts and lives.

Methodists understood the camp meeting as sacred space, indeed, as one itinerant put it, "like a heaven on earth." As Taves has shown, this extends typological interpretation beyond Scripture and into the present. "If the presence of God in the camp meeting made the camp a type of heaven," she notes, "Methodists were then free to envision the heavenly camp in light of the Old Testament types," centered on the tabernacle in the wilderness and the temple in Jerusalem.[35] This overlapped with the emerging theology of the shout tradition in Methodism, which drew upon God's presence in Jerusalem in terms of the Ark of the Covenant, Ezekiel's prophecy of judgment, Jesus' triumphal entry, Pentecost, and the coming New Jerusalem. In every case the response of God's people as they came into God's presence was to shout.[36]

By the second half of the nineteenth century the shout theology and the altar theology of Phoebe Palmer were being interwoven and taken up into a Shekinah theology. Developed by British Methodist William Cooke, it argued that just as the Shekinah or presence of God dwelt in the Temple, so that same presence after Pentecost now dwells in the church and each believer.[37] This theology also emphasized other biblical accounts of God's presence, most notably "in the burning bush and in the pillar of cloud and fire."[38] The Holiness movement made ample use

33. Cited in ibid.
34. Taves, *Fits, Trances, and Visions*, 239.
35. Ibid., 114–15.
36. Ibid., 113.
37. Ibid., 236.
38. Ibid., 238.

of this imagery to extend the typology to their meetings. Describing a tent meeting led by John Inskip in Sacramento, his biographers noted that "though there was no visible pillar of cloud or fire resting upon it, an *invisible* presence which one could feel, was there, and pervaded the place."[39] The thirteenth day of that meeting was even more notable: "A wonderful power came upon all. Many were stricken down under the mighty shock." But most distinctive was a visible manifestation, "a haze of golden glory encircled the heads of the bowed worshippers—a symbol of the Holy Spirit."[40] Such occasional visible manifestations will also be reported by Pentecostals, though the invisible felt presence would remain much more common.

Pentecostals built upon this inherited Shekinah/Tabernacle theology, reframing it in light of the baptism of the Spirit. When the "Spirit would fall upon the congregation" at Azusa Street, Frank Bartleman wrote, "God was in His holy temple. . . . The Shekinah glory rested there. In fact some claim to have seen the glory by night over the building. I do not doubt it."[41] In a series of articles in *The Apostolic Faith* (the first authored by Seymour and the remaining unsigned), the Holiness tabernacle theology was reworked to support the Pentecostal distinction between entire sanctification and the Baptism of the Spirit. These articles, Taves notes, argued that these three distinct experiences were "prefigured in the tabernacle's two altars and the Holy of Holies." The brazen altar (the place of sacrifice) prefigured conversion, the golden altar (the place of consecration) prefigured sanctification, and the Holy of Holies (which only the sanctified could enter) prefigured Spirit baptism[42] Thus each of the three Christian experiences brought one ever more deeper into the presence of God.

Cecil M. Robeck Jr. argues that in a different way the image of the Jerusalem temple is an apt description of worship at Azusa Street. Drawing on Samuel Terrien's *The Elusive Presence*, Robeck notes that most of the Protestant churches in Los Angeles were similar to the worship of the Jewish diaspora, in which God is primarily encountered through the spoken word. But Azusa Street and the revivals it produced were more like

39. Cited in ibid., 238.
40. Cited in ibid., 239.
41. Cited in ibid., 337.
42. Ibid., 338.

worship in the Jerusalem Temple, involving all the senses in an encounter with the awesome glory of God.[43]

Such an encounter could not be experienced without producing profound effects. As Robeck notes, this intense encounter with God "was a life-changing moment, a transformative time that produced a tangle of responses. There were those who, 'surrounded by [His] glory' at the mission, broke into dance. Others jumped, or stood with hands outstretched, or sang or shouted with all the gusto they could muster. Others were so full of awe when they encountered God that their knees buckled—they fell to the floor, 'slain in the Spirit.' Some spoke, rapid-fire, in a tongue they did not know, while others were struck entirely speechless."[44] To the outside observer much of this was simply exhibitionist behavior or mass hysteria. But as Robeck argues, it is the testimonies of the participants that tell what has happened within them that provide explanation. For all their diversity, Robeck says, "They speak of a personal quest for a divine encounter that put them in direct touch with the God they worshipped."[45]

As Dale Coulter has shown, it was this quest for divine encounter that led William Seymour to revision the theology he inherited from Charles Parham, thereby placing Pentecostalism on more solid spiritual ground. In contrast to Parham's narrower understanding of Spirit baptism as the gift of foreign tongues for end-time mission, Coulter argues that Seymour "understood that bearing witness involved much more than tongues. It encompassed visions, prophesies, revelations, and loving actions toward others, all of which stemmed from being caught up in the arms of the Beloved."[46]

Early Pentecostals like Seymour, G. B. Cashwell, and G. F. Taylor "offered a successful revisioning of Parham's theology of Spirit baptism by placing it in a larger framework of union between bride and bridegroom . . ."[47] Spirit baptism was now located in the divine encounter, and its central effect was affective transformation. It was love more than tongues that was the impetus for mission and power for renewal. Spirit baptism did not simply enable witness, it made the church itself a witness to the life of the age to come. Thus, for Seymour, "The ecstatic embrace of

---

43. Robeck, *Azusa Street Mission*, 131–32.

44. Ibid., 131.

45. Ibid., 186.

46. Coulter, "Spirit and the Bride Revisited," 309.

47. Ibid., 307. What Coulter calls the "Seymour-Cashwell trajectory" received its most comprehensive treatment in G. F. Taylor's *The Spirit and the Bride*.

Spirit baptism is a proleptic participation in the eschaton . . . the rapture of encounter anticipates the final rapture. . . . Seymour held together a view of sanctification as deliverance from sin and beautification of the soul with a view of Spirit baptism as ecstatic embrace and charismatic gifting."[48]

In the decades ahead, Pentecostals would themselves yearn for a renewal of these kinds of encounters with God. As William Faupel has shown, it was the desire for God to "tabernacle" with his people that was a primary motivation underlying the emergence of the Latter Rain Movement among Canadian Pentecostals in the 1940s. The key insight was that God inhabits the praise of God's people. This "led to the conviction that 'praise' produces the divine presence—an 'atmosphere' in which 'supernatural' manifestations can take place. 'Praise' would become the 'key' to crossing the threshold into the tabernacle of the Lord."[49] While its distinctive doctrinal teachings would prove to be highly controversial, this teaching on praise would have an enormous influence on later Pentecostals and Charismatics.

Dreams and Visions

Personal encounter with God was not only sought at love feasts, camp meetings, and Pentecostal revivals. It was an expected feature of everyday life, and while it often took the form of a gentle sense of God's guidance or direction, it frequently took the more definite form of dreams and visions. John Wigger's claim that "it may not be an exaggeration to say that this quest for the supernatural in everyday life was the most distinctive characteristic of early American Methodism"[50] describes this entire tradition, from Wesley's movement to the Pentecostals and Charismatics of the twentieth century

It would be hard to underestimate how pervasive the experience of dreams and visions were. Especially common, according to Henry Rack, were "visions of Christ crucified and bleeding for sinners,"[51] as well as visions of judgment. Some seeking Christian perfection even had visions of the persons of the Trinity. Rack concludes that "the visions appear to have

48. Coulter, "Spirit and the Bride Revisited," 309.
49. Faupel, "Everlasting Gospel," 465.
50. Wigger, *Taking Heaven by Storm*, 110.
51. Rack, *Reasonable Enthusiast*, 434.

the function of dramatizing their concerns and resolving their problems, and so marking stages in their spiritual pilgrimages. Visions of judgment brought conviction of sin; visions of the Crucified Christ brought forgiveness and joy; visions of the Trinity a kind of beatific vision open only to the perfect in love."[52] "It should be said," Rack notes, "that the majority of these cases occurred in those not habitually subject to special mystical experiences."[53]

Dreams and visions could also be instrumental in calling Methodists into preaching. This was especially true for women, for whom taking on a culturally proscribed role was made less difficult through receiving a specific calling from God in this manner. Mary Bosanquet Fletcher had such a dream, and the story of her calling and subsequent ministry was well known to nineteenth-century Methodists on both sides of the Atlantic. She often used dreams as content for her preaching as well as for guidance (a fact that embarrassed one early nineteenth-century editor of her writings, who apologized for her interest in dreams and sought to recast her preaching ministry as a series of domestic chats).[54] On one occasion recorded by Mary Taft, the seventy-one-year-old Fletcher preached a sermon incorporating a dream she had of the Tree of Life. The tree included within it a human form, and the sap of the tree ran from the root and trunk throughout the branches, producing very green leaves. However, in some branches the sap ran quite slowly, blocked by knots in the branches. "She informed us, that the dream was immediately explained to her. She said the trunk and roots represent God the Father. The human form within the trunk [was] Jesus Christ. The sap represents the Holy Spirit. The branches and leaves the church. The knots and crooked parts . . . were the remains of un-belief, self-will, carnality, etc."[55]

In America, as John Wigger has shown, "a great many early Methodists believed in the efficacy of prophetic dreams, visions, and supernatural impressions and were not afraid to base day-to-day decisions on such phenomena."[56] Most dramatic were those dreams that led to conversion. Thomas Rankin, one of the missionaries sent to America by Wesley, was converted after a series of dreams and visions, most notably a vision of

52. Ibid.
53. Ibid.
54. Mack, *Heart Religion*, 128.
55. Cited in ibid., 247.
56. Wigger, *Taking Heaven by Storm*, 106.

his doomed soul in hell followed by one of Christ as Savior.[57] Benjamin Abbott had dreams in which he was given a tour of both hell and heaven, but it was seven years later that the words of a preacher brought those dreams again to his mind and he experienced conversion.[58] Freeborn Garretson, probably the leading figure in early American Methodism after Asbury, was a strong believer in dreams, visions, and divine healing. He provides many detailed accounts of dreams in his journal, one of which was a tour of hell designed to increase his fervor to reach sinners with the gospel of salvation. His wife Catherine also had numerous vivid dreams and visions, and likewise recorded them in her journal.[59]

Wigger notes that "Methodist willingness to accept divinely inspired impressions, dreams, and visions as evidence of the work and call of God circumvented conventional assumptions about education, social standing, gender and race."[60] This made them especially attractive to African Americans. When George White became free after the death of his master he began attending Methodist meetings which led to conviction of sin and eventually conversion in 1791. Through "a number of vivid prophetic dreams and visions," he received a call to preach and obtained an exhorters license in 1805. After experiencing sanctification and learning to read and write, he sought a preacher's license. He was turned down four times, likely due to his race, until he finally was licensed to preach in 1807.[61]

African American women did not have doors for official recognition readily open to them, either in the Methodist Episcopal Church or the new African American Episcopal and African American Episcopal Zion denominations. But that did not deter them from responding to callings from God, received often in the form of dreams and visions. Zilpha Elaw heard a voice say, "Thou must preach the gospel; and thou must travel far and wide"; Julia Foote had a vision of an angel holding a scroll that read, "Thee have I chosen to preach my gospel without delay."[62] Dreams, visions, and supernatural impressions filled both Elaw's and Jarena Lee's

57. Ibid., 113.

58. Ibid., 53–54.,

59. Ibid 106–7.

60. Ibid., 129–30.

61. Ibid., 131–32.

62. Elaw, *Memoirs*, 82, and Foote, *Brand Plucked from the Fire*, 200, cited in Stanley, *Holy Boldness*, 102.

accounts of their ministries as well as African-American males like John Jea.[63]

Dreams and visions were a common feature of Holiness spirituality as well. Phoebe Palmer believed impressions, dreams, and visions to be significant sources of divine guidance, and as Charles White notes, they "were an important part of her spiritual life."[64] Palmer, however, believed all such experiences "must not be taken at face value" but "tested by the Bible." If the dream or vision neither reinforces Scripture nor is contradicted by it, then she considers the circumstances. A dream that follows a prayer asking for divine confirmation could be trusted; one that seems increasingly unreal after asking for divine confirmation should be discarded.[65]

Late nineteenth-century Holiness leader Martin Wells Knapp actually wrote a book on such experiences titled *Impressions* which may have had an influence on William Seymour when he studied at God's Bible School in 1900. Cecil Robeck argues that "Seymour must have found some resonance in the way Knapp wrote about the need to take visions, dreams, and internal voices seriously, while warning his readers to discern the spirits in order to recognize which manifestations came from God."[66]

Seymour would soon have ample opportunity to aid others in such discernment, as dreams and visions were common at the Azusa Street Mission. Even before the revival broke out, Edward Lee, who had been attending the meetings led by Seymour in the home of Richard and Ruth Asberry, told of a vision he had of the apostles Peter and John speaking in tongues.[67] At the revival itself, one of many striking testimonies was that of Lucy Leatherman. Seeking the baptism of the Spirit, with Lucy Farrow laying hands upon her, Leatherman began praising God. Then, as Robeck recounts, "she received a vision of her savior, Jesus, in the heavens. In that vision she began to move closer to him. She became so small she was 'swept into the wound in His side.'"[68] This decentering of self and focus on Christ was a common feature of these testimonies. Leatherman was

63. Wigger, *Taking Heaven by Storm*, 122–23.
64. White, *Beauty of Holiness*, 116.
65. Ibid., 116–17.
66. Robeck, *Azusa Street Mission*, 33–34.
67. Ibid., 66.
68. Cited in Ibid., 182.

transformed, finding her "rest" in Christ. Telling the Lord she wanted the "gift of the Holy Ghost," she reported that "the heavens opened and I was overshadowed, and such power came upon me and went through me." Angels then ministered to her, one loosening her vocal chords and turning her praise into an unknown tongue.[69] Such stories of visions frequent the pages of *The Apostolic Faith* as well as the written accounts of participants.

A Reasonable Enthusiasm?

As many Methodists moved into the middle class toward the mid-nineteenth century they became uneasy with an earlier tradition that so willingly embraced dreams, visions, and falling under the power of the Spirit. Nathan Bangs embodies much of this move to respectability. He began his ministry in 1801 as an awakening preacher in Canada, and prophetic dreams influenced his early ministry. By 1810 in New York, however, he became an ardent opponent of enthusiasm, and insisted on more orderly meetings. But as John Wigger notes, "Bangs believed that his campaign against enthusiasm was validated by a prophetic dream in which he slew a great serpent symbolizing the 'enemy' of order." Bangs was not against religious experience itself, only those practices that hindered Methodism's growing respectability.[70]

While some sought to distance themselves entirely from these phenomena, and others like Bangs sought simply to tamp down those deemed offensive to more genteel culture, the proponents of these forms of experience were faced with a different task. They sought a way to theologically discern the authentic from the inauthentic, the supernatural from the natural, and the divine from the demonic. Palmer, Knapp, Seymour, and others were not simply accepting every reported dream or vision as from God, but insofar as was possible tested them by Scripture and circumstance. The deepest reflection on this problem came from John Wesley himself.

Wesley's accounts of persons crying, shouting and falling, along with his emphasis on a witness of the Spirit and Christian perfection, led his critics to call him an enthusiast. Certainly by their definition he was, although by his own theologically crafted definition he was not. "The rub

69. Ibid., 182–83.
70. Wigger, *Taking Heaven by Storm*, 189.

of the matter," writes David Hempton, "was that Wesley accepted as a general proposition that God regularly and strikingly intervened in the created order to advance his purposes and protect his servants, whereas most critics did not, at least not in the same way."[71]

Historians use the term "enthusiasm" more broadly than Wesley, and find it an appropriate label for the movement he birthed. Yet even they recognize it was an enthusiasm of a distinctive kind. Wesley's own belief in supernatural intervention was qualified by his empiricist inclinations; he was, as Hempton says, "in a peculiar sense, a reasonable enthusiast, but an enthusiast for all that."[72] His Methodism "occupied a position of creative tension between the apparent polar opposites of enlightenment and enthusiasm,"[73] tempering "enthusiasm with discipline, and rugged individualism with communal accountability."[74] Thus, as Phyllis Mack observes, Wesley's "writings on the subject show him trying to walk a fine line between the Pietist's receptivity to divine experience and the scientists' skepticism about these intangible and ultimately unverifiable events."[75]

Hempton was not the first to call Wesley a reasonable enthusiast—Stephen Gunter had used the term, and it was the title of Henry Rack's influential biography of Wesley.[76] Yet with Ann Taves I'm inclined to think "that this sells Wesley short."[77] Wesley's theological reflections were more than a precarious navigation between enlightenment and enthusiasm; in some ways they were able to transcend them both.

The bedrock theological issue for addressing the problem of enthusiasm is how we know God. For Wesley, as we saw in chapter three, the answer is faith understood as a spiritual sense, which "gives us eyes to see" and removes the "veil" between us and God. Since faith is itself a work of the Holy Spirit, only those who have received that gift can truly know, that is, experience the presence of God. The claim that we can know God today with the same directness as those in the apostolic age

71. Hempton, *Methodism*, 35.

72. Ibid., 41.

73. Ibid., 49.

74. Ibid., 34.

75. Mack, *Heart Religion*, 224.

76. Gunter, *Limits of "Love Divine"*, and Rack, *Reasonable Enthusiast*.

77. Taves, *Fits, Trances, and Visions*, 54.

makes perfect sense to persons who have this living faith, but can only appear to be enthusiastic presumption to those who have not.

There is a postmodern sensibility in this way of describing things. In contrast to Enlightenment assumptions, postmodernism denies universal foundations for knowledge and the objectivity of reason. We are all already part of a distinctive culture, already living out of implicit cultural narratives, already shaped by context. We retain our freedom, but significant change occurs only through a paradigm shift that reconfigures the tacit assumptions out of which we think and act, or through a conversion from our cultural narrative to another that makes better sense of reality. Wesley is suggesting something more than this but not less: through conversion to Christ one really does enter a new world that both encompasses and transcends the world from which we come.

But Wesley insists not only that we can know God in this experiential manner, he also insists God acts in ways that range from imperceptible to dramatic. He provides theological guidance for discerning divine causality from that which is demonic or merely human.

We can begin examining that guidance by summarizing the careful comparison by Ann Taves of Wesley and Jonathan Edwards. Most important for discerning a true work of God was their agreement "on two fundamental points regarding these phenomena: first, that they were no sure sign or evidence of salvation and, second, that the witness of the Spirit . . . must be tested by the fruit of the Spirit."[78] That is, intense emotion or falling to the ground neither proves it is a work of God (v. enthusiasts) nor proves that it is not (v. rationalists). The main evidence is emergence of or growth in fruit of the Spirit, most centrally love for God and neighbor. Thus, Wesley warns, "let none ever presume to rest in any supposed testimony of the Spirit which is separate from the fruit of it."[79]

While having this in common, they disagreed on the manner in which God caused these phenomena. Edwards expended much philosophical energy distinguishing between what is due to "primary causation (effects arising directly from supernatural action) and secondary causation (effects arising naturally as indirect effects of supernatural action)," increasingly privileging the first over the second. Thus for Edwards visions and involuntary bodily movements were naturalistic by-products of divine action rather than a direct result of that action.[80]

78. Ibid., 53.

79. John Wesley, "The Witness of the Spirit II," *Wesley's Works* 3:297.

80. Taves, *Fits, Trances, and Visions,* 56.

Wesley did not make that distinction. He readily admitted that dreams, visions, and bodily phenomena could be the result of weak minds, but to consider them all as such would contradict the clear teaching of Scripture. "God does now," he insisted, "as aforetime, give remission of sins and the gift of the Holy Ghost, even to us and our children; yea, and that always suddenly, as far as I have known, and often in dreams or the visions of God."[81] While Wesley is willing to accept that some awakening phenomena are natural, indirect effects of God's action, he nonetheless believes many dreams, visions, and the like a direct result of divine activity.[82] Thus while Edwards sought to clearly distinguish divine and natural phenomena, Wesley was far more open to God acting in and through nature.

Taves argues that something of this same difference between Edwards and Wesley is found over a hundred years later, in the conflict between Charles Parham and William Seymour over the Azusa Street revival. Like Edwards, Parham distinguished between manifestations that were supernatural and natural. Apart from speaking in tongues, Parham (also like Edwards) discouraged physical manifestations at his meetings." But what was unusual at his meetings was common at Azusa Street. There he judged the manifestations to be more hypnotic than divine, and most of the tongues inauthentic. Surprisingly, though, Taves notes that Parham did believe that, in his own words, "it is possible for God to speak through the subconscious mind by His Holy Spirit's power."[83] Here we see a more Wesleyan sense of God working directly in and through the natural mind.

Seymour and Frank Bartleman "viewed a much wider range of experiences as authentic" than did Parham, interpreting them in terms of the tabernacle tradition discussed earlier.[84] They were more in tune with John Wesley's assertion that much of these manifestations are directly due to divine causality, as they are in Scripture, although some are spiritual or natural counterfeits.

Wesley provides his own advice for discerning what is truly of God in his sermon "The Nature of Enthusiasm." In it Wesley describes enthusiasm as "a religious madness arising from some falsely imagined influence or inspiration of God; at least from imputing something to God

81. John Wesley, *Journal*, May 20, 1739, *Wesley's Works* 19:60.

82. Taves, *Fits, Trances, and Visions*, 57.

83. Ibid., 330–31.

84. Ibid., 332.

which ought not to be imputed to him, or expecting something from God which ought not to be expected from him."[85] He then offers a typology of the various forms enthusiasm might take. There are "those who imagine they have the *grace* which they have not," not only the "fiery zealot" but the far more numerous "who imagine themselves Christian and are not."[86] This latter group includes the nominal or formal Christians; that is, those most apt to accuse Wesley of enthusiasm. Wesley thus forcefully challenges the usual categories: his critics define imaginary religion as having intense emotion, while Wesley links it with claiming to be Christian while not seeking holiness or having a transformed heart. For him, both the intemperate zealot and the respectable but unholy churchgoer imagine they are Christian when they are not.

A second form of enthusiasm includes "those who imagine they have such *gifts* from God as they have not," such as "the power of working miracles," and "those who in preaching and prayer imagine themselves to be so influenced by the Spirit of God as in fact they are not."[87] A subset of these are those who expect to receive directions from God in "an extraordinary manner. I mean by visions or dreams, by strong impressions or sudden impulses of the mind. I do not deny that God has of old time manifested his will in this manner, or that he can do so now. . . . But how frequently do men mistake herein!"[88] Wesley argues that in inquiring what is the will of God we are not to wait for it in dreams, visions, or impressions but to find it in Scripture.[89] Even in particular cases in which Scripture has no specific guidance, we still have the "general rule, applicable to all particular cases: 'The will of God is our sanctification'"[90] Thus "instead of saying on any particular occasion, 'I want to know what is the will of God,' would it not be better to say, 'I want to know what will be most for my improvement, and what will make me most useful.'"[91]

A third form of enthusiasm "is that of those who think to attain the end without using the means, by the immediate power of God." While not at all ruling out God's exerting immediate power, Wesley insists it is

---

85. John Wesley, "The Nature of Enthusiasm" 12, *Wesley's Works* 2:50.

86. Ibid., 13–17, 2:50–52.

87. Ibid., 18–19, 2:52–53.

88. Ibid., 21, 2:54.

89. Ibid., 22, 2:54.

90. Ibid., 23, 2:54.

91. Ibid., 26, 2:56.

when we begin to *expect* God to act in that manner and neglect the means of grace in which God has promised to be present that we have fallen into enthusiasm.[92] Therefore," he urges, "constantly and carefully use all the means which he has appointed to be the ordinary channels of his grace."[93]

What Wesley is calling enthusiasm here is not the *having* of dreams, visions, impressions, but *expecting* that they are the normal and preferred manner of encountering the presence of God. Indeed, it is precisely Scripture and other means of grace that enable persons to discern more accurately whether such an experience is or is not from God.[94]

While warning his Methodists not to over value dreams and visions, he at the same time was concerned with undervaluing them. In returning to Everton in 1759, Wesley noted that whereas before there had been many cases of trances and persons crying out or falling down, now there were none, although many were refreshed with the peace of God. Reflecting on this Wesley concludes, "The danger *was*, to regard *extraordinary* circumstances too much, such as outcries, convulsions, visions, trances, as if these were *essential* to the inward work, so that it *could not* go on without them. Perhaps the danger *is*, to regard them too little, to condemn them altogether: to imagine they had nothing of God in them, and were an hindrance to his work."[95]

In contrast to both of these errors Wesley provides his own assessment of what happened in that earlier Everton revival: "1. God suddenly and strongly convinced many that they were lost sinners; the natural consequence whereof were sudden outcries and strong bodily convulsions: 2. To strengthen and encourage them that believed, and to make his work more apparent, he favoured several of them with divine dreams, others with trances and visions: 3. In some of these instances, after a time, nature mixed with grace: 4. Satan likewise mimicked this work of God, in order to discredit the whole work . . ."[96] It is as unwarranted to deny the work of God in causing such phenomena as it is to assert that all of it is of God.

Wesley expands his thinking to the general patterns of awakenings themselves in his 1783 sermon "The General Spread of the Gospel." There he observes that when the truths of the gospel were proclaimed "in any

92. Ibid., 27, 2:56.

93. Ibid., 39, 2:59.

94. This is central to my argument in Knight, *Presence of God.*

95. John Wesley, *Journal,* November, 25, 1759, *Wesley's Works* 21:234.

96. Ibid.

large town, after a few days or weeks there came suddenly on the great congregation . . . a violent and impetuous power . . ." which "frequently continued, with shorter or longer intervals, for several weeks or months. But it gradually subsided, and then the work of God was carried on by gentle degrees . . ."[97]

In the same manner he believed God would continue to work in the future: "At the first breaking out of his work in this or that place there may be a shower, a torrent of grace. . . . But in general it seems the kingdom of God will not 'come with observation', but will silently increase wherever it is set up, and spread from heart to heart, from house to house, from town to town, from one kingdom to another."[98]

The critics of the awakening were in error when they discounted dreams, visions, and falling as not the work of God, for the fruit of transformed hearts and lives proved otherwise. But it was equally erroneous to insist God's work had ended when these phenomena subsided, when it in fact was only just beginning.

If we think of the experienced presence of God as one form of heaven below, then there will always be the temptation in religious awakenings to collapse the "not yet" into the "already," and insist that God is only present in direct and unmediated ways. This Wesley does not do. He maintains an optimism of grace while warning against presumption, and honors the freedom of God to act as God decides while directing expectancy toward encountering divine presence where it has been promised, in the means of grace. Wesley's heirs have always been at their wisest and strongest when they acknowledged God's presence whenever and however they experienced it, while seeking it where God has promised to meet them.

97. John Wesley, "The General Spread of the Gospel" 15, *Wesley's Works* 2:491–92.
98. Ibid., 17, 2:493.

CHAPTER 10

The Redemption of Our Bodies

Dr. Hamilton brought with him Dr. Monro and
Dr. Gregory. They satisfied me what my disorder
was and told me there was but one method of cure.
Perhaps but one natural one, but I think God has
more than one method of healing either the soul
or the body.[1]

—JOHN WESLEY

WHETHER CATHOLIC OR PROTESTANT, Calvinist or Wesleyan, theologically orthodox Christians understood biblical accounts of healing as
actual occurrences through the power of God. Their disagreement was
over whether such miracles could occur in the present. Roman Catholics
believed they could and did occur, especially in and through saints. The
absence of such miracles in Protestantism, in their view, undermined
Protestant claims to be a true church. Many Protestants followed Calvin
in arguing that miracles were limited to the apostolic age, and later claims
for such things as healing were largely if not totally false.

But not all Protestants agreed. Jane Shaw has demonstrated that
in England the "doctrine of the cessation of miracles did not, perhaps,
become as fixed in the sixteenth and seventeenth centuries as historians
have often presumed."[2] In fact, the practice of healing through prayer was
common among both Primitive Baptists and the Society of Friends; and

1. John Wesley, *Journal*, May 18, 1772, *Wesley's Works* 22:323–24.
2. Shaw, *Miracles in Enlightenment England*, 49.

a number of Anglicans began to defend miraculous healing in the present as biblical while not endorsing every reported instance of it.

It is no surprise that Wesleyans, beginning with John Wesley himself, would with their optimism of grace be drawn to healing through prayer as well. But for them there were larger issues at stake. If God is love, and clearly has the power to heal, then what might we realistically hope for in relation to illness and other afflictions? If healing is for today, is it a possibility through prayer or more a certainty through promise, provided one met the conditions for receiving? Ultimately, this takes Wesleyans beyond the miraculous to the fundamental issue of God's attitude toward our physicality: if God provides in the new creation for the redemption of our bodies, then surely the health and healing of the body in this age should be a matter of theological and practical concern.

Medicine and the Miraculous

John Wesley's concern for health and healing was not in itself unusual for an Anglican priest. By the eighteenth century it was expected that conscientious High Church clergy of an Arminian persuasion would include dispensing medical care and advice (or "physic"), especially to the poor, as part of their pastoral duties. Like others of his generation of clergy, as Deborah Madden shows, "Wesley felt a *duty* and obligation to practice physic."[3] What was distinctive in Wesley was the *scope* of the healing expected, whether occurring through medicine or prayer. As Randy Maddox put it, "While most Christians shared the conviction that God would provide full healing of body and spirit at the resurrection, Wesley's emphasis on the degree to which *both* dimensions of divine healing can be experienced *in the present* was less common."[4] While Wesley's optimism of grace opened avenues of hope beyond that of most other Arminian clergy, Calvinists commonly moved in the other direction. Not only did they have even lower expectations for God's healing ministry to the body than they did for the sanctification of the heart, it was Anglican Calvinists who were most opposed to a model of ministry that included medical advice within its cluster of responsibilities.[5]

---

3. Madden, *"Cheap, Safe and Natural Medicine"*, 47.

4. Maddox, "Reclaiming the Eccentric Parent," 17.

5. Ibid.

What Wesley did in effect was to reimagine that model of ministry within his connection of societies and preachers. Those designated "visitors of the sick" were to procure advice for society members regarding the health of their souls and bodies; the preachers were to actually dispense advice to the sick, much as would an Anglican priest. As most lacked a university education, Wesley's program for training his preachers included medical texts.[6]

Wesley believed God healed both through medicine and prayer, and took a decidedly empirical approach to each. Underlying all of this was a holistic theology of creation, which emphasized the interrelation of body and soul. We will first examine Wesley's practice of healing, followed by its theological underpinnings.

For a number of years, beginning in 1747, Wesley operated free dispensaries in London and Bristol. As he later recounts, Wesley was "in pain for many of the poor that were sick; there was so great expense, and so little profit." Finding neither hospitals nor physicians could provide effective care, "At length I thought of a kind of desperate expedient. 'I will prepare, and give them physic myself.'" Renewing his own study of medicine, and enlisting the assistance of an apothecary and surgeon, Wesley offered to those "who were ill of chronical distempers (for I did not care to venture upon acute)" to come "and I would give them the best advice I could, and the best medicines I had."[7]

Wesley's more enduring answer to this pressing need was his publication in 1747 of *Primitive Physic: An Easy and Natural Way of Curing Most Diseases*, which went through multiple editions and revisions in his lifetime and continued to be widely used by Methodists in both Britain and America well into the latter nineteenth century. An expansion of his 1745 *A Collection of Receipts for the Use of the Poor*, Wesley increased his list of maladies from 63 to around 250,[8] as well as adding extensive advice for healthy living. Its purpose, as Deborah Madden succinctly puts it, was to serve as "a manual designed to help the laboring poor stave off disease by regulating their lifestyle through regimen, as well as self-medicating safely when they became sick."[9]

---

6. Ibid., 18.

7. John Wesley, "A Plain Account of the People Called Methodists" XII.1–3, *Wesley's Works* 9:275–6.

8. Holifield, *Health and Medicine in the Methodist Tradition*, 32.

9. Madden, "Saving Souls and Saving Lives," 6.

The "primitive" in *Primitive Physic* refers to an approach to piety and medicine that, in Madden's words, "drew on the tradition of Primitive Christianity to meet the physical and spiritual needs of the poor in eighteenth-century England."[10] Wesley was inspired by the patristic ideal of the physician who refused payment and sought to serve the poor,[11] in contrast to those physicians in his day who extended treatments to maximize profit, or otherwise demonstrated their motives were more financial than benevolent.

Wesley's perspective is well illustrated by this incident in 1757: "Calling on a friend, I found him just seized with all the symptoms of a pleurisy. I advised him to apply a brimstone plaster, and in a few hours he was perfectly well. Now, to what end should this patient have taken a heap of drugs, and lost twenty ounces of blood? To what end? Why, to oblige the Doctor and Apothecary."[12] But this did not mean Wesley had disdain for physicians as a whole or for medical science. He based his remedies on "authoritative medical sources"[13] and drew "from an array of eighteenth-century European medical sources and celebrated physicians."[14] Thus Wesley united the ideal of medical service of Primitive Christianity with the most effective remedies discovered and utilized by eighteenth-century medicine.

The *Primitive Physic* was characterized by plain language, cheap and safe remedies, and empirical method. Whereas, Wesley notes, physic in the ancient world "was wholly founded on experiment,"[15] that is, what actually worked, in the modern world persons "of learning began to set experience aside, to build physic upon hypothesis, to form theories of diseases and their cure and to substitute these in the place of experiments."[16] As the language became more technical, the remedies more complex, and the theories more speculative, "physic became an abstruse science, quite out of the reach of ordinary men."[17] Both profit and honor conspired to keep medical knowledge in the hands of physicians and away from com-

10. Madden, *"Cheap, Safe and Natural Medicine"*, 20.

11. Ibid., 102.

12. John Wesley, *Journal*, February 16, 1757, *Wesley's Works* 21:86.

13. Madden, *"Cheap, Safe and Natural Medicine"*, 111; see also 103.

14. Ibid., 116.

15. John Wesley, Preface to *Primitive Physic: Or, an Easy and Natural Method of curing most Diseases* (1791 ed.) 7, *Wesley's Works* (Jackson) 14:310.

16. Ibid., 8, 14:310.

17. Ibid., 9, 14:310.

mon people.[18] This Wesley sought to reverse by providing persons with an accessible guide that enabled them to tend to common medical needs.

As noted in a postscript to the 1755 edition, Wesley sought in the *Primitive Physic* "to set down cheap, safe, and easy medicines; easy to be known, easy to be procured, and easy to be applied by plain, unlettered men."[19] Thus Wesley largely omits in this edition "the four Herculean medicines, opium, the bark, steel, and most preparations of quicksilver" as too dangerous to use without the oversight of physicians.[20] Wesley also objects to compound medicines as too costly, usually ineffective, and potentially dangerous, offering instead more simple remedies.[21] His recommendations included such common remedies as "air, water, milk, whey, honey, treacle, salt, vinegar, and common *English* herbs,"[22] together with, as Madden notes, "a range of ingredients commonly used by eighteenth-century physicians, such as vitriol, tartar, tar-water, balsam of peru, balsam of tolu, gum storax, and gum guaiacum."[23] While condemning the widespread and excessive use by physicians of such extreme treatments as bleeding, purging, and blistering their patients, Wesley was an enthusiastic advocate of the healing power of low doses of electricity, which "comes the nearest an universal medicine, of any yet known in the world,"[24] and possessed an electrifying machine for that purpose.

We have seen Wesley's preference for a more traditional experimental method to those physicians who "build physic upon hypothesis" and then use their theories as the basis of treatment. Indeed, as Brooks Holifield notes, "The medical theorists who occupied the university chairs believed that medicine could become a science only when its practicioners achieved clarity about fundamental principles, which would

---

18. Ibid., 10, 14:310.

19. John Wesley, Postscript to *Primitive Physic* (1755), 2, in ibid., 14:316.

20. Ibid., 3, 14:316–17.

21. Deborah Madden notes that "modern medicine takes for granted the positive synergy effect produced by a combination of drugs, but it was generally true that eighteenth-century compounds could be protracted and dangerous" (*"Cheap, Safe and Natural Medicine"*, 128).

22. Wesley, Postscript to *Primitive Physic* (1755), 4, *Wesley's Works* (Jackson) 14:317.

23. Madden, *"Cheap, Safe and Natural Medicine"*, 120.

24. John Wesley, Postscript to *Primitive Physic* (1760), *Wesley's Works* (Jackson) 14:319.

become axioms that enabled one to deduce practical rules for therapy."[25] Wesley sided with the more traditional "empirick" physicians, for whom experimentation is the primary avenue to discover effective treatment. Thus, as Madden states, "the remedies contained within *Primitive Physic* are empirically based from beginning to end."[26] By 1760 Wesley was adding "the word *tried* to those [remedies] which I have found to be of the greatest efficacy."[27]

Equally important as the suggested remedies was Wesley's advice for healthy living. He urged his readers to "abstain from all mixed, all high-seasoned food. Use plain diet, easy of digestion; and this as sparingly as you can, consistent with ease and strength. Drink only water, if it agrees with your stomach; if not, good, clear small beer. Use as much exercise daily, in the open air, as you can without weariness. . . . To persevere with steadiness in this course is often more than half the cure."[28] This is then followed by a more detailed list of rules largely taken from one of Wesley's favorite sources, Dr. George Cheyne.[29]

In addition to both remedies and regimen Wesley adds "that old unfashionable medicine, prayer."[30] In his 1769 *Advices with Respect to Health*, a critical abridgment of a work by Dr. Samuel Tissot, Wesley concludes the Preface thus:

> I have only to add, (what it would not be fashionable for a Physician to believe, much less to mention,) that as God is the sovereign disposer of all things, and particularly of life and death, I earnestly advise every one, together with all his other medicines, to use that medicine of medicines,—prayer. . . . At the same time, then, that we use all the means which reason and experience dictate, let us seek a blessing from Him who has all power in heaven and earth, who gives us life and breath and all things, and who cannot withhold from them that seek Him any manner of thing that is good.[31]

---

25. Holifield, *Health and Medicine in the Methodist Tradition*, 32–33.

26. Madden, *"Cheap, Safe and Natural Medicine"*, 111; see also 126.

27. Wesley, Postscript to *Primitive Physic* (1760), *Wesley's Works* (Jackson) 14:317.

28. Wesley, Preface to *Primitive Physic*, 15, in ibid., 14:313–14.

29. For a detailed analysis of Wesley's prescription for a healthy regimen, see Madden, *"Cheap, Safe and Natural Medicine"*, 155ff.

30. Wesley, Preface to *Primitive Physic*, 15, *Wesley's Works* (Jackson) 14:314.

31. John Wesley, "To the Reader," in *Advices with respect to Health: Extracted from a late Author* (1767), 9, *Wesley's Works* (Jackson) 14:258–59.

One important role of faith and prayer, Madden notes, is as an avenue for God to provide "comfort and tranquility of mind," thus counteracting those passions that so often are the source of bodily disorder.[32] But Wesley could also insist—as he did in response to a medical treatise advocating a coupie of extreme remedies—"I know a Physician that has a shorter cure than either one or the other."[33] God can and does cure illness through prayer.

Wesley's *Journal* is sprinkled throughout with accounts of miraculous healing, from as early as 1736 until the last month for which he made entries, October, 1790. In some he is relating stories told to him by others which he finds credible; most directly involve Wesley himself, often joining in prayer with others. The following is one such account from 1742: "When I came home they told me the physician said he did not expect Mr. Myrick would live till the morning. I went to him, but his pulse was gone. He had been speechless and senseless for some time. A few of us immediately joined in prayer. (I relate the naked fact.) Before we had done his sense and his speech returned. Now, he that will account for this by *natural causes*, has my free leave. But I choose to say, This is the power of God."[34]

Here is another almost forty years later, in 1782: ". . . Mr. Floyde lay in a high fever, almost dead for want of sleep. This was prevented by the violent pain in one of his feet, which was much swelled, and so sore, it could not be touched. We joined in prayer that God would fulfil his word, and 'give his beloved sleep'. Presently the swelling, the soreness, the pain were gone. And he had a good night's rest."[35] Wesley not only prayed for others, but multiple times for himself and his brother Charles. On three different occasions he prayed for his horse which had become lame, and the horse was cured.[36]

There is no single pattern to these accounts. In some instances prayer is offered on behalf of the sick; in others it is those who are ill who pray for their own healing. Moreover miraculous healing didn't always come by prayer; Robert Webster notes that Wesley also believed "in the

---

32. Madden, *"Cheap, Safe and Natural Medicine"*, 186.

33. John Wesley, *Journal*, June 26, 1772, *Wesley's Works* 22:339.

34. John Wesley, *Journal*, December 20, 1742, *Wesley's Works* 19:306.

35. John Wesley, *Journal*, April 26, 1782, *Wesley's Works* 23:239.

36. See, for example, John Wesley's *Journal* entries for May 19, 1728; March 21, 1741; May 10, 1741; March 17, 1746; September 19, 1750; October 16–22, 1756; September 2, 1781; May 23, 1783.

healing efficacy of the eucharist."[37] Thus Wesley had no set formulas for how God heals, nor did he insist on faith on the part of the sufferer as a precondition. What he does believe is healing is a manifestation of the love of God in this age, and the occurrence of miracles is one of the marks of genuine Christianity.[38] Wesley thus decidedly rejected the cessationist claim that miracles only occurred during the apostolic age.

While believing in healing through supernatural means, Wesley did not simply accept every report as true. As Jane Shaw has noted, Wesley sought to examine "miraculous and supernatural phenomena along the lines of the experimental method." His is a prime example of "the attempt to negotiate a middle way between an excessive rationalism or a too-ready 'enthusiasm', by using the experimental method to investigate the evidence for contemporary miracle claims, and appealing to probability rather than certainty."[39] This experimental method marked Wesley's approach to the miraculous just as it did for his identification of effective medical remedies.

Inward and Outward Health

Wesley's concern for health was rooted in a holistic vision not only of the human person but of creation as a whole. In the original creation, Wesley says, "Whatever was created was good in its kind, suited to the end for which it was designed, and adapted to promote the good of the whole and the glory of the great Creator."[40] All was harmoniously interrelated—"Every part was exactly suited to the others"[41]—and no evil existed that would mar that harmony. What was true for creation as a whole was also true for humanity. Soul and body were mutually dependent, and both were harmoniously united, such that the intentions of the heart were faithfully enacted in and through the body.

The fall into sin disrupted the harmony of the entire creation; what it did not disrupt is the interdependence. Thus the various components of the created order conflict with one another even as they cannot exist apart from one another. Before the fall, says Wesley, humanity "was

---

37. Webster, "'Health of Soul and Health of Body,'" 222.

38. Ibid., 221.

39. Shaw, *Miracles in Enlightenment England*, 179.

40. John Wesley, "God's Approbation of His Works" 1, *Wesley's Works* 2:387.

41. Ibid., I.14, 2:396.

the great channel of communication between the creator and the whole brute creation"; but when through sin humanity turned from God and was no longer capable "of transmitting those blessings, that communication was necessarily cut off."[42] Thus through no fault of their own, the animals were brought into a lower state, and their interdependence was now marked by violence.

Humanity moved from immortality to mortality, and the "heavens, the earth, and all things contained therein, conspire" in carrying out this divine judgment. As a result, the "seeds of weakness and pain, of sickness and death, are now lodged in our inmost substance; whence a thousand disorders continually spring, even without the aid of external violence." The earth we inhabit, the creatures we share it with, the air we breathe all carry with them threats to our lives; even "the food we eat daily saps the foundation of life which cannot be sustained without it."[43]

But the disharmony is not only with external creation; it has seriously disrupted the relation of soul and body. The body, although remaining an amazingly wonderful gift of God, has become corruptible and

> very frequently hinders the soul in its operations, and at best serves it very imperfectly. Yet soul cannot dispense with its service, imperfect as it is. For an embodied spirit cannot form one thought but by the mediation of its bodily organs. For thinking is not (as many suppose) the act of a pure spirit, but the act of a spirit connected with a body, and playing upon a set of material keys. . . . Hence every disorder of the body, especially of the parts more immediately subservient to thinking, lays an almost insuperable bar in the way of its thinking justly.[44]

To put it in terms used in earlier chapters, a disordered body is a source of those mistaken ideas and misjudgments that lead to involuntary transgressions and undermine holiness of life.

But just as bodily illness can hinder persons from enacting love, spiritual problems can have emotional and physical repercussions. As Maddox notes, Wesley considered many minor cases of what was termed "nervous disorders" were actually the result of persons sensing they were not as God would have them to be, and therefore "medical treatment

---

42. John Wesley, "The General Deliverance" II.1, *Wesley's Works* 2:442.

43. Wesley, Preface to *Primitive Physic*, 2, *Wesley's Works* (Jackson) 14:308.

44. John Wesley, "On the Fall of Man" II.2, *Wesley's Works* 2:405–6.

alone would not be sufficient to restore" them to health.[45] Wesley relates the story of a woman who had pain in her stomach for which numerous medicines had no effect. The root of her problem was grief over the loss of her son. Her dispositions had bodily effect; the appropriate remedy in her case was the love of God.[46]

In the coming new creation God will restore and even enhance the harmony of the original. The harmony of body and soul will be restored, as there will be no sickness, death, or sin. But as we have seen, Wesley also holds to an optimism of grace in this age, in which we can anticipate a measure of healing of both body and soul. The soul can be restored to the image in which it was created, to once again love as God loves. As for the body, through healthy regimen, medicine, and prayer, we can, as Wesley says in *Primitive Physic*, lessen the "inconveniences which cannot be wholly removed . . . and prevent in part the sickness and pain to which we are continually exposed."[47]

Wesley rejected the prevailing spirituality, rooted in Puritanism and largely embraced by his brother Charles, that sickness was sent by God and was more to be borne in submission than removed. While this piety did not prevent the seeking of medical care, it (in Maddox's words) "could create the subtle suggestion that strong concern for comfort or healing reflected lack of faith."[48]

John Wesley's view was more complex. Sickness or tragedy could certainly turn us to God in dependence, but it could also evoke bitterness toward God. Good health and other blessings could lead to a false sense of self-sufficiency, but also to profound gratitude toward God. In other words, the spiritual result of bodily affliction depends much on our response to it. But in turning toward God in the face of illness Wesley was more prone to encourage expectant faith than passive submission, grounded in a deep sense of God's love. Thus his advice to Alexander Knox: "It will be double blessing if you give yourself up to the Great Physician, that He may heal soul and body together. And unquestionably this is His design. He wants to give you . . . both inward and outward health."[49]

---

45. Maddox, "John Wesley on Holistic Health and Healing," 16.

46. Holifield, *Health and Medicine in the Methodist Tradition*, 20–21.

47. Wesley, Preface to *Primitive Physic*, 3, *Wesley's Works* (Jackson) 14:308.

48. Maddox, "John Wesley on Holistic Health and Healing," 11.

49. Cited in Maddox, "Reclaiming the Eccentric Parent," 17.

Perseverance and Expectant Faith

Early Methodist spirituality after Wesley encompassed both gratitude to God for healing by whatever means as well as encouraged perseverance in faith when illness persisted. The prevailing evangelical understanding of sickness as providentially used by God to chasten, instruct, or test, was a common assumption among Methodists. Yet this belief was not seen as incompatible with the use of medicine or earnest petition to God for relief, often envisioned as occurring through natural means.

But for some, this strong sense of God's presence in daily life fueled an expectation of divine intervention that included miraculous healing. In England, where the Wesleyan Methodists under the leadership of Jabez Bunting were moving toward greater social respectability, belief in divine healing was found more in secessionist bodies like the Primitive Methodists. Early Primitive Methodism embraced both healing and exorcism, and miraculous healings marked the ministries of such preachers as Elizabeth Smith and John Oxtoby. Especially well received among the poor, where illness abounded due to their working and living conditions, and medical care was scarce, the Primitive Methodists brought hope for healing as well as a new sense of community and dignity.[50]

Early American Methodists, as John Wigger has said, "rarely prayed for divine healing," as they understood disease to be "a product of God's providence, sent to test one's faith."[51] Francis Asbury, whose frequent bouts of ill health were largely addressed through medical treatment, was perhaps the exemplary model of a faith that persevered in ministry in spite of sickness. Yet as Wigger has also shown, divine healing was not unknown among American Methodists. The autobiographies of James P. Horton, Sampson Maynard, and Billy Hibbard included accounts of divine healing, "and Valentine Cook, Philip Gatch, Noah Fiddler, and Joshua Thomas gained reputations as healers whose prayers sometimes brought miraculous results."[52] Rebecca Cox Jackson, a free African American itinerant preacher who eventually left her African Methodist Episcopal Church for the Shakers, "claimed an extraordinary gift of healing, along with other supernatural powers."[53]

50. Robinson, *Divine Healing*, 117–21.

51. Wigger, *American Saint*, 305.

52. Wigger, *Taking Heaven by Storm*, 108.

53. Ibid., 123. See also Robinson, *Divine Healing*, 125–26.

This same mix of views marked the early Holiness movement. Phoebe Palmer, who suffered chronic health problems throughout her ministry,[54] understood periods of suffering as meant to test or instruct, while at the same availing herself of medical care (her husband Walter was a homeopathic physician). She also turned to God in prayer. While writing the *Way of Holiness* she was so seriously ill that Harold Raser wonders if she thought of it as a kind of last will and testament.[55] On one occasion she says that she "was taken unexpectedly ill" with "alarming symptoms." "I realized a perfect resignation to the will of God," she records, "but felt that he did not chide me when I asked, that if consistent with his will, the hand of disease might be arrested. . . . The Lord heard and answered the petition, and I found myself surprisingly better in the morning . . ."[56]

During a much more serious illness, one lasting several days and marked by fever and severe pain, Palmer initially sought sustaining grace and to accept God's will for her, be it life or death. But it was suggested to her mind that "'all are yours, whether life or death:' 'Ask what you will, and it shall be done unto you;'—it *will* be according to the will of God."[57] She initially resisted, thinking this suggestion was not of God, but was finally convinced and "dared not resist longer." She renewed her full consecration to God, and prayed that if it would glorify God, "let me live!" "At once," she wrote, "I felt I should recover"—and the symptoms were rapidly removed.[58]

In these accounts Palmer presupposed that God permits sickness for a purpose, but that one can nonetheless turn to God in prayer and find healing. The healing she found was not understood as miraculous, but wrought by the power of God exercised through natural means.

But others in the early Holiness movement did believe in miraculous healing. B. T. Roberts, founder of the Free Methodist Church, anticipated later Pentecostal claims that the gifts of the Spirit, including the gift of healing, were to be permanent features in the life of the church. Healing "was to run down through all ages, to the end of the world"; "persons

54. Raser, *Phoebe Palmer*, 72.
55. Ibid., 165.
56. Palmer, *Way of Holiness*, 227.
57. Ibid., 261.
58. Ibid., 363.

who have received the gift of healing," he argued, "have appeared from time to time, in the church, in all ages."[59]

What had been lost in all of these early Methodist responses to illness was John Wesley's nuanced theology of creation, fall, and new creation. Nonetheless, in early Methodism as a whole the Wesleyan optimism of grace and value placed on bodily health remained, and was in tension with the dominant evangelical piety of submission to sickness. Out of that tension would come a new theology of healing that would spread throughout the Holiness movement in the late nineteenth century.

---

59. Cited in Snyder, *Populist Saints*, 798–99.

CHAPTER 11

Holiness and Healing

God now heals bodily sickness, precisely as He now
heals soul sickness, by His power alone, unaided by
any means whatever; and . . . He does it through and by
the virtue of the perfect Atonement of Jesus Christ.

—R. KELSO CARTER (1884)[1]

. . . healing by faith in this age is a matter of special
favor from God, and is always peculiarly under the
guidance and leading of the Holy Spirit. In very many
cases it is certain that no healing is granted, no matter
how consecrated the person may be.

—R. KELSO CARTER (1897)[2]

THE HOLINESS MOVEMENT HAD insisted in good Wesleyan fashion that
salvation is for the present as much as for the age to come, and its goal is
not pardon but holiness. The love that will one day reign in fullness can
even now fill the hearts and govern the lives of Christians. The promise of
holiness had already been won by Christ, and only awaited its reception
through consecration and faith.

But if the age to come includes redemption of our bodies as well as
our souls—if the "physical body," as R. Kelso Carter put it, "is not a cage"

1. Carter, *Atonement for Sin and Sickness*, 18–19.
2. Carter, *"Faith Healing" Reviewed*, 117.

157

for the soul but "is to be offered to God as a sacrifice," is indeed a temple of the Holy Ghost[3]—then does it not stand to reason that God would, even in this age, care for our physical as well as our spiritual health? The theological connection between an optimism of grace and bodily health had fallen out of sight in much of the Holiness movement by the mid-nineteenth century. Its rediscovery would energize a healing movement that would lead large numbers of Christians from a piety of passive resignation to one of active service, especially on behalf of the poor and hopeless.

The Emergence of the Divine Healing Movement

The roots of this new healing theology are found in the ministry of Ethan O. Allen. He had survived childhood tuberculosis (then called consumption) but the ill effects persisted into adulthood. In 1846, having received entire sanctification at a meeting of Methodist class leaders, Allen then said, "Brethren, if you will pray for me, I believe that this mighty power that has come upon me will heal my lung." While such a request was far from normal, the class leaders did so on the basis of Mark 16:17–18, and Allen was instantly healed.[4]

Allen then undertook the first full-time healing ministry in America, focused on those who were impoverished, incurable, or had mental disorders. A quiet, even shy person, Allen's long ministry—he died in 1903—took him to poor houses and homes throughout the northeast, and he became a revered figure among those in the healing movement in the last decades of the nineteenth century.

As a layperson without theological training, Allen drew his understanding of healing directly from Scripture. Sickness, he believed, was the work of Satan, either directly or indirectly, and hence was not sent by God. Thus he would often begin by casting out the evil spirit causing the illness before actually praying for healing (anticipating practices found later within some Pentecostal and Charismatic healing ministries). He did allow that illness is sometimes due to divine chastening, calling for self-examination and repentance; hence he spent time with persons to

3. Carter, *Atonement for Sin and Sickness*, 228.

4. MacArthur, *Ethan O. Allen*, 14, 19, cited in Chappell, "Divine Healing Movement," 88–89.

first discern their spiritual condition in order to uncover any barriers to healing.

Allen did not anoint with oil or claim to be an elder in the church as in James 5:14–16, but called for the expectant and confident faith of Mark 16:17, both in the recipient of healing but even more so in himself as the one praying for healing. When healing came, Allen expected it to be instantaneous. He also rejected the use of doctors and medicine, instead urging persons to trust in God alone. Given that the underlying source of sickness was Satan, physicians were seen by Allen as trying to address the physical issues without first dealing with the spiritual. This focus on the spiritual condition linked sanctification to healing; eventually Allen developed a four-fold gospel of salvation, sanctification, healing, and premillennial eschatology that anticipated that of A. B. Simpson.[5]

A second key figure at the beginning of the healing movement was Sarah Mix. An African-American from Connecticut, she was brought up a Baptist, converted in an African Methodist Episcopal Church, and became an Adventist upon marrying her husband Edward. She had a family history of consumption, lost all of her children to lung disease at young ages, and by 1877 had symptoms of it herself.

When Ethan Allen, accompanied by Mr. and Mrs. Loomis, arrived in her hometown to pray for a Mrs. Whitney, Sara Mix joined in the prayer. This led Allen to inquire into Mrs. Mix's health, and when she described her condition, Allen prayed for her as well. Then she recounted, "At that moment I believed I was healed, the room was filled with the glory of God, so much so that sister Loomis fell to the floor as one dead, and I was so overwhelmed with the power of God, I felt everything like disease was removed; I felt light as a feather. . . . I leaped for joy into the other room, shouting victory in the name of Jesus."[6]

Sara Mix received not only her healing that day but also her calling to ministry. She and her husband Edward first traveled with Allen, then set up their own healing ministry. When she could not personally be with someone, she would by mail set a definite time in which she and that person would agree in prayer. Although her ministry was relatively short—after three years of good health the tuberculosis returned, and she died in 1884—her impact was significant.

5. Chappell, "Divine Healing Movement," 87–89, 100–103; Robinson, *Divine Healing*, 126–29.

6. Mix, *Faith Cures*, 39, cited in Hardesty, *Faith Cure*, 10.

The Mixes' theology would become mainstream in the healing movement. Edward Mix taught that, in Paul Chappell's words, "the curse of sin . . . fell upon both the soul and the physical body," and that Christ brings both salvation and healing, received by faith.[7] Sarah Mix urged those who were sick to "pray believing and then *act faith*. It makes no difference how you feel, but get out of bed and begin to walk by faith."[8] This echoes Phoebe Palmer's understanding of faith as needing no further evidence than the promise of God in Scripture, now being applied to the promise of healing.

These were indeed the exact words Sarah Mix wrote to Episcopalian Carrie Judd in 1879. Contracting spinal fever as a teenager after a serious fall in 1876 on a snow-covered sidewalk in Buffalo, New York, Judd became an invalid, unable to turn herself over in bed, and considered by physicians an almost hopeless case. Her father read a newspaper account of Mrs. Mix, and with some reluctance Carrie authorized a letter on her behalf. Following Sarah Mix's advice, she set aside her medications, and prayed for faith, while her family prayed in another room and Edward and Sarah Mix prayed in Connecticut. Filled with peace, she found she was able to turn herself and sit up in bed unassisted. With her nurse's help, she rose to sit in a chair, and within a month had regained strength to walk downstairs.[9]

Carrie Judd Montgomery would become one of the leading advocates of divine healing, as well as a bridge between the Holiness and Pentecostal movements. In the opening editorial of her periodical *Triumphs of Faith*, which was devoted to both holiness and healing, Montgomery urges her invalid readers to lay hold of the promised blessing of healing by faith: "Our part is simply to reckon our prayer as answered, and God's part is to make *faith's reckonings real*. This is by no means a question of *feeling* faith, but of *acting* faith. . . . What is true of . . . spiritual healing is likewise true of physical healing. . . . Christ bore our sickness as well as our sins, and if we may reckon ourselves free from one, why not from the other?"[10] The influence of Phoebe Palmer and Sarah Mix is clear in this passage, as is the parallel Montgomery draws between entire sanctification and healing.

7. Cited in Chappell, "Divine Healing Movement," 94.

8. Judd, *Prayer of Faith*, 9–11, cited in Hardesty, *Faith Cure*, 8.

9. Hardesty, *Faith Cure*, 8. An extensive study of her ministry and theology was published after this manuscript was completed. See Miskov, *Life on Wings*.

10. Cited in Dayton, *Theological Roots*, 126.

While Ethan Allen was beginning his pioneering ministry in America, a separate healing movement was emerging among pietists in Europe. In 1843 Lutheran pastor Johann Christian Blumhardt found himself faced with a case of demonic possession for which his theological training had not prepared him. Through struggle and prayer, Katharina Dittus was delivered, and the departing demon's cry "Jesus is Victor!" became the centerpiece of Blumhardt's theology. This event led to a religious awakening in the community that for Blumhardt included a healing ministry, eventually leading to his establishing the Bad Boll Healing Home in 1852 as a center for those seeking counseling and prayer.[11] Blumhardt believed "sin is the cause of sickness," and thus "the forgiveness of sins and healing stand in an inner relationship to one another."[12] Christ is victorious over Satan and sin, and thereby sickness as well.

Of more immediate impact in America was the ministry of Dorothea Trudel. Growing up in the Swiss village of Männedorf, her hard-drinking father continually left the family impoverished. With no money for doctors, in times of illness Trudel's pious Lutheran mother would turn to God in prayer, often with positive results. In 1851 Trudell, now an adult, was managing a flower business and had four workers turn ill. The doctor who was called was unable to restore them to health. Yet when Trudell herself layed hands on them and prayed, they all recovered.[13] As word spread of this event, more and more persons came to Männedorf for counsel and healing, and more healings occurred. Trudel began to obtain additional houses to accommodate the growing numbers. After her death, Samuel Zeller, her chosen successor, continued the work, which eventually expanded to ten healing homes.[14]

Trudel and Zeller grounded their practice of healing on James 5:14–16; hence prayer was accompanied by anointing with oil and the laying on of hands. Their theology was based on Isaiah 53:5 ("He was wounded for our transgressions and bruised for our iniquities, and with his stripes we are healed.") along with Matthew 8:17 and I Peter 2:24, which they understood to mean that healing no less than salvation is accomplished

---

11. Robinson, *Divine Healing*, 52–65.

12. Bodamer, "Life and Work of Johann Christian Blumhardt," 34–44, cited in Dayton, *Theological Roots*, 121.

13. Robinson, *Divine Healing*, 70–72.

14. Ibid., 72–75.

by the atonement of Christ. This teaching would become both one of the most central and controversial in the healing movement.[15]

Trudel, based on her initial experience with healing, thought medicine unnecessary and even detrimental to faith. Zeller, on the other hand, was not dismissive of medicine, although emphasizing that in their work they stay close to Scripture and use only prayer.[16] There was no claim by either that the failure to receive healing was due to lack of faith; rather healing is a sovereign act of God. Hence it can be instantaneous or gradual when it occurs. When healing does not occur, it can be because the illness was sent by God to encourage dependence on grace or the seeking of sanctification, and in some cases infirmities must simply be borne in faith. Thus Trudel and Zeller always ministered to a person's spiritual relationship with God before they addressed the need for healing.[17]

Trudel's ministry may have had its greatest long-term impact through a man she never met. Charles Cullis was a devout Episcopalian and homeopathic physician in Boston who in 1862 became concerned for impoverished persons dying of consumption with no place to stay. Later that same year Cullis attended Phoebe Palmer's Tuesday Meeting for the Promotion of Holiness in New York City, where he received entire sanctification. Two years later, after a widespread fund raising drive throughout Boston, Cullis opened his consumptive home where the dying patients could live in comfort and receive medical care, as well as be introduced to the gospel of salvation. The numbers of applicants soon led to expansion, and by 1871 Cullis had four consumptive homes as well as an orphanage, deaconess home, out-patient dispensary, the Willard Tract Repository Publishing house, a library, an evening college, and a local church, as well as holding a Tuesday Meeting to promote holiness in his home.[18] In this Cullis stood in a tradition reaching back to the benevolent societies of the earlier nineteenth century, to Wesley's Methodists, and ultimately to the array of institutions for spiritual and social needs founded by pietists such as August Hermann Francke.

The seeds of his faith-healing ministry were planted in the late 1860s when he wondered if his ministry should "extend to the cure of disease

---

15. Ibid., 79.

16. Ibid.

17. Chappell, "Divine Healing Movement," 46–48.

18. Ibid., 107–26.

as well as the alleviation of the miseries of the afflicted."[19] Challenged by James 5:14–15, Cullis wondered if the promise of healing remained true today. He asked Christian leaders if anyone knew of cases of divine healing, and he was given *The Life of Dorothea Trudel*, which convinced him that healing could indeed occur now as it had in the New Testament. In 1870 he anointed with oil and prayed for Lucy Drake, who had a brain tumor that had almost totally immobilized her for five months. She was able to rise and walk, and within three months the tumor was gone.[20]

By 1871 Cullis was sharing his discovery of healing by faith with a wide range of Holiness leaders, including William Boardman, John Inskip, William McDonald, A. J. Gordon, Daniel Steele, R. Kelso Carter, and A. B Simpson, as well as providing encouragement to Carrie Judd. Inskip himself received healing through Cullis' ministry, as later did Simpson.[21] While divine healing was not accepted or emphasized by all segments of the Holiness movement, it became a central feature of much of it.

In 1881 Cullis began holding weekly prayer meetings for the sick at his Beacon Hill Chapel, as well as camp-meeting style healing services at the Methodist campground at Old Orchard Beach in Maine. Soon he had also opened a Faith Cure home modeled after that of Dorothea Trudel.[22]

As with all of these early healing practitioners, Cullis did not have a fully developed theology of healing. He understood divine healing as a promise of God to the church, and was impatient with those who were unsure if it was God's will that they be healed. For those who were not believing Christians, Cullis would first call for faith in Christ for their salvation, which then could be extended to trust for healing.

Like most of the other healing pioneers, Cullis believed doubt undermined the faith necessary for healing. While he saw reliance on doctors and medicine as a danger to full reliance on Christ, he at the same time cautioned against extreme promises to never again take medicine as a sign of faith. "No one knows," he counseled, "what his spiritual condition will be in six months, a year, or even three weeks from now."[23] Cullis continued to provide free prescriptions and medical care to the poor, as

19. Cited in ibid, 127.

20. Ibid., 127–29.

21. Robinson, *Divine Healing*, 167.

22. Ibid., 168–69.

23. Cullis, *Faith Healing*, 18, cited in Robinson, *Divine Healing*, 170.

did missionaries he supported in other countries.[24] As healing was often gradual, Cullis urged persons not to let continued symptoms lead to doubt: "You may have the symptoms of your disease, but count the work of God done, and leave the symptoms with God."[25]

Not everyone who sought healing was healed. In some cases, Cullis believed, it's because their requests were inappropriate; the promise was for the healing of disease, not new teeth or restored limbs. Sometimes persons viewed the faith cure as just another avenue of treatment, and lacked the deep faith necessary for divine healing. And in some cases it is simply God's appointed time for them to die, and in that case "you will have no faith to get well." When criticized by a minister for those cases when healing did not occur, Cullis shrewdly responded, "Were all the people converted that you preached to last Sunday? . . . We are praising God for victory, not defeat!"[26]

Healing in the Atonement

While the varied theological insights of healing pioneers like Cullis and Trudel were persuasive to many, it remained for others who they had influenced to develop more comprehensive theologies of healing. These were supplied by William Boardman, R. Kelso Carter, A. J. Gordon, A. B. Simpson, and in Europe, Otto Stockmayer. While not identical in specifics and nuance, there was nevertheless a strong consensus among them all.

Their most obvious point of agreement was their rejection of cessationism, the teaching that miracles such as healing were only for the apostolic age. Since Calvin this had been the dominant view among Protestants, although as we have already seen, it was never universally accepted, most notably not by John Wesley. As Robert Bruce Mullin has shown, this precarious division of "history into a biblical epoch and a post biblical epoch, each having distinctively different rules of evidence and probability," faced severe challenges in the second half of the nineteenth century.[27] By the 1880s, for different reasons, both theological liberals and the proponents of the healing movement were denying the cessa-

24. Chappell, "Divine Healing Movement," 141.

25. Baer, "Perfectly Empowered Bodies," 70, cited in Robinson, *Divine Healing*, 170.

26. Cullis, *Faith Healing*, 30, 31, cited in Robinson, *Divine Healing*, 172.

27. Mullin, *Miracles and the Modern Imagination*, 30.

tionist claim that New Testament miracles were solely for the purpose of demonstrating the divinity of Jesus or apostolic authority, and hence now unnecessary. As to why there are no claims that the full range of Jesus' miracles were replicated in the present, healing theologians made a critical distinction. Healing, they argued, was not technically a miracle like walking on water or stilling a storm, but a common privilege of the church for all ages, alongside salvation.[28] The church was not promised power over storms, but it was promised deliverance from both sin and sickness through faith.

A second common theme was their rejection, in the words of Heather Curtis, of "the ideal of sanctified suffering that demanded passive forbearance in the face of sickness and somatic distress," advocating instead "an alternative devotional ethic that uncoupled the longstanding link between corporeal suffering and spiritual holiness."[29] It was Charles Wesley's assumption of the necessity of suffering for growth in sanctification that John Wesley had similarly denied. The model of sanctification held up by the healing theologians was not passive endurance, but active service, presupposing the necessity of at least a degree of good health.

Curtis illustrates this shift in spirituality with the remarkable story of Jennie Smith. From the age of fifteen, when she wrenched her back, Smith was an invalid, suffering "countless ailments, including typhoid and bilious fever, spinal disease, inflammation of the stomach and bowels, paralysis, paroxysm in her limb, a withered arm, blindness, and nervous prostration." Physicians used a range of extreme and painful heroic measures to treat these problems, adding greatly to her suffering. But as she wrote in *Valley of Baca: A Record of Suffering and Triumph* (1876), Smith saw her afflictions "as blessings sent or permitted by God for her benefit and for the good of others." "Perfect submission," she wrote, meant "passively to endure pain"—indeed, to suffer in any way that would bring glory to God.[30] Her Methodist Episcopal pastor in his introduction to the book praised Smith's "submission to the divine will, which has led thousands of Christians who have known her to a loftier trust in God."[31]

But Smith did want to be well, and had begun hearing from some that her resignation to suffering was not an example of faith but inadequate

28. Ibid., 95.

29. Cited in Curtis, *Faith in the Great Physician*, 6.

30. Ibid., 1.

31. Ibid., 2.

faith in God as healer.[32] By 1878 Smith had become convinced that God's will for persons was not prolonged suffering but health, and she sought prayer for her own healing. At least twelve persons, including her physician and the local Methodist and Presbyterian ministers, gathered together to pray for her. With expectant faith Smith waited, and after two hours made her own prayer, offering her body to God. She became "conscious of a baptism of strength. . . . I felt definite strength come into my back, and into my helpless limb." She raised herself, and then for the first time in sixteen years stood up and walked. Her pain was gone and her back and limbs were strong again. She published the story of her remarkable recovery in *From Baca to Beulah* and soon became an itinerant evangelist, preaching salvation and temperance to "railroad men," a ministry she continued until her death in 1924.[33]

As they had for John Wesley, accounts such as this provided the healing movement with empirical evidence that God does heal through prayer in the present day. They not only strengthened an optimism of grace and expectant faith for healing, but modeled active service for God as a response to healing. "When confronted with the testimonies of those who claim healing," Kimberly Alexander observes, "one is at once impressed with the fact that those healed had an immediate sense of their need to serve the Kingdom of God." This focus on mission that marked Holiness and early Pentecostal healing ministries, she adds, would shift in the second half of the twentieth century to a "focus on 'what God has for me.'"[34]

These testimonies also illustrate another central tenet of healing theology that was in continuity with Wesley: God's loving care is as focused on this world as it is on the next, and on our bodies as well as our souls. A. J. Gordon rejected the denigration of the body in cessationest theology, arguing that divine healing is a "pledge and foretoken" of the resurrection of the body, as sanctification is of the holiness of heaven.[35] "The heresy of death-worship," he complained, "has supplanted the doctrine of resurrection with a multitude of Christians, because they have allowed . . . departing to be with Christ, to take the place of the final victory, the coming of Christ, to quicken our mortal bodies by his Spirit that

32. Ibid.

33. Ibid., 5.

34. Alexander, *Pentecostal Healing*, 51.

35. Gordon, *Ministry of Healing*, 52, cited in Van De Walle, *Heart of the Gospel*, 127.

dwelleth in us."[36] Although not directly an element in their theologies of healing, it is striking how so many healing ministries were motivated by a very this-worldly love for the poor, including those of Allen, Cullis, Gordon, and Simpson, again in continuity with Wesley's own motivation for a ministry of health and healing.

Yet the theology of the healing movement, at its heart, is characterized more by discontinuity with Wesley than by what they held in common. Most significant was the different way they understood the relation between medicine and prayer. While Wesley saw them as two complementary methods God uses to heal, the healing theologies, to different degrees, placed medicine and prayer in tension, with the latter as God's preferred manner of healing. This tension was grounded in their two most distinctive doctrines: healing in the atonement and the prayer of faith. The first had to do with the divine promise of healing, and the second with how that promise is received.

A. J. Gordon, with his customary caution, argued that "in the atonement of Christ there seems to be a foundation laid for faith in bodily healing. . . . We have Christ set before us as the sickness-bearer as well as the sin-bearer of his people." Gordon then connects this atoning work with its eschatological fulfillment: "We hold that *in its ultimate consequences* the atonement affects the body as well as the soul of man. Sanctification is the consummation of Christ's redemptive work for the soul; and resurrection is the consummation of his redemptive work for the body. And these meet and are fulfilled at the coming and kingdom of Christ."[37] Gordon makes clear what is often implicit in many of the other healing theologies, that the atonement provides a measure of the healing that will be fully found in the age to come.

Most of the other healing theologians were far more bold in their statement of the doctrine. R. Kelso Carter argued that "the Atonement has provided for the body all that it has provided for the soul";[38] A. B. Simpson held that "Christ literally substituted His body for our body," providing for the consequences of sin, be they spiritual or physical.[39] Thus healing for the body came to be seen as a promise of God parallel to salvation of the soul. This was made explicit by R. L. Stanton, whose *Gospel*

36. Gordon, *Ministry of Healing*, 195, cited in Mullin, *Miracles and the Modern Imagination*, 96.

37. Gordon, *Ministry of Healing*, 3rd ed., 16, cited in Hardesty, *Faith Cure*, 93.

38. Carter, *Atonement for Sin and Sickness*, 17.

39. Simpson, *Lord for the Body*, 78, cited in Van De Walle, *Heart of the Gospel*, 131.

Parallelisms: Illustrated in the Healing of Body and Soul, was published by Carrie Judd Montgomery. Stanton argued that "the atonement of Christ lays a foundation equally for deliverance from sin and for deliverance from disease; that complete provision has been made for both."[40]

But to say the promises are parallel is not to say that are of equal significance. It does mean, as we shall see, that healing for the body is received in much the same manner as salvation. But salvation, especially sanctification, is the greater gift. This corresponds to their common understanding of the root of sickness. While sickness may be permitted by God "as a corrective," says Carter, "Sickness and sin are alike the work of the devil."[41] But in addition to its Satanic rather than divine origin, there is also the sense in most healing theologies that sin is at the root of sickness. Hence for many sufferers, dealing with sin and their broken relationship with God is the precondition for healing.

A. B. Simpson uniquely carries this atonement theology beyond the cross to the resurrection. He argues that "there is something higher even than the cross. It is the resurrection of our Lord. There the gospel of healing finds the fountain of its deepest life. The death of Christ destroys it—the root of sickness. But it is the life of Jesus that supplies the source of health and life for our redeemed bodies. The body of Christ is the living fountain of all our vital strength."[42] Through the Holy Spirit, the believer is united with the risen Christ. This brings more than a restoration to health. It is not, Simpson says, "an old man made well" but "a renewing of life,"[43] a divine life that, in Bernie Van De Walle's words, "lifts those in whom it dwells to a quality of physical life beyond the ordinary." Through "the indwelling of Christ" the believer "receives not only remedial divine healing but ongoing divine health."[44]

It is in the second distinctive doctrine of the healing theologians, on faith and the prayer of faith, that the parallels with the Holiness movement's teaching on sanctification are most clearly seen. As with Holiness theologies in general, the exercise of faith included both trusting in God and an action as a sign of that trust.

40. Stanton, *Gospel Parallelisms,* 13, cited in Dayton, *Theological Roots,* 126.

41. Carter, *Atonement for Sin and Sickness,* 227.

42. Simpson, *Gospel of Healing,* 27, cited in Van De Walle, *Heart of the Gospel,* 134.

43. Simpson, *Lord for the Body,* 44, cited in Van De Walle, *Heart of the Gospel,* 134.

44. Van De Walle, *Heart of the Gospel,* 135.

Faith is understood as a gift of God, a work of the Holy Spirit. Both Carrie Judd and A. B. Simpson say they only became sicker when they depended on their own exertions of faith rather than on God. "Our very faith is but the grace of Christ Himself within us," Simpson argued. "We can exercise it, and thus far our responsibility extends; but He must impart it."[45] Much as Keswick theology would argue for sanctification, faith is not an exertion of our will but a removal of self to enable the Holy Spirit to come in and provide divine strength. The trust is not in our having faith, but in Christ and his atonement.

Healing "comes to us by faith," says Simpson. "It is not the faith that heals. God heals, but faith receives it."[46] To exercise faith is to trust that healing is the promise and will of God. "If the Lord Jesus has purchased healing for you in his redemption," Simpson argues, "it must be God's will for you to have it . . ."[47] Thus, Simpson insists, it "is not enough to believe that [one] may be healed, or to believe in God's power to do this; but [one] must definitely claim the blessing, count upon it, confess it, and commit [oneself] to it by going forth to reckon upon it, and act as if it were a reality."[48] Carter makes a similar claim "There is no more necessity for us to be sick than to sin," he argues. "If then we are wholly the Lord's, and rest in His Word, we may enjoy health of body and of soul."[49] The language of consecration and faith in the word of God echoes Phoebe Palmer, but Carter's claim that healing is now available and receivable by faith is not significantly different from the more Keswick-sounding theology of Simpson.

While faith is described in terms of dependence or resting, it is nonetheless an acting faith. If one really believes the promise, then one

45. Simpson, "Gospel of Healing," *Triumphs of Faith*, 257, cited in Curtis, *Great Physician*, 95. This emphasis on faith as a distinctive gift from a transcendent God was designed to distinguish the divine healing movement from the "mind cure" philosophies of New Thought and Christian Science, which in different ways emphasized the spiritual over the physical and the power of belief over materiality, including sickness. These mind cure philosophies completely contradicted the positive evaluation of embodiment within the divine healing movement. On the various mind cure traditions, see Taves, *Fits, Trances, and Visions*, 212–25.

46. Simpson, *Four-Fold Gospel*, 62.

47. Simpson, *Gospel of Healing*, 59, cited in Van De Walle, *Heart of the Gospel*, 141 n. 135.

48. Simpson, *Friday Meeting Talk*, 1:35, cited in Van De Walle, *Heart of the Gospel*, 141.

49. Carter, *Atonement for Sin and Sickness*, 231–32.

must act on that faith regardless of symptoms that may persist. "If I say that I believe a certain thing, my actions must testify to that belief,"[50] wrote Carrie Judd. Echoing Phoebe Palmer's teaching on faith for entire sanctification, Judd argued, "If, after prayer for physical healing, we reckon the work as already accomplished in our bodies, we shall not fear to *act out* that faith, and to make physical exertions which will justify our professed belief in the healing."[51] While Judd was perhaps the most emphatic proponent of an acting faith, it became standard teaching among the healing theologians.

Doubt was the great enemy of faith, and persistence of symptoms was the primary occasion for doubt. "The foundation of the doctrine of faith-healing is the Word of God, and not visible results," Carter argued. "*Apparent* failures count for nothing."[52] "Healing in Scripture was not always instantaneous," he noted, so "we must not be discouraged if the answer appears to be delayed, but diligently seek for possible hindrances in ourselves."[53] Carter finds in Scripture "three vital reasons for an imperfect or a gradual healing":

1. The absence of the complete "touch" [of Jesus].

2. Imperfect consecration, requiring time for the entrance of the light and the deepening of the work.

3. Neither comprehending nor apprehending God's plan.

"But when we come to Jesus," he concludes, "when the conditions are all met, when we touch, we are certainly healed."[54]

Part of what Carter has addressed here is the question of whether healing is instantaneous or gradual. Chappell argues that there was actually a difference among healing practitioners on this issue. Many "believed healing, like entire sanctification, was an experience of the supernatural intervention of God and always occurred instantaneously," and "if it did not, it was due to a lack of faith or existing sin on the part

---

50. Judd, "Faith Without Works," *Triumphs of Faith* 1 (October 1881) 145–46, cited in Curtis, *Great Physician*, 91.

51. Judd, "Faith's Reckonings," *Triumphs of Faith* 1 (January 1881) 1–4, cited in Curtis, *Great Physician*, 92.

52. Carter, *Atonement for Sin and Sickness*, 234.

53. Ibid., 237.

54. Ibid., 212.

of the sick person."[55] This is the position of Carter. On the other hand, those who had a "Keswickian view of sanctification" often "believed there was a point at which God touched the person, but that the actual physical healing or recovery would occur gradually." Thus, "one could receive the healing instantaneously, but must continue to exercise faith in order to experience a full recovery."[56] This was the view of Cullis, Judd, and Simpson, among others.

Kimberly Alexander has found a similar distinction between healing theologies of the "Wesleyan-Pentecostals" in the tradition of Parham and Seymour, and the "Finished Work" Pentecostals who follow Durham. Wesleyan-Pentecostals, she argues, understood grace for healing as immediately available much as Palmer did for sanctification, but there was "a move back to Wesley's original intent of *crisis-process*, at least where healing is concerned."[57] Thus healing could be both instantaneous and gradual. This could even more be seen as a recovery of *Palmer's* original intent, in which entire sanctification, immediately received, was lived out daily through consecration and faith. From this angle, instantaneous healing was the beginning of growing in and maintaining health. For "Finished Work" Pentecostals, healing was accomplished on the cross. "Just as one reckoned that the work necessary for salvation was done," Alexander says, "the Spirit-filled believer also reckoned that healing had been accomplished." Healing was claimed "in the name of Jesus," and one acted in faith without regard to symptoms.[58] Gradually the symptoms would disappear in accordance with the healing that had already occurred.

Both groups of Pentecostals "held that a person who had real faith would not consult a doctor or use medicine," for this "would show a lack or weakness in faith." Divine healing was through faith in Jesus *alone.*[59] This widespread consensus among early Pentecostals was rooted in the teaching both of Parham and the Azusa Street revival, and was an inheritance from the healing movement.

Yet there was more nuance among healing theologians than some of their more straightforward statements would indicate. For most, reliance

55. Chappell, "Divine Healing Movement," 74.

56. Ibid., 74–75.

57. Alexander, *Pentecostal Healing*, 205–6.

58. Ibid., 213.

59. Ibid.

on doctors and medicine depended on the nature and degree of one's faith. A. J. Gordon wrote of a Lutheran pastor who "would not allow any remedy to come between him and his God," and rejoiced when others likewise had an "unreserved faith" that enabled them to dispense with physicians. Yet that same pastor "never regarded it as a sin in any one to take medicine or consult a doctor, when they had not the special faith to do without them."[60]

Similarly, R. Kelso Carter argued that "physicians are mercifully provided for those who cannot trust God alone,"[61] knowing "that only a small percentage of the sick will trust in Him."[62] But he also insisted that nowhere in the Bible is there even a single case of a person being healed of disease through medicine. "The Bible," he says, "never advises us to trust in any one or anything but in God."[63] God's "means and medicines are threefold,—prayer of faith, laying on of hands, anointing with oil in the name of the Lord."[64]

Of all the healing theologians, A. B. Simpson perhaps has the strongest language against medical means: "Our healing must be wholly of God or not of grace at all. If Christ heals he must do it alone. This principle ought to settle forever the question of using [medical] means in connection with faith for healing . . ."[65] According to Van De Walle, part of Simpson's concern was that the credit for healing be given to Christ alone. If both divine and medical means are used, persons will most naturally credit the medical for the healing. But, Van De Walle also notes, the ultimate problem was that an attempt to depend on both medical means and Christ," is a manifestation of unbelief."[66]

Yet even Simpson's view is not as stark as it seems. Faith for healing is itself a gift of God, he says, and not an exertion of our will to believe. Until one has such a faith, where one has confidence in the healing provided in the atonement, then one is not ready to lay aside doctors and medicine and step out in faith.[67] Thus Simpson writes, "We have nothing

60. Cited in Robinson, *Divine Healing*, 193.
61. Carter, *Atonement for Sin and Sickness*, 228.
62. Ibid., 157.
63. Ibid., 133; see also 148.
64. Ibid., 191.
65. Cited in Robinson, *Divine Healing*, 183.
66. Van De Walle, *Heart of the Gospel*, 140.
67. Robinson, *Divine Healing*, 184.

to say against the use of remedies as far as those are concerned who are not ready to trust their bodies fully to the Lord. For them it is well enough to use all the help that nature and science can give, and we cheerfully admit that their remedies have some value as far as they go. . . . Unless they have been led to trust Christ entirely for something higher and stronger than their natural life they had better stick to natural remedies."[68] Thus, unlike John Alexander Dowie, Simpson never ridiculed persons who sought medical help.[69]

While Wesley had seen both medicine and prayer as means of healing by God, the healing theologians instead portrayed medicine at best as an inferior means of healing provided out of love for unbelievers or Christians with weak faith. There are several reasons for this difference in sensibility.

Although both understood the root of sickness to lie in the Fall, for Wesley that did not mean sin was always the direct cause of sickness (although it might be). The Fall disrupted the entire creation in such a way that disease and other afflictions were the result, and both medicine and prayer were potential remedies. For the healing theologians the cause of sickness was ultimately spiritual; hence physicians were at best alleviating symptoms rather than addressing the underlying issue of sin. This made sanctification and the prayer of faith far superior to medical approaches.

Second was the state of medicine itself. As Nancy Hardesty has helpfully shown, "Nineteenth-century medicine was deeply divided and largely ineffective," with most treatment of illness occurring in the home. Only later, during the early twentieth century, did medicine become the profession we think of today.[70]

Among the various approaches were the "regulars" who practiced the sort of heroic medicine that so afflicted Jennie Smith: "bleeding, blistering, and purging."[71] Based on the eighteenth-century theory of Dr. Benjamin Rush, illness was believed to be caused by imbalances in the body; hence the goal of treatment was to restore bodily equilibrium by radical therapies designed to deplete the body of overabundance. As Curtis notes, even though by the 1830s regulars themselves were beginning to challenge this theory, heroic therapies were widely used well

---

68. Simpson, *Four-Fold Gospel*, 47–48.

69. Robinson, *Divine Healing*, 184–85.

70. Hardesty, *Faith Cure*, 73.

71. Ibid., 74.

into the latter part of the century.[72] Another approach was that of the "Thomasonians" and "botanics" (or "empirics") who drew upon herbal remedies. The "homeopathic" physicians (like Charles Cullis and Phoebe Palmer's husband, Walter) had a more philosophical basis for their theories, and hence appealed especially to the more educated upper classes. A central principle of treatment was the "law of similar, that like cures like," and in contrast to the heroic approach of the regulars recommended small dosages (with little or no side effects). There was widespread acrimony between physicians, and between and within medical schools, around these competing approaches, occasionally even leading to violence.[73]

Given the state of medicine in the nineteenth century, it is no wonder that many found the promise of divine healing a welcome alternative. Moreover, many who sought divine healing did so after first consulting physicians, often to no avail. While Wesley rejected heroic therapies in his day and adopted an approach that ignored theories and advocated those remedies that seemed to work, in the nineteenth century medicine was so entrenched in competing theories that many were tempted to avoid it entirely.

A third concern identified among some Pentecostals by Kimberly Alexander may have also worked to undermine confidence in physicians. In many ways echoing a critique by Wesley, Church of God Pentecostal A. J. Tomlinson (who compared medicine to poison) offered an almost Marxist critique of "doctors who become rich through the suffering of others."[74] Alexander cites a telling comment by another Church of God writer, Mrs. B. L. Shepherd: "You can look at the doctors and see that they live better than most any laboring class of people. They have finer homes and more of the world's goods and it is all because the gospel standard has not been preached and practiced enough by Christians. . . . We have the Great Physician and we should put our case in His hands and leave it there."[75] That these sentiments were not more widespread may be due to physicians like Charles Cullis and others who themselves demonstrated a sacrificial concern for the poor.

---

72. Curtis, *Great Physician*, 29–30.

73. Hardesty, *Faith Cure*, 74–75.

74. Alexander, *Pentecostal Healing*, 227. See also Wacker, *Heaven Below*, 191–92.

75. *Church of God Evangel* 10.34 (August 23, 1919) 3, cited in Alexander, *Pentecostal Healing*, 110.

The Promise of Healing and the Freedom of God

In 1885, a twenty-one-year-old missionary named Charlie Miller arrived in Africa to work alongside Methodist Bishop William Taylor, a renowned figure in the Holiness movement. When Miller contracted malaria, he refused any medical remedies, "testifying freely and continually," as R. Kelso Carter relates, "that his trust was only in God, asserting that a 'steady faith wins,' and declaring he did not have the fever, until his last conscious cry" to call the doctor, "as he was simply choking to death."[76] He had fought the fever for three weeks, and after another week of delirium, he died.[77]

Miller's death strengthened the critics of the healing movement even as it provoked theological reassessment among many of its friends. Writing twenty years after publishing his earlier *The Atonement for Sin and Sickness*, Carter now questioned the theology he had then so forcefully defended. He saw Miller's death as "a solemn object lesson to all who held the extreme theory [of healing], and has often been pondered upon by the writer of the book which (he deeply mourns) perhaps helped Miller to take the position he did."[78] Bishop Taylor who did not hold to an extreme theory of healing, had urged Miller to avail himself of the medical care that likely would have saved his life. While he did believe (in Curtis' words) "that Christ's atonement included a provision for bodily as well as spiritual restoration," he nonetheless cautioned that "the work of physical redemption would not be completed until the resurrection." To link the healing of body and soul together in such a way that bodily cures depended on human faith rather than God's decision was a theological error that could have tragic consequences.[79]

Bishop Taylor identified the issue that is at the heart of the healing theologies. Is bodily healing promised in the same way as sanctification? Is it provided in the atonement, only awaiting our obtaining it through a consecrated faith? Without some qualification, the claim that healing is in the atonement tends to resolve the eschatological tension in favor of the "already" at the expense of the "not yet," at least as far as sickness is concerned.

76. Carter, *"Faith Healing" Reviewed*, 126.

77. Curtis, *Great Physician*, 194.

78. Carter, *"Faith Healing" Reviewed*, 126–27.

79. Curtis, *Great Physician*, 195.

Herein lies the difference between Wesley and the healing theologians. When they speak of healing as available today through the prayer of faith, and maintain that such healings are normal occurrences in the church, they and Wesley are not far apart. But when healing is understood as always attainable through the cross of Christ, the healing theologians take an optimism grace much further than did Wesley. To put it in terms used in chapter 6, the healing theologians emphasize God's faithfulness to the point of making it a guarantee of healing for those who meet the conditions, and thereby reduce God's freedom to a degree unacceptable to Wesley.

When healing proponents like Carter and William McDonald began to publish their revisions of what had become the standard healing theologies, they did so by way of a greater emphasis on God's freedom. The motivation for Carter's *"Faith Healing" Reviewed After Twenty Years* was more than tragic deaths such as Charlie Miller's. His own experience played a role as well. Originally healed of heart disease through the prayers of Charles Cullis in 1879, Carter had continued to turn to prayers for a number of aliments, always receiving a partial if not complete healing. But in 1887 he had an attack of nervous prostration, and despite many prayers, including that of Cullis, there was no healing. It was only through finally taking medicine that Carter was cured and returned to active and fruitful ministry. Carter wrote that *"he had a right to praise God for sending him to that physician, and he did so with all his heart. What matters the method? It is God who ordains and directs."*[80] This is exactly the position held by John Wesley a century earlier.

The central thesis of Carter's revised theology was this: "That the Atonement of Christ covers sickness and disease as well as sin, is but to say the effects are necessarily embraced in the root cause. There was and could be no error there. But the claim that ALL the results of the Atonement are NOW open to the present living Christian is a grave mistake."[81] Thus Carter denies only "the absolute right of any believer to claim healing at any time because of Jesus' sacrificial offering of Himself for us. It says not one word against the 'prayer of faith,' but strongly endorses it."[82]

This in turn leads Carter to readjust the relation of the "already" to the "not yet." Some are indeed "HEALED BY THE DIRECT POWER

---

80. Carter, *"Faith Healing" Reviewed*, 153–58; quote on 157–58. Carter's italics.

81. Ibid., 167. Carter's capitalization.

82. Ibid., 124; see also 92.

OF GOD IN THIS DAY OF GRACE," but nevertheless "the very great majority of those who now seek healing by faith do not receive the literal answer. They are not healed."[83] The problem with his earlier book, Carter now argues, "is that it loses sight of God's times and seasons and dispensations in the effort to secure at once all the provisions of his 'will.'"[84] All the blessings of God will indeed be ours through the atonement, but the physical world itself will not be changed until the return of Christ.[85] In the meantime, in this age in which we suffer various forms of disease, "God always expects us to do for ourselves what we know or think we can do," including following rules to stay well and when ill availing ourselves of both medicines and prayer.[86] The close similarity of this with Wesley's theology is evident.

Even as proponents of healing like Carter were moderating their theologies, others on the more radical side of the Holiness movement were holding on to the older view, only for their successors to moderate it in later decades. D. S. Warner, founder of the Church of God (Anderson, Indiana), had taken a nuanced position on divine healing, arguing that the sanctified believer should not resort to physicians, but could properly use "natural remedies" as well as prayer. But after Warner's death in 1895, E. E. Byrum strongly argued that healing was purely by the prayer of the elders in the church, and the use of natural remedies was due to weak faith.[87] While strongly advocating healing in the atonement, Byrum himself began to moderate his views on such things as medicine for children, and by 1926 C. W. Naylor was advocating a renewed emphasis on the freedom of God's will. Naylor was himself bedridden and suffered lifelong pain. His abiding joy in spite of his condition was held up as an example of an advanced spirituality, even as Naylor himself saw other persons healed through his prayers at his bedside.[88]

Pentecostalism was also birthed with a radical healing theology. Charles Parham suffered a number of ailments throughout his childhood and early adulthood, receiving healing through prayer and renewed commitment to God. Although interpreting his recovery from rheumatic

---

83. Ibid., 62–63. Carter's capitalization.
84. Ibid., 69.
85. Ibid., 59, 66.
86. Ibid., 124–25.
87. Stephens, *Who Healeth All Thy Diseases*, 80–81.
88. Ibid., 169–70.

fever at age nine to be a call by God to ministry,[89] in college in 1891 he decided instead to become a physician. The rheumatic fever returned, producing intense pain and almost taking his life. Parham repented, and received a partial healing that left him unable to walk normally. It was only after renewing his commitment to preach the gospel that he received complete healing. He later observed that "the devil tried to make us believe that we could be a physician and a Christian too."[90] From 1893–1900 Parham was essentially a healing evangelist, proclaiming healing in the atonement and warning against the use of medicine as lack of faith. However, he was also aware that roughly half of the illnesses he encountered were psychosomatic, calling for a change in attitude; it was the other more serious conditions that required the prayer of faith.[91]

Parham's basic theology of healing was largely assumed at Azusa Street and among most early Pentecostals. The Apostolic Faith declared "All sickness is the work of Satan, and we have just as much right to look to Jesus for the health of these bodies as for the saving and sanctifying of our souls."[92] Kimberly Alexander has shown in detail how every early Pentecostal denomination proclaimed that the atonement provided for healing, and most understood reliance on doctors and medicine to be inimical to faith.[93] Healing was largely a practice within local churches, through prayer and often accompanied anointing with oil and laying on of hands. Over time the opposition to medicine would wane among mainstream Pentecostals, and their theology would, like that of R. Kelso Carter, move more in the direction of Wesley's emphasis on divine freedom.

The next wave of Pentecostals who popularized the more radical view were the healing evangelists. The earliest was Maria B. Woodworth-Etter, whose mass meetings began to draw widespread attention in 1885. She was, as Joshua McMullen has shown, a link between the Wesleyan/Holiness and Pentecostal movements: her roots were in the United Brethren and Winebrennarian Church of God, and she was steeped in Wesleyan Holiness thinking, but in 1912 she became a Pentecostal. Her revivals were marked by physical manifestations of the presence of

---

89. Goff, *Fields White Unto Harvest*, 25.

90. Ibid., 28–29, citation on 28.

91. Ibid., 43.

92. *Apostolic Faith* I:4 (Los Angeles: December, 1906), 2.

93. Alexander, *Pentecostal Healing*.

God—healings, dreams, visions, and trances in which persons were slain in the Spirit—which she took to be nothing more than what was common to both Wesley's movement and early American Methodism. They were certainly prominent features of early Pentecostalism. Her style of healing was confrontational, commanding the spirit of infirmity to leave the person who was afflicted.[94]

Woodworth-Etter was followed by F. F. Bosworth and Aime Semple McPherson and then, in the 1940s, by a new generation of healing evangelists, the most prominent of which were William Braham and Oral Roberts. All proclaimed that healing is accomplished in the atonement, and faith as the essential condition for receiving the promise. They also taught that the healing evangelist is God's anointed, a message somewhat in tension with the more normal congregation-centered practices of local Pentecostal churches. The mass revivals and theology of healing evangelism were widely promoted by Gordon Lindsay's periodical *The Voice of Healing*, and eventually would spread worldwide.[95]

But this resurgent teaching of the more radical view was not without its critics within Pentecostalism. Donald Gee, a major mid-century figure in international Pentecostalism known for his avoidance of extremes—he was called the "Apostle of Balance"[96]—published his own assessment in 1952 in *Trophimus I Left Sick*. There he argued that while healing evangelists urge persons to claim by faith the healing provided in the atonement, many who do so nonetheless find no relief from their illnesses. While not denying healing is provided in the atonement, Gee argued, as Carter had done over sixty years earlier, that Scripture promised no absolute guarantee that believers would be healed.[97]

Gee's critique presaged a shift that would soon occur throughout much of Pentecostalism still committed to the healing in the atonement theology. As Gary McGee notes, the message that "healing in the atonement" is "always available to those with sufficient faith, with resort to medicine and doctors as implicit sign of unbelief" would yield "over time" to "a more holistic understanding that saw medical science as a gift from God . . ." The most prominent expression of this more moderate theology was in 1978, when Oral Roberts founded his City of Faith

94. McMullen, "Marie B. Woodworth-Etter"; see also Alexander, *Pentecostal Healing*, 177–79.

95. See Harrell, *All Things Are Possible*.

96. Bundy, "Gee, Donald," 662.

97. McGee, *Miracles, Missions, and American Pentecostalism*, 196.

hospital, specifically designed "to show how belief in the miraculous healing with medical treatment could 'round out the totality of healing for the whole man.'"[98]

Of course, the state of medicine itself was more advanced and reliable in the latter twentieth century than it had been at the end of the nineteenth. It was also much more widely available in places like America than it was a century earlier. But even among the poor throughout the world that gravitated toward divine healing, the motive was less a rejection of medicine than finding ways to cope in its absence.

As mainstream Pentecostals and others influenced by the healing evangelists were moderating their theologies of healing, a new Word of Faith movement began proclaiming an even more extreme version of the atonement theology. The roots of this movement lie with E. W. Kenyon, an earlier twentieth-century figure whose theological outlook was shaped by the Higher Life wing of the Holiness movement. But Kenyon also drew upon ideas found within New Thought, a mind cure movement he deemed heretical, but which had, he believed, nonetheless recovered some elements of biblical truth the church had neglected.[99] Kenyon developed a very distinctive form of Finished Work theology (using the term earlier than William Durham), in which he sharply contrasted a faith based on sense knowledge from one based on the revelation knowledge contained in the word of God. Kenyon argued that believers should demand healing in the Name of Jesus, and then act on that faith through positive confession. It is a spiritual law, he believed, that we become what we confess, so to confess our healing based on revelation knowledge was to eventually become healed.[100] By the mid-twentieth century Kenneth Hagin and a host of other Word of Faith proponents would further radicalize Kenyon's theology, extend it to prosperity as well as healing, and spread it across the globe.[101]

There are signs that even this eccentric version of healing in the atonement theology is beginning to moderate. If it does, it will likely

---

98. Ibid., 197.

99. Simmons, *E. W. Kenyon*, xii. Simmons' work is more balanced than McConnell's *A Different Gospel*, which makes New Thought the primary source of Kenyon's theology.

100. Ibid., 164–73.

101. For a clear summary and critique of Word of Faith theology, see Barron, *Health and Wealth Gospel*.

follow the path of its healing theology predecessors in not equating the use of medicine with weak or absent faith.

But there is a deeper theological issue that runs through all these various healing theologies, from Ethan O. Allen and Sarah Mix to the present day. Kimberly Alexander highlights it in her contrast between the Wesleyan/Holiness and Finished Work strands of early Pentecostalism. For the Wesleyan/Holiness stream, "every act of healing is viewed first of all as a sign of the coming Kingdom," a foretaste or earnest of the resurrection in which we now participate.[102] Within the Finished Work tradition "healing was accomplished on the cross," "a work already done," waiting to be appropriated by faith.[103] For virtually all these early Pentecostals, healing was one of the signs found in the longer ending of Mark (16:20), a text mostly ignored by the nineteenth-century healing movement. The difference, says Alexander, was in "how the *signs* were interpreted. Are these signs of the inbreaking Kingdom or are they signs of a work already finished? Consistently the two groups saw the signs as pointing to two different directions. For the Wesleyan camp, the signs were the inbreaking of the Kingdom to come; for the Finished Work camp, they pointed backward to the cross."[104] All Pentecostals believed healing was provided in the atonement, but clearly that took on different meanings in these two models of healing.

Although as Alexander shows the theological claim that healing is in the atonement does not necessarily lead to an overly-realized eschatology, it nonetheless has a strong tendency to do so. This is the temptation that runs through all the healing theologies, and perhaps the reason what Carter called the extreme view continually re-asserts itself against those who seek to qualify what it seems to promise. The fundamental theological error was to understand divine healing as parallel to sanctification, when as Wesley knew and Carter discovered they are neither identical in significance nor received by believers with the same certainty. All too often, the result of this equation was to turn the possibility of healing into a given, and expectant faith into presumption.

What is needed is a theology of healing that maintains the tension between God's faithfulness and freedom, and between the "already" and "not yet." In this John Wesley's theology has much to commend it. As I

---

102. Alexander, *Pentecostal Healing*, 203–4.

103. Ibid., 212–13.

104. Ibid., 234.

noted in an earlier work, for Wesley, "Healing was important, because it was important to a loving God who will ultimately put an end to sickness and death. But it was not as important as salvation itself. . . . Consequently to elevate healing to the level of salvation is as great an error as to ignore it. Prayer for healing should be a natural and normal feature of the Christian community, but it always in service to the greater goal of growing in love."[105]

105. Knight, *Future for Truth*, 178. On 176–78 I summarize a typology of late twentieth-century Charismatic healing theologies that I develop more extensively in "God's Faithfulness and God's Freedom."

CHAPTER 12

The Church as Witness

... houses of worship should be, not like the first class
car on a European railway, for the exclusive, but like
the streets we walk, free for all. Their portals should
be opened as wide for the common laborer, or the
indigent widow, as for all the assuming, or the wealthy.

—B. T. ROBERTS[1]

... the color line was washed away in the blood.

—FRANK BARTLEMAN[2]

WESLEYANISM BY ITS VERY nature tends to fuel discontent with the condition of the church, much as it does with the condition of persons. At the root of this discontent is a vision of holiness, or what it would mean for God's will to be done on earth as it is in heaven. If there is anywhere the love and righteousness of God should be manifested, it should be in that community that is termed by Paul the body of Christ. Yet all too often, the church seems to mirror the culture more than the kingdom of heaven.

The bias in Wesleyan and Pentecostal movements is that the apostolic church most faithfully reflected the kingdom of heaven in its life and mission. While even it was by no means perfect, apostolic Christianity

1. Roberts, "Free Churches," cited by Cullum, "Gospel Simplicity," 102.
2. Bartleman, *Azusa Street*, 54.

served as a basis for critique and a model to emulate. For many, the recovery of apostolic faith and love would also lead to recovery of apostolic power. The ultimate goal of this "primitivist" or "restorationist" impulse was not to return to the past, but by way of the early church to anticipate the future kingdom of heaven.

The most common strategy was that pioneered by Pietism of calling existing churches to renewal. But when churches or denominations resisted that call, new communities would be established. The sadly repeated story is that these new communities, though initially impacting the surrounding culture, eventually succumb to the same accommodation that marked their predecessor bodies. Yet the vision of holiness and optimism of grace does not die, but continues to inspire movements calling the church to renewal.

Renewing the Church

When John Wesley and his colleagues considered in conference the question of "God's design in raising up the Preachers called Methodist," their answer was "to reform the nation, particularly the church, and to spread scriptural holiness over the land."[3] This succinct mission statement could be applied to the movement as a whole. The entire structure, from the preachers to the societies with their small groups and spiritual discipline, was to hold before people and the church the promise of justification and sanctification, and to enable their appropriation in hearts and lives. The result would not only be Methodist societies that communally embody this new life of love, but eventually the renewal of the church itself.

In taking this approach to renewal, Wesley is following the path laid out by the Pietists. Philip Jacob Spener's lay-led *collegia pietatis* (colleges of piety) were designed to renew the hearts and lives of seventeenth-century German Lutherans through prayer and studying Scripture. This strategy of *ecclesiola in ecclesia* (little churches within the larger church) spread throughout Europe, and was introduced in England by German Reformed Pietist Anthony Horneck in the second half of the seventeenth century.[4]

3. John Wesley "Minutes of Several Conversations" (Q.3), *Wesley's Works* (Jackson) 8:299.

4. On the role of Horneck, see Kisker, *Foundation for Revival*.

Yet Wesley's *ecclesiola* were distinctive in that they were specifically designed to enable persons to move along the way of salvation. Every Methodist, from awakened sinners to those perfected in love, belonged to a class meeting, which had as its purpose keeping persons accountable to the discipline, and thereby focused on both God and the neighbor. The band, which was the other major group, helped persons to grow in sanctification. In addition, penitent groups aided those who had fallen away through loss of faith to regain what they had lost, and select societies (or select bands) were for those well advanced in sanctification or who had attained Christian perfection. The larger society meetings, which met quarterly, were occasions for teaching, exhortation, and testimony.[5] The assumption was that as persons were renewed, so too would be the church.

This assumption is rooted in Wesley's understanding of what constituted a church. Drawing on Ephesians, Wesley defines the "catholic or universal church" as "All the persons in the universe whom God hath so called out of the world . . . to be 'one body,' united by 'one spirit'; having 'one faith, one hope, one baptism; one God and Father of all, who is above all, and through all, and in them all.'"[6] The church, put simply, is the congregation of believers, and "is called 'holy' because every member thereof is holy, though in different degrees, as he that called them is holy."[7]

Wesley therefore declined to insist on that part of the Articles of Religion of the Church of England that describes a church as where "the pure word of God is preached, and the sacraments be duly administered." This would exclude all Roman Catholics along with many others from the church catholic even when they conform to the Ephesian definition.[8] The church, then, is neither co-extensive with its membership rolls nor defined by its worship practices, but consists of all those who are aiming for or growing in holiness.

The holiness of the church, Wesley believed, has been threatened throughout history by the "mystery of iniquity." Since the Fall, sin spread

---

5. For analyses of the purpose and practice of Wesley's varied groups, see Watson, *The Early Methodist Class Meeting*. For a comparison with Pietist and Moravian groups, see Snyder, *Signs of the Spirit*.

6. John Wesley, "Of the Church" [I] 14, *Wesley's Works* 3:50. This understanding is especially prominent in the later Wesley. For an account of the changes in Wesley's ecclesiology over time, see Oh, *John Wesley's Ecclesiology*.

7. Ibid., [III] 28, 3:55–56.

8. Ibid., [I] 18–19, 3:52.

throughout the world, including Israel itself, and while the sanctifying work of God never fully disappeared, neither did it stem the tide of ungodliness.[9] In Jesus Christ, God provided a way out of this condition, and indeed Pentecost "was the dawn of the proper gospel day," in which "a proper Christian church," manifesting righteousness, peace, and joy, was established.[10] But the mystery of iniquity soon infected the apostolic church, of which the New Testament bears abundant witness, leading to partiality for one group over another, zeal for particular opinions coupled with lack of mutual forbearance, tolerance of overt sinful behavior, and desire for wealth.[11]

The mystery of iniquity continued to plague the church throughout post-apostolic history. In the first three centuries following the apostolic age there were seasons in which true Christianity revived, often in times of persecution. But what could not be accomplished by persecution was done with great effectiveness by Emperor Constantine. As he "poured in a flood of riches, honours, and power upon the Christians, more especially upon the clergy," Wesley argues, a "grand blow was struck at the very root of that humble, gentle, patient love, which is . . . the whole essence of true religion."[12] The disease of sin now spread unchecked throughout the church, and even the Protestant Reformation, which brought needed reforms in doctrine and practice, did not reverse it.[13] While there have certainly been individual examples of true Christianity in all ages,[14] the witness of the church as a whole has been anything but. Indeed, Wesley insists the primary reason the gospel has so little credibility to those outside the church is "the lives of Christians."[15]

It is this deplorable condition of the church that Wesley believed God was curing in the eighteenth-century awakening, and had raised up the Methodists as key agents in that mission. Yet the mystery of iniquity was not so easily defeated, and in his later years Wesley began to see it among his own Methodists. In his 1787 sermon "On God's Vineyard" he asks what more could God have done for the good of the Methodists than

---

9. John Wesley, "The Mystery of Iniquity" 1–6, *Wesley's Works* 2:452–53.

10. Ibid., 11, 2:455.

11. Ibid. 14–21, 2:456–60.

12. Ibid., 27, 2:462–63.

13. Ibid., 29, 2:465.

14. Ibid., 30, 2:466.

15. John Wesley, "The General Spread of the Gospel" 21, *Wesley's Works* 2:495.

what already has been done through doctrine, spiritual helps (e.g., the classes and bands), discipline, and protection by the King of their freedom to preach the gospel? Given all of this, would it not be reasonable to expect that God's Methodist vineyard would produce excellent grapes? Wesley himself expected as much. Having witnessed the transformation of hearts and lives at the movement's inception, "I could expect nothing less than all these would have lived like angels here below; that they would have walked as continually seeing him that is invisible; . . . living in eternity, and walking in eternity."[16]

But instead of an increase of faith and love spreading throughout the entire church, the Methodists brought forth wild grapes: error, enthusiasm, pride, judging and condemning one another, all subversive to love for God and neighbor. It also brought forth love of the world, manifested in a desire for possessions and wealth.[17]

Two years later Wesley offers another diagnosis of what has compromised Methodist witness. "The Methodists," he argued, "grow more and more self indulgent, because they *grow rich*;[18] they "are deplorably wanting in the practice of Christian self-denial."[19] True Christianity, he fears, "has a tendency, in the process of time, to undermine and destroy itself," for the diligence and frugality it encourages eventually produces riches, which in turn "beget pride, love of the world, and every temper that is destructive of Christianity."[20] The solution is one he recommended almost three decades earlier: not only gain all you can and save all you can, but also give all you can, most especially to the poor.[21]

The threat of riches to true Christianity is not only at the heart of Wesley's historical and contextual analysis of the condition of the church, but is also seen as central to the teaching of Jesus. Wesley echoes that teaching in a series of sermons published throughout his ministry: Upon Our Lord's Sermon on the Mount VIII (1748), Self-Denial (1760), The Use of Money (1760), The Danger of Riches (1781), On Riches (1788), Causes of the Inefficacy of Christianity (1789), and The Danger of Increasing Riches (1790), among others. His focus on this topic in the latter

16. John Wesley, "On God's Vineyard" 5.1, *Wesley's Works* 3:514–15.

17. Ibid., 5.2–3, 3:515.

18. John Wesley, "Causes of the Inefficacy of Christianity" 16, *Wesley's Works* 4:95.

19. Ibid., 14, 4:94.

20. Ibid., 17, 4:95–96.

21. Ibid., 18, 4:96.

years of his ministry is indicative of the deteriorating spiritual condition among Methodists themselves.

Wesley is not concerned in these writings to advance a particular economic theory. His focus is resolutely spiritual—on the desires of the heart. When a desire for material abundance governs our heart and life, then it undermines generosity toward the neighbor, including the poor. At the same time we lose our desire to seek God and God's righteousness, as life is now centered on possessions and material well-being. That is, a desire for riches—which Wesley understands as a desire for more than is necessary—directly subverts love for God and one's neighbor, which is the heart of sanctification. Where our treasure is, so will our hearts be as well.

Wesley is well aware that for Christians to live this way is to run counter to widely accepted cultural norms. He argued in a 1788 sermon that if one lives by faith—by knowing and trusting in God—then one walks by faith as well. Those who do "regulate all their judgments concerning good and evil, not with reference to visible and temporal things, but to things invisible and eternal."[22] Thus he challenges his readers, "by what standard do you judge the value of things? . . . which do you judge best,—that your son should be a pious cobbler, or a profane lord? Which appears to you most eligible,—that your daughter should be a child of God, and walk on foot, or a child of the devil and ride in a coach and six? . . . do you 'seek' in the general tenor of your life, 'the things that are above,' or the 'things that are below'?"[23] The "things" that are "above" and "eternal" are God and the love which Jesus Christ revealed. To faithfully seek those things—to live and walk in eternity—is to embody in this age heaven below.

Wesley's vision of the entire church renewed in holiness—Protestant, Catholic, Orthodox, and Coptic—is consistent with this. In terms of the *order* with which those in the churches embrace inward and outward holiness, Wesley believes "God will observe the same order which he hath done from the beginning of Christianity." All shall know God, "not from the greatest to the least (this is that wisdom of the world which is foolishness with God) but 'from the least to the greatest,'" so that praise will belong to God alone. But while the poor and common people are generally the first to embrace the promise of holiness, no one is left out

22. John Wesley, "The Difference Between Walking by Sight, and Walking by Faith" 14, *Wesley's Works* 4:54.

23. Ibid., 15, 4:55–56.

of the gospel. "Before the end," Wesley says, "even the rich shall enter into the kingdom of God. Together with them will enter in the great, the noble, the honourable; yea the rulers, the princes, the kings of the earth. Last of all the wise and learned, the men of genius, the philosophers, will be convinced that they are fools; will 'be converted and become as little children, and enter into the Kingdom of God.'"[24]

The *nature* of the church will then mirror that of the kingdom of God. Everyone shall know God, "from the least to the greatest." "The grand Pentecost shall 'fully come,'" and the devout in every nation "shall 'all be filled with the Holy Ghost.'" They will then be like the church in Acts 2: faithful to apostolic doctrine, in fellowship with one another, and continue to break bread together and pray. Filled with abundant grace, and united in spirit, the church will then manifest in its very life the love that governs the kingdom of God. None will say that any of their possessions are their own, "but they will have all things in common." No one among them will have need, for those "possessed of lands or houses will sell them," distributing the proceeds to everyone in accordance with their need. At the same time, "their desires . . . and passions, and tempers will be cast in one mould, while all are doing the will of God on earth as it is done in heaven."[25]

Charles Wesley shares the same vision of the church renewed in this remarkable hymn:

> Which of the Christians now
>> would their possessions sell?
> The fact you scarce allow,
>> the truth incredible:
> that saints of old so weak should prove
> and as themselves their neighbor love.
>
> Of your abundant store
>> you may a few relieve,
> but all to feed the poor
>> you cannot, cannot give,
> houses and lands for Christ forego,
> or live as Jesus lived below.

24. John Wesley, "General Spread," 19, *Wesley's Works* 2:493–94.
25. Ibid., 20, 2:494–95.

> Jesus, thy church inspire
>> with apostolic love,
> infuse the one desire
>> to store our wealth above,
> with earthly goods freely to part,
> and joyfully sell all in heart.[26]

For the Wesleys the Acts 2 church was itself a model of heaven below, with this exception: the presence of sin still defiled the church, in the form of Ananias and Sapphira's love of money, and the partiality that led to neglect of widows of one group by another. This time, John Wesley believed, the renewed church would have a purer eschatological character, whose life together would be governed solely by love.[27]

How well did early Methodism embody this vision of a holy community? We have already seen John Wesley's despair at upwardly mobile Methodists who, instead of being a leaven for the church, now needed to be leavened themselves. Yet there are still important ways Methodism did reflect something of the reality of heaven below. Phyllis Mack, in her insightful study of everyday persons in Wesley's movement, speaks of the loneliness experienced by many who became Methodists, due to death of loved ones, estrangement from parents, separation from family, neglect by fathers and abuse by husbands.[28] Certainly this was not their sole motivation for joining. "But the fact is," Mack argues, "that many of their perceived sins before justification—anger, lust, snobbery, hypocrisy, lying—involved flawed social relationships, while in Methodism, they encountered a theology and practice in which salvation was felt and described as a vastly increased capacity to love."[29] It is as a community of love for God and one another that Methodism at its best embodied heaven below. Though falling short of the Wesley brothers' vision it nonetheless enabled participants to experience in this life a real anticipation of the love that will fully reign in the age to come.

After Methodism itself became a denomination on both sides of the Atlantic, it gradually lost its character as a renewal movement. Class meetings became too large to be effective, and discipline was neglected, until after a long period of decline in the nineteenth century they finally

26. Hymn 4:1–3, Kimbrough, *Songs for the Poor*.

27. John Wesley, "General Spread," 20, *Wesley's Works* 2:495.

28. Mack, *Heart Religion*, 75–76.

29. Ibid., 81.

disappeared from Methodist life entirely in America and England (although they did continue in some form in both African American and Caribbean Methodism).

The Pietist strategy of renewal was freshly appropriated by the nineteenth-century Holiness movement, now directed at the main Methodist denominations themselves as well as those in other theological traditions. Phoebe Palmer's Tuesday Meetings were a bit like Wesley's societies, including teaching, exhortation, discussion, and testimony. They lacked the small groups and spiritual discipline, although in her day that was considered already to be a feature of Methodist churches.

After the Civil War, the Holiness camp meeting became a new agent of church renewal. With the success of the first Holiness camp meeting in Vineland, New Jersey, in 1867, the National Camp Meeting Association for the Promotion of Holiness was formed under the leadership of John S. Inskip. Camp meetings themselves had long been an accepted and honored institution among Methodists since the early decades of the nineteenth century. While the original camp meetings placed their focus on conversion, the Holiness camp meetings were centered on entire sanctification, and therefore on a Christian audience.

From the Holiness perspective, post-bellum Methodism was in dire need of renewal. In 1873 Asbury Lowery defended the use of extraordinary agents of renewal such as Holiness camp meetings by providing a searching analysis of the state of the church. Expanded "ecclesiastical machinery" had put the focus more on externals than spirituality, while spiritual means of grace such as camp meetings were neglected. Holiness literature, including the writings of Wesley and Fletcher, were no longer read. Large numbers of unconverted persons were being accepted into membership, and "respectable vices" were tolerated. Methodism had also become increasingly wealthy and popular. "We are numerous, wealthy, educated, and damagingly respectable," Lowery warned. "From these sources, influences are constantly springing adverse to holiness."[30] The wealth and power of mainline Methodism would only accelerate in the 1880s.[31] From the Holiness perspective, Methodism was now seemingly reliving the time when Emperor Constantine wounded holiness through pouring riches and power on the church, a fate Wesley had feared for his Methodists.

30. Cited in Dieter, *Holiness Revival of the Nineteenth Century*, 109.
31. Ibid., 171.

Predictably, many in Methodism did not see the need for renewal. They argued that Methodism itself was a Holiness movement, irregular institutions like Holiness camp meetings were unWesleyan and schismatic, and the Holiness movement as a whole was more in the enthusiast tradition of George Bell than that of John Wesley.[32] The very success of Methodism as the dominant form of Christianity in nineteenth-century America, a prominence recognized by American presidents, seemed to refute the need for renewal. So while a potent force for renewal in the 1870s, the Holiness movement by the 1880s began to face stiffer opposition that eventually led to its marginalization in mainline Methodism.

Coming Out

The late-nineteenth-century Holiness movement was not the first to face the dilemma of what to do when a church or denomination resists renewal. It was a live issue in John Wesley's day, as some of the Methodist preachers would have been happy to leave the Church of England and begin a new denomination. Charles Wesley feared that his brother would capitulate to their pressure and consent to separation. But John would not separate, although he would take a number of irregular actions to meet the missional needs of the movement, actions that would greatly disturb Charles.

John Wesley addressed the issue in his 1786 sermon "On Schism." There he argued that schism "is evil in itself," for separation "from a body of living Christians with whom we were before united is a grievous breach of the law of love." Love by its very nature unites, so it is only when "love grows cold" that separation becomes thinkable.[33] Schism also produces evil fruit: "unkind tempers," "evil surmising," "severe and uncharitable judging" in the heart leading in turn to "evil words" and "unrighteous actions."[34] The act of separation both flows from and engenders a loss of that love which is at the heart of sanctification.

Wesley writes this to warn those who take separation lightly, ready to leave "a Christian society with as much concern as they go out of one room into another."[35] He can countenance separation in only one

---

32. Ibid., 108, 110, 113.
33. John Wesley, "On Schism" [II] 11, *Wesley's Works* 3:64
34. Ibid., [II] 12–14, 3:65.
35. Ibid., [II] 18, 3:68.

instance: that one cannot "continue therein with a clear conscience," that is, "without sin."[36] In that case it is continued participation that subverts sanctification and therefore necessitates leaving. Consistent with his central theological commitment, Wesley makes holiness centered in love both the reason separation is evil as well as the grounds for the one instance it is permissible.

It cannot be said that all separations from mainline Methodism meet this criteria. The earliest ones in America were conflicts over polity, driven more by American democratic and egalitarian impulses within a clergy-centered denomination with an episcopal polity. The first major defection, of the Republican Methodist Church in 1792, was argued on that basis; of greater significance was the separation of the Methodist Protestant Church in 1830, which was a more thoroughgoing attempt to democratize the church, including the elimination of bishops and providing for lay representation in conference. The counterargument to these democratizers was missional: the current structure of conferences consisting of itinerating preachers under episcopal appointment was the most effective way to reach persons with the gospel and oversee those responsible for their nurture. The egalitarianism of the new denominations had their limits. While the Republican Methodists had been antislavery, the later Methodist Protestants refused to extend voting rights to their African American members.

Of course, such racism was increasingly found within the Methodist Episcopal Church itself as it grew in membership and respectability. This would eventually provoke some African Americans to leave that denomination entirely to form new ones: Peter Spencer's African Union Church (1813), Richard Allen's African Methodist Episcopal Church (1816), and James Varick's African Methodist Episcopal Zion Church (by 1824). While not willing to tolerate overt racism, outright separation was often a last resort, taken with reluctance, after measures to provide a degree of autonomy for African Americans within the denomination were rejected.

The story of Richard Allen illustrates this. Born a slave, Allen was converted by Methodists in 1777 at age seventeen, and began attending class meetings. When his master was convicted of the sin of slavery, also by Methodist preaching, he allowed Allen to buy his freedom. Allen then became a Methodist preacher, joining the staff of St. George's, a large interracial church in Philadelphia. But in 1792, when the all-white trustees

36. Ibid., [II] 17, 3:66.

segregated the seating and tried to forcibly remove African Americans from a section of the church, Allen led a walkout. He began building a new church, led by African Americans alone. Although he had the support of Bishop Asbury, white church leaders fought him all along the way, even in court. By 1796 Allen was convinced he and his church could no longer remain within the denomination, and in 1816 he joined with other churches across the country to establish the AME Church.[37]

The racism Allen experienced at St. George's was in sharp contrast to the spirit of Methodism as he had originally encountered it. Russell E. Richey describes that spirit as expressed in the popular evangelical language "of sermon, of class, of love feast, of camp meeting, of prayer." Such language was often found in accounts in the journals of early Methodists, in which "Preachers spoke with freedom; words uttered in great liberty produced tears; hearts were melted; souls found mercy and were closely knit in love; a new community of 'brothers' and 'sisters' defined itself over against the world and its distinctions of sex, class, position, and race that ruled therein; this new community reoriented itself toward Zion."[38] In light of this ethos, the actions of the white trustees and conference officials in Philadelphia represented a religion diametrically opposed to the Methodism Allen had joined.

Allen saw himself as a faithful follower of Wesley, and understood sanctification as a work of the Spirit that purifies the heart of sin and fills it with love. But holiness is not only for the heart, it must be lived out. That was what the Methodist Episcopal Church was failing to do. The underlying reason, he believed, was that many in the church now sought respectability rather than sanctification.

Of course, Allen was not alone among American Methodists in making this most Wesleyan critique. Frances Asbury himself echoed Wesley's warning against abandoning a commitment to holiness for earthly possessions, upward mobility, and cultural conformity. "Respectable," said Asbury. "Ah! There is death in that word."[39] But Allen was unique in seeing the root of the problem at the founding of the denomination in 1784, with its ordinations, gowned clergy, and other trappings of respectable religion. "I have thought," Allen said, that "religion has been declining in

37. On Richard Allen's story, see Newman, *Freedom's Prophet*, and Dickerson, "Richard Allen and the Making of Early American Methodism."

38. Richey, *Early American Methodism*, 84.

39. Cited by Wigger, "Where Have All the Asburys Gone?" 68.

the church ever since."[40] Writing fifty years later, Allen argued that once they lost "the simplicity of the Gospel that was among them," the Methodists began to "conform more to the world and the fashions thereof," and now "fare very little better than the people of the world." They had altered the discipline "considerably from what it was." Allen "would ask for the good old way, and desire to walk therein."[41]

This move to respectability began to transform Methodism from a movement that welcomed the poor and was open to all races to a denomination that mirrored the culture, including racism. As Dennis C. Dickerson has argued, the new denominations founded by Allen and others were designed to recover authentic Wesleyanism and its "egalitarian/evangelical" ethos.[42] Indeed, notes Russell Richey, "In important respects, Black Methodists . . . may preserve and represent Methodism more faithfully than white."[43]

Indicative of his Wesleyan commitments, Dickerson notes, "Allen drew a sharp line of demarcation between church and culture," intending African Methodism to avoid the pursuit of wealth and power that had compromised the witness of the Methodist Episcopal Church. Second, like Wesley, "Allen contended the fruit of faith was charity."[44] This is lived out not only in care for the poor and needy, and doing good to all, but in working to change racist structures in church and society and resolute opposition to slavery. The church must itself model this in its own life if it is to have the vision, motivation, and credibility to work for social reform.

James H. Cone, in his analysis of the role of the Holy Spirit in Black worship, makes explicit the theological insight of African American leaders like Allen. Cone argues that at its heart, a "black congregation is an eschatological community that lives as if the end of time is already at hand." In worship the Holy Spirit "authenticates the peoples' experience of freedom by empowering them with courage and strength to bear witness in their present existence to what they know is coming in God's own

40. Allen, *Life Experiences and Gospel Labors*, 13–14, cited in Dickerson, *Liberated Past*, 21.

41. Allen, *Life Experiences and Gospel Labors*, 28, cited in Dickerson, *Liberated Past*, 23.

42. Dickerson, *Religion, Race, and Region*, 15.

43. Richey, *Early AmericanMethodism*, 60.

44. Dickerson, "Richard Allen and the Making of Early American Methodism," 76.

eschatological future."[45] In worship people live out their true identities in the kingdom of God in contrast to how they have been defined and humiliated in white racist society.[46] It was their inability to do this due to the decision to racially segregate the seating at St. George's that led Allen and others to leave and start a new congregation, and their inability to do that free of white control that caused them to separate and form a new denomination. Even the majority of African Americans who remained in the Methodist Episcopal Church began to worship in predominantly black local churches for much the same reasons.

Cone sees black worship as actualizing the story of salvation among African Americans. In light of this, he argues, it is easy to understand why Wesleyan teachings on justification and sanctification were so compelling for persons like Richard Allen. While "the failure of White Methodism" to adhere to Wesley's opposition to slavery "led to the creation of a white spirituality that is culturally determined by American values and thus indifferent to oppressed black people's struggle for social justice," black people refused "to reconcile racism and social injustice with the experience of conversion and new birth." Thus, Cone concludes, it is not "possible to be sanctified and a racist at the same time."[47] Amanda Berry Smith, writing in 1893, makes the same point in a more nuanced way: "Some people don't get enough of the blessing to take prejudice out of them, even after they are sanctified."[48]

A somewhat similar pattern can be found among the Wesleyan Methodists. We shall look at the theology of their founder, Orange Scott, in the next chapter. But here we can say that their ecclesiological vision united the democratizing tendencies exemplified by the Methodist Protestants with a commitment to holiness that had strong egalitarian and abolitionist implications.

One major branch of Wesleyan Methodists were located in upstate New York, and in the 1840s was part of a widespread, radical commitment to holiness and abolitionism involving local churches from many traditions. As Douglas M. Strong has shown, the Wesleyan Methodists, like the other antislavery churches in that area, "linked advocacy for civil rights to the advocacy for greater spiritual democracy within the

---

45. Cone, "Sanctification and Liberation," 175.

46. Ibid., 176.

47. Ibid., 188.

48. Smith, *Autobiography*, 226, cited in Stanley, *Holy Boldness*, 81.

churches."[49] Thus Wesleyan Methodists were opposed to all hierarchies of privilege, whether due to class, gender, or ecclesiastic authority. Strong notes how they "resisted the pervasive racial prejudice of the period," and welcomed African Americans into their churches "as equals."[50] With regard to church structure, New Yorkers like Luther Lee disagreed with founder Orange Scott, who favored retaining a modified episcopacy. Lee feared such authority as a threat to individual conscience and the freedom to live out one's holiness commitment through social reform, and while wanting to maintain a translocal connection argued for a more congregational polity.[51]

A decade later upstate New York was the scene of another conflict over the nature of the church. The focal issue was renting pews, a fundraising practice Methodists had borrowed from other denominations. The closer the pew was to the front of the church, the more it cost to rent it. Thus the most prominent, well-to-do families would parade down the aisle of the church each Sunday, to sit in a place that had become a sign of their importance. In some churches, inability to pay would mean having to stand in the back of the church.

B. T. Roberts saw this as not only a betrayal of Wesleyan holiness but a denial of the gospel of Christ. During the 1850s he wrote a series of articles criticizing what he would come to call "New School Methodism." The church, he argued, should not be making distinctions that God does not make. How can we invite non-believers to worship and then deny them a seat when they arrive?[52]

Roberts lifted up the camp meeting by comparison. While many churches in New York "say in effect to the rich 'sit thou here in this good pew for thou art able to pay for it' and to the poor 'here take this bench, or go get a seat in the gallery,' we are in danger of forgetting that in the presence of God, worldly distinctions are lost. But at the camp meeting, the rich and poor meet together and feel as they cannot in many of our sanctuaries that 'the Lord is Maker of us all.'"[53]

The issue of pew rentals was the sign of a much deeper problem. Roberts criticized the increasingly common life-style of "splendid houses,

49. Strong, *Perfectionist Politics*, 99.

50. Ibid., 101.

51. Ibid., 102, 104–5.

52. On Roberts, see Snyder, *Populist Saints*, and Cullum, "Gospel Simplicity."

53. Cited by Snyder, "B. T. Roberts' Early Critique of Methodism," 125.

elegant furniture, parties of pleasure, ornaments of gold, and costly apparel" by Methodists who claim allegiance to the one of whom it was said "He who was rich became so poor, that he had not where to lay his head."[54] In addition to wealth, Roberts also took Methodists to task for the de-emphasis or abandonment of class meetings, camp meetings, and love feasts, and reducing conversion to doing good works.

Roberts' goal in making this case was to renew the church. But because he and his allies were expelled from their conference they linked up with likeminded Methodists in the upper middle west to found the Free Methodist Church. Much like Wesley, Roberts understood the church to be a community of persons who were entirely sanctified or earnestly seeking sanctification. "The true church," he said, "is holy; not in name merely, but in reality."[55] The mission of the church is to "preach the gospel to the poor" and "maintain the Bible standard of Christianity."[56] A church that ignores the poor is not a church, for it is not apostolic. A church that adheres to the Bible cannot but be radical, for the Bible is "a radical book" that demands sin be abandoned at once, not tolerated over time; it calls for radical obedience, not "halfway measures."[57] Should the church once again recover such holiness, Roberts argued, it "would bring Paradise back to earth." [58]Thus Roberts was an abolitionist, an advocate for women's rights, and a consistent friend of the poor and of farmers threatened with losing their farms.

Opposition to pew rentals was not limited to Roberts or to Methodism. Even earlier the revivalism of Charles Finney had become the seedbed for egalitarian protest. As Ted A. Smith notes, "In the 1820s space within the churches in the United States came heavily coded with distinctions," most often reflected in seating patterns that segregated men and women, black and white, and pew rentals that segregated by class and income. Maintaining these distinctions were essential foundations for cultural respectability, yet camp meetings and Finneyite revivals "crossed every one of these lines of demarcation."[59] Out of this came the Free Church movement, leading to the founding of the First Free Presbyterian

54. Ibid., 133.

55. Snyder, *Populist Saints*, 795. See also Dayton, "'Good News to the Poor,'" 85.

56. Snyder, *Populist Saints*, 800.

57. Ibid., 790–92. See also Kostlevy, "Benjamin Titus Roberts and the 'Preferential Option for the Poor,'" 51–67.

58. Cited in Snyder, *Populist Saints*, 548.

59. Smith, *New Measures*, 154.

Church in New York City in 1830, increasing to four by 1835[60] (Finney for a while pastored the Second Free Presbyterian Church). Lewis Tappen, a financier ally of Finney's, sought to renovate the Chatham Street Theater to turn it into a church. Tappen, says Smith, "wanted every single seat in the church to be equally good, and for every person to be free to choose where to sit." "Free church spaces," Smith argues, "sought not so much to transgress distinctions as to abolish them,"[61] and thereby redefine cultural respectability itself.

This attempt to redefine culture respectability took a more radical turn with the late-nineteenth-century Holiness movement. Convinced that anyone could be used by God, Holiness proponents like D. S. Warner, H. C. Morrison, and W. E. Godbey envisioned an interracial, egalitarian church and ministry. Many new denominations, such as the Holiness Church formed in California in the 1880s, were interracial from their inception.[62] As Randall J. Stephens has shown, Holiness evangelists even brought these egalitarian practices to the South, with black and white preachers, both men and women, often addressing interracial crowds. These racially mixed gatherings evoked strong opposition from mainstream white Methodist and Baptist periodicals, which commonly idolized the Confederacy, upheld Southern sectionalism, and asserted that blacks were both racially inferior and an abiding threat to whites. Some of the reaction turned violent, with tents or churches burned and preachers beaten by mobs—some of which were led by anti-Holiness preachers.[63] Likewise, the leading role of women in the Holiness movement was denounced as subversive of the patriarchal order assumed as both scriptural and natural by most Southern Baptists and Methodists.[64]

Yet even in this harsh cultural terrain, most Holiness preachers maintained an optimism of grace. J. Livesey, a white Southern evangelist, urged white ministers to both preach and "indoctrinate" their congregations in "the Wesleyan teachings on the subject of holiness." Holiness would not only cure whites of their "undue assumption of superiority" toward blacks, but more importantly identify African Americans "as redeemed and sanctified MEN—as common heirs with all the saints."[65]

60. Ibid., 156.
61. Ibid., 159.
62. Kostlevy, "Holiness Church (HC)," 147.
63. Stephens, *Fire Spreads,* 82–92.
64. Ibid., 93–97.
65. Cited in ibid., 86–87.

And while the opposition to the Holiness movement was indeed fierce, the number of remarkably changed lives were many.

This radical Holiness vision of the church culminated at Azusa Street. "From the beginning," Cecil M. Robeck notes, William Seymour "envisioned it becoming a multiracial multiethnic congregation. While having a strong African American influence, the Azusa Street Mission became one of "the most racially inclusive, culturally diverse groups to gather in the city of Los Angeles at that time."[66]

If, as Seymour believed, the real sign of Spirit baptism was love, then that love should produce a community marked by mutual care and respect across all lines of class, race, gender, and age.[67] "The Pentecostal power," says *The Apostolic Faith*, "is just more of God's love. . . . Pentecost makes us love Jesus more and love our brothers more. It brings us all into one common family."[68] It was not only love that served to unite, but also empowerment: "No instrument that God can use is rejected on account of color or dress or lack of education. This is why God has so built up the work."[69]

In addition to Spirit baptism, there was also a distinctly christological grounding for this new community. "It is the Blood of Jesus," declared *The Apostolic Faith*, "that brings fellowship among the Christian family. . . . It makes all races and nations into one common family in the Lord and makes them all satisfied to be one. The Holy Ghost is the leader and He makes all one" just as Jesus prayed they would be.[70]

The unity at Azusa Street was also seen as preparatory for the second coming: "One token of the Lord's coming is that He is melting all races and nations together. . . . He is baptizing by one spirit into one body and making up a people that will be ready to meet Him when He comes."[71] For Seymour and many of his coworkers, the nature of the Christian community at Azusa Street was an anticipation of and preparation for the coming of Christ and his kingdom. As Steven J. Land put it, for early Pentecostals, "Continuity with one's racial, cultural and/or denominational identity might be disrupted and altered by discontinuous Spirit

---

66. Robeck, *Azusa Street Mission and Revival*, 88.

67. Jacobsen, *Thinking in the Spirit*, 79.

68. *Apostolic Faith* II: 13 (May 1908), 3.

69. *Apostolic Faith* I: 3 (November 1906), 1.

70. *Apostolic Faith* I: 7 (April 1907), 3.

71. *Apostolic Faith* I: 6 (February-March 1907), 7.

baptism. In establishing experiential, pneumatic continuity with the first century church of Pentecost one was forced to consider conformity with the church of the end, the holy Bride made up of all races, tongues, and nationalities."[72]

This experienced discontinuity is evident in many of the testimonies. White Holiness evangelist G. B. Cashwell traveled to Azusa Street from North Carolina, but his racial prejudice—and perhaps his sense of cultural propriety—made him averse to having African Americans lay hands on or pray for him. Back at his hotel room, Cashwell said he underwent a "crucifixion" in which he "had to die, to many things, "including his racial prejudice." Returning to Azusa Street, he asked Seymour and others to lay hands on him. It was several days later that he received his "Pentecost."[73] Cashwell would become the "Pentecostal Apostle to the South," bringing the Pentecostal message to all races.

With that message also came the same reconstruction of Christian community in the South that was evident at Azusa Street. "Racial and gender divisions among converts were . . . not as clearly demarcated as they were in society at large and in the mainline churches,"[74] says Randall Stephens; in fact, "black and white southern pentecostals . . . attended tent revivals together, shared pulpits, and wrote in each other's newspapers. On occasion a white man would minister to a mixed congregation, and other times a black woman would do the same."[75] The same phenomenon was occurring in Pentecostal gatherings all across the nation.[76]

This is not to say that there was no ambiguity in racial attitudes, even at Azusa Street. Their tasting of the world to come occurred within this world, of which they all remained very much a part. This meant some white Pentecostals might genuinely embrace greater racial equality while at the same time continue to have paternalistic attitudes about other races. Even Seymour has been accused of discrimination against Latinos, although, as Charles R. Fox has noted, the evidence is unclear and such a stance would contradict much of what else we know about Seymour.[77]

---

72. Land, *Pentecostal Spirituality*, 67.

73. Robeck, *Azusa Street Mission and Revival*, 217–18.

74. Stephens, *Fire Spreads*, 209.

75. Ibid., 211.

76. See, for example, Bundy, "G. T. Haywood," 237ff.

77. See the discussion in Synan and Fox, *William J. Seymour*, 140–46. It is clear that in 1909 Latinos left Azusa Street en masse. Fox believes the primary reason was most

What is clear is that white racial assumptions and their accompanying paternalism quickly reappeared in ministries to and with Latino Pentecostals, as Arlene Sánchez-Walsh has shown.[78] Yet what struck, indeed shocked, many outside observers was not lingering paternalism but the early interracial unity of the movement.

As we have seen, the cultural context in which all this was happening was hostile: "The times were unforgiving," as Grant Wacker so aptly put it.[79] Mainstream newspapers routinely published crudely racist cartoons and filled their accounts with racist language and allusions—immensely offensive to most Americans today, but completely normal in the early twentieth century. While social reform was not high on the agenda of early Pentecostals—politics was often derided—the countercultural nature of their meetings and ministries was enough to spark outrage.

As Stephens notes, for Pentecostals the "revival emanating from Azusa offered a type of spiritual liberation that its converts believed transcended more immediate forms of social liberation."[80] Steven Land argues that Pentecostals had no need to "play the game of the power elites." "The Church," they believed, "was a community on the way to the kingdom; this world was not home." It was the community that was "the Spirit's strategy for transforming the world and them with it."[81]

The response to this interracial movement was strong and harsh. Within Pentecostalism, Charles Parham most notably opposed the interracial character of Azusa Street, moving from white paternalism to a more bitter form of racism.[82] But it was those outside the movement that posed the greater threat. Besides ridicule in the press, Pentecostals were threatened, their meetings broken up, and they were sometimes beaten by mobs, just as had been done to their Holiness cousins.

Eventually, the racial segregation patterns of American society reasserted themselves against early Pentecostals, as they had against the early Methodists. C. H. Mason, an African American Pentecostal who led the explicitly interracial Church of God in Christ, was forced to see most

---

likely theological: their adoption of Oneness (non-Trinitarian) teachings in contrast to Seymour's emphatic Trinitarianism.

78. See Sánchez-Walsh, *Latino Pentecostal Identity*, and her nuanced account and analysis in "Borderlands Mission."

79. Wacker, *Heaven Below*, 226.

80. Stephens, *Fire Spreads*, 214.

81. Land, *Pentecostal Spirituality*, 180.

82. Wacker, *Heaven Below*, 231–32.

of his white members leave for the Assemblies of God, and permitted interracial congregations that remained to voluntarily divide by race.[83] Even Seymour by 1914 reluctantly abandoned the interracial governance at the Azusa Street Mission and restricted directors positions to "people of Color" in order to reduce racial conflict, for which he blamed both whites and blacks.[84] The effect was to temper their optimism of grace for the short term, but not to discount their vision of what the church would be like if it reflected heaven below.

Catholic Spirit?

The tension between seeking to renew denominations in holiness and leaving those denominations in order to faithfully embody holiness took on new urgency within the late-nineteenth-century Holiness movement. "Holiness was a reformatory principle," Melvin Dieter notes, yet "how to most effectively apply its purifying principles to the churches so they might in turn be restored to the hoped-for primitive holiness and power, was by no means clear to them, and certainly not to the churches." The difficulty and irony was that "the principles of perfect love which were to make all the sanctified one" often instead created divisions.[85]

The problem was not new. The insistent evangelism of the eighteenth-century awakening had divided denominations and local churches into "new lights" and "old lights" even as it also fostered interdenominational cooperation. Now the Holiness movement was having the same effect, as would the Charismatic movement in the second half of the twentieth century. The analogy with the Charismatics is more precise, for both began as movements to renew existing denominations, found unity in a common experience across denominational lines in spite of doctrinal differences, and were thereby accused by their opponents of denominational disloyalty.

As opposition to the Holiness movement began to harden in the Methodist mainline (and remained as hard as ever in many non-Methodist bodies), the Holiness movement began to fragment over both renewal strategy and ecclesiastical vision. A large segment of the movement, centered in the National Camp Meeting Association, continued to see

---

83. Daniels, "Charles Harrison Mason," 269. See also Thuston, "C. H. Mason."

84. Wacker, *Heaven Below*, 231.

85. Dieter, *Nineteenth Century Holiness Movement*, 200–201.

themselves as agents of renewal within Methodism and other denominations. Another segment continued the process of reluctantly leaving their denominations to form new ones, most notably the Church of the Nazarene and Salvation Army. But a sizeable number on the radical wing of the movement began to question denominationalism itself.

The beginning of this critique of denominationalism is found in the 1877 address by J. P. Brooks to a national Holiness convention. Brooks warned against linking the promotion of holiness too closely with Methodism, as this dampened its reception by those outside Methodism. Instead, he argued, "it would seem wise . . . to hold forth and enforce holiness as an altogether Catholic doctrine—Catholic because belonging . . . not to one sect, but to all . . ."[86] While sects are often understood as schismatics who leave a parent denomination, here Brooks is describing denominationalism itself as sectarian, as having broken the unity of the primitive church. The implication is that to restore that unity, denominational loyalty must be curtailed if not abandoned. This tendency was only strengthened by Brooks' insistence that holiness evangelists not be impeded in their work by denominational opponents, remaining free to preach anywhere and everywhere even if opposed by local pastors[87]—a stance with obvious echoes to that of John Wesley.

A second element in this new antisectarian argument has to do with the nature of holiness itself. At a camp meeting in 1873 Methodist John Inskip had warned against letting speculative creedal issues undermine unity in holiness. Dr. Edgar M. Levy, who was Baptist, argued at that same meeting that "at last we have discovered the basis for Christian unity. The sanctification of the believers of every name, create unity . . . as no creed has ever been able to accomplish. A unity not in ordinances; a unity not in church government; a unity not in . . . forms of worship; a unity not in mere letter of creed—but in . . . the baptism of the Holy Spirit."[88] While creeds and practices divide, holiness by its very nature unites.

As more radical leaders in the Holiness movement develop these ideas, they are frequently tied to the theme of recovery of the primitive church in these last days, a manifestation of a new Pentecost that presages the second coming of Christ. What remains often implicit is how the holiness and unity of the church is itself a present anticipation of that

86. Cited in ibid., 185.

87. Ibid., 185–86.

88. Cited in ibid., 203.

holiness and unity that will mark believers in the kingdom of heaven. Denominationalism was understood to be a product of sin, and hence would have no place in the new creation nor in a present church renewed in holiness.

The antisectarian impulse among the radicals took two distinct forms. Martin Wells Knapp developed a strategy of "associationalism," seeking a union for those "members of the New Testament Church, which exists in different denominations, and which probably can never be united in one denomination, however pure."[89] Knapp's growing estrangement from his native Methodism was fueled by the ecclesiastical insights of his friend and ally Seth Cook Rees. In his *The Ideal Pentecostal Church*, published in 1897, Rees drew upon Acts 2, in the words of William Kostlevy, to describe "a church free from sexual distinctions, generous to those in need, joyful and demonstrative in worship, united in service, and committed to missionary outreach," as well as to divine healing.[90] Knapp's own vision of the church, outlined in *Lightning Bolts from Pentecostal Skies* (1898), carries this vision even further, to a radical understanding of stewardship and property based on the church formed after Pentecost, in which "they would sell their possessions and goods and distribute the proceeds to all, as any had need" (Acts 2: 45). "New Testament stewardship is not like renting a farm or store and paying the owner a per cent," Knapp argued, "It acknowledges the proprietorship of Jesus Christ, labors solely under His instructions, and renders all to Him who owns it."[91]

Thus, when Knapp founded God's Bible School in Cincinnati in 1900 he deeded the campus to God and named himself as trustee. The school was radically egalitarian, promoting the leadership and ministry of women and had an interracial student body. God, he believed, would supply the needs of those who recognized divine proprietorship, and all profits beyond necessities were to be given away. As with the Acts 2 church, "accumulation of property for self is absolutely prohibited." This is an even more radical version of what the Wesleys argued in the eighteenth century, now actually put in practice. Knapp wanted his school to be a witness to the world, a community shaped by Pentecostal

89. Cited in Thornton, "God's Trustee," 152.
90. Kostlevy, *Holy Jumpers*, 29.
91. Cited in ibid., 32.

principles.[92] Implicit in this is that it would thereby also be a witness, in terms of this age, of the kingdom of heaven.

Knapp's associational strategy of bringing together persons irrespective of denomination was in contrast to the antidenominational approach of Daniel S. Warner. Beginning his ministry in the anticreedal Church of God (Winebrennarian) denomination in 1867, Warner a decade later received what he called a "new commission" from God. "The Lord showed me," he wrote in his journal in 1818, "that holiness could never prosper upon sectarian soil encumbered by human creeds and party names, and he gave me a new commission to join holiness and all truth together and build up the apostolic church of God."[93] Breaking with both the denominational reform strategy of the mainstream holiness associations and leaving his own denomination in 1881, Warner sought to be faithful to what he saw, in Barry Callen's words, "was God's intended alternative, a Spirit-unified gathering of all God's people." God intends for the church to be visible, and "surely there is a better way of showing it to the world than settling for a network of quarreling and divisive denominations."[94] The "Church of God" would make the invisible church, hidden within many denominations, visible to the world. With the Church of God united in holiness, Callen notes, the "lines of denomination, race, sex, and social status are to be discounted, even ignored in the face of the transforming grace of God."[95]

When William Seymour traveled north from Louisiana, he encountered the interracial holiness vision embodied in both Warner's Evening Light Saints and Knapp's God's Bible School, and this would in turn shape his Pentecostal vision of the church. Meanwhile Warner's own holiness group would become the Church of God (Anderson, IN).

This vision of a single, unified, holy Church of God, not divided by creeds and doctrines, caught the imagination of many in the Holiness movement. Some advocates of holiness had faced discipline or expulsion for deviating from the teachings of their denominations; other experienced doctrinal differences as an impediment to the unity they felt with other holiness adherents across denominational lines.

92. Cited in Thorton, "God's Trustee," 155.
93. Cited in Callen, "Daniel Sydney Warner," 142.
94. Ibid., 143.
95. Ibid., 146.

Richard G. Spurling was one of these. When along with his father he left the Baptist church after refusing to conform to an element of doctrine, they formed the Christian Union in 1886. Although this new congregation was the beginning of what would become the Church of God (Cleveland, TN), it is Spurling's original vision that is of interest here. This is found in his little booklet called *The Lost Link*, written in 1896 and later published in 1920.[96]

Spurling's central thesis is "that love is the law on which Christ built the church."[97] Using the analogy of a railroad, Spurling describes love of God and love of neighbor as "the golden rails that reach all the way to heaven and on which every wheel must roll." The drive wheels of the engine were "the law of liberty and equality,"[98] and the fuel is the Holy Spirit. But Satan convinced the church that "other fire will run this engine as well as fire from heaven," and it would roll better on "wooden rails (men-made creeds)."[99] In this way the church abandoned the law of love, which then became the "lost link."

The fall into creedalism historically occurred with Emperor Constantine and the promulgation of the Nicene Creed in 325 CE. While not defending Arianism, which the Nicene Creed sought to combat, Spurling argued that this event "gave birth to creeds, and every creed has made a sect or denomination."[100] The ill effects of creeds are evident throughout history: "instead of unity it makes division; instead of peace they make strife; instead of unity they bring discord; instead of love they bring hatred."[101] While creeds may indeed contain some truth, "no uninspired man or men can make an infallible creed."[102] One simply cannot follow a creed and at the same time let the Holy Ghost "guide into all truth."[103]

Instead of trying to "reform from creeds to God's law," Luther, Wesley, and Alexander Campbell sought "to reform the creeds to a purer standard of faith." They failed to see that "God's law wasn't a creed

---

96. On Spurling, see Jacobsen, *Thinking in the Spirit*, 50–56, and Beaty, *R. G. Spurling*.

97. Jacobsen, *Reader in Pentecostal Theology*, 162.

98. Ibid., 163.

99. Ibid., 164.

100. Ibid., 167.

101. Ibid., 169.

102. Ibid., 165.

103. Ibid., 168.

system," and hence did not recover the lost link.[104] But the good news of God is restoring the church "with an outpouring of the Holy Ghost as never seen since apostolic days." "Built by Christ," Spurling says, "here on earth," in "God's quarry," every stone that does not spoil, "when perfected through suffering like Jesus was," will fit perfectly in the temple of God in the heavenly Jerusalem.[105] Thus to abandon creedalism and recover the lost link of love will enable the church now on earth to become fit for the age to come.

John Wesley had addressed this same issue over a hundred years earlier in his sermon "Catholic Spirit." There he too recognizes that the two "general hindrances" to Christians loving one another is "that they all can't think alike" and "they all can't walk alike,"[106] that is, they are divided by both belief and practice. Yet, Wesley asks, "Although a difference in opinions or modes of worship may prevent an entire external union, yet need it prevent our union in affection? Though we can't think alike, may we not love alike?"[107]

Wesley's argument involves a call for both humility and faithfulness. With regard to the first, Wesley notes that while every person "necessarily believes that every particular opinion" he or she holds is true, no one can know this for certain. It is "the necessary condition of humanity" to be ignorant of much, and be mistaken in some things. Our problem is that we do not know wherein our mistakes lie.[108] We should therefore no more insist on others embracing our opinions or modes of worship than they should insist on us embracing theirs as a precondition for loving one another as fellow Christians. Wesley thus roots denominational differences in finitude rather than sin; the sin comes in using those differences as a reason not to love.

But Wesley does not say that those differences are of no consequence. A catholic spirit is not "an indifference to all opinions" (a "speculative latitudinarianism"), an "indifference" to modes of worship (a "practical latitudinarianism"), or "an indifference to all congregations" (denominations). A person of a catholic spirit "is fixed in his congregation as well as his principles," firmly adhering to those doctrines and practices believed to be most faithful to God. But while remaining faithful to his or her best

104. Ibid., 166.

105. Ibid., 165.

106. John Wesley, "Catholic Spirit" 3, *Wesley's Works* 2:84.

107. Ibid., 4, 2:82.

108. Ibid., I. 4, 2:83–84.

understanding, the heart is enlarged toward all, not only all Christians, but all humanity. "This," says Wesley, "is catholic or universal love."[109]

Wesley does acknowledge certain doctrines as Christian essentials, such as belief in God as divine governor of the world and in Jesus Christ as Savior and Lord. But these beliefs are inextricably interwoven with the tempers of the heart—most especially faith in God and love for God and neighbor—that they evoke and shape.[110] Elsewhere he will expand his list of essentials to include such things as original sin, justification, and sanctification, doctrines that are necessary because they convey the soteriological promises of God.

For Wesley, it is not the absence of denominations or creeds that anticipates heaven below. These are an inescapable feature of living as finite creatures in this age. The greatest manifestation of heaven below is a love that transcends the limitations of denomination and creed, and witnesses to a unity in spite of differences in belief and practice, a unity that is ultimately grounded in God's love for us in Christ.

As we have seen, desire for wealth and social respectability, recognition of societal distinctions of race and class, and acrimony due to differences over belief and practices all decisively prevent a community from being governed by that love. Church history, including the history of Wesleyanism and Pentecostalism, is filled with churches and denominations founded with great hope, yet sadly accommodating to such cultural norms within a generation or two. Yet this has not dampened the optimism of grace of those who have caught a vision of heaven below, and call the church to open itself to God's transforming power and become yet again a vibrant witness to the love revealed in Jesus Christ.

109. Ibid., III. 1–4, 2:92–94.
110. Ibid., I. 12–18, 2:87–89.

CHAPTER 13

The Gospel to the Poor

I bear the rich, and love the poor . . .

—JOHN WESLEY[1]

Turn the poor out of a church, and you turn Christ out.

—B. T. ROBERTS[2]

. . . the first service of a Holy Ghost baptized church is to the poor . . .

—PHINEAS BRESEE[3]

WHILE CHRISTIAN PERFECTION WAS not the first or only anticipation of heaven below, for John Wesley it was certainly its ultimate manifestation. But as we have seen, holiness of heart, if it really does image the love of God, must necessarily be expressed through holiness of life.

Theodore Runyon notes two aspects of Christian perfection that are essential for living it out. First, "we are not just to receive but reflect this perfect love into the world," in order to fulfill "the vocation to which we are called."[4] That vocation includes sharing with others the promise of full salvation through Jesus Christ as well as addressing the full range

1. John Wesley, Letter to Ann Foard (September 29, 1764), cited by Outler, *Wesley's Works* 1:17 n. 22.
2. Cited by Snyder, *Populist Saints*, 551.
3. Cited by Dayton, "'Good News to the Poor,'" 90.
4. Runyon, *Exploring the Range of Theology*, 184.

of human needs. Secondly, "God's perfect love is a *critical principle*" that forms our consciences such that we abhor "whatever is destructive of persons or society or the good creation."[5] As a critical principle Christian perfection gives us a kind of eschatological vision, a perspective from the standpoint of the promised new creation. It enables us to see that which contradicts God's love, and to envision new realities in which God's will is done on earth as it is in heaven. The strength of Christian perfection, Runyon argues, "lies in its capacity to mobilize the believers to seek a future that surpasses the present."[6]

Holiness indeed proved itself to be a powerful motivation for both compassionate ministries and movements of social reform. From Wesley's day to the early twentieth century, holiness advocates promoted a wide range of causes, from rescue missions, education, job training and prison ministries, to calls for temperance reform, women's rights, and the protection of the economic well-being of farmers and labor. There are more of these ministries than can be adequately considered in this chapter. We will examine the two that are arguably the most prominent: the antislavery movement and ministry to the poor. They will provide illustrations of how an optimism of grace and a vision of heaven below have ramifications for the wider society.

Slavery Is Sin

From their time as missionaries in the Georgia colony in the mid-1730s, John and Charles Wesley were opposed to slavery. While it was not yet legal in Georgia, they encountered slavery in neighboring South Carolina. The Wesleys were appalled not only at the barbarity of some slave owners but by the degradation fostered by the system itself, both to the inherent human dignity of those enslaved and to the moral character of their masters.

It was not until 1770 that John Wesley gave sustained attention to the issue. Upon telling Granville Sharp, an Anglican known for fighting slavery through the English legal system, of his desire to write against slavery, Sharp provided Wesley with a collection of antislavery writings. Among them were several by Quaker activist Anthony Benezet. A

5. Ibid., 186.
6. Ibid.

three-way correspondence developed between Wesley, Sharp, and Benezet that led to Wesley's publication of *Thoughts Upon Slavery* in 1774.

Drawing about half of his material from that of Benezet, Wesley's
short, inexpensive tract had an immediate impact on Methodists and
non-Methodists alike. Like Benezet, he made his argument to a broad
public, basing it on natural law rather than Scripture. After a brief over-
view of contemporary African civilization, Wesley relates the degrading and brutal process of procuring, transporting, selling, and utilizing
slaves, including their deaths due to inhumane conditions on slave ships
and the torture they face at the hands of owners. Wesley then challenges
arguments in favor of slavery based on natural order and economic necessity, and concludes with a pointed exhortation to slave traders and
slave owners, appealing to their humanity while warning them of a just
God who will judge everyone according to their works.[7]

There are a number of theological assumptions implicit in Wesley's
argument. First, he can appeal to the consciences of his readers because
he believes that, fallen as they are, they nonetheless through prevenient
grace have a sense of right and wrong sufficient to see the evil of slavery.
Thus, as Irv Brendlinger has noted, "the great evil of slavery . . . could
not be dismissed on the grounds that people are ignorant of right and
wrong, or that they were devoid of feelings." They had both a capacity to
empathize or share in the suffering of others, and an ability to distinguish
benevolence from cruelty.[8]

Second, Wesley believes in human equality. "Liberty," he argued, "is
the right of every human creature, as soon as he breaths the vital air; and
no human law can deprive him of that right which he derives from the
law of nature." Thus, he continues, if "you have any regard to justice, (to
say nothing of mercy, nor the revealed law of God) render unto all their
due."[9] Here Wesley grounds human equality in the law of nature; much
more frequently it is based on our being created in the image of God. In
fact, as Brendlinger notes, there were several bases for human equality
in Wesley's theology: all are created in God's image, all are equally fallen
into sin, all equally receive God's grace, and all are endowed with im-
mortal souls. Wesley not only argues for a common humanity, but denies

7. For an insigtful analysis of Wesley's argument, see Runyon, *New Creation*,
176–82.

8. Brendlinger, *Social Justice Through the Eyes of Wesley*, 88.

9. John Wesley, "Thoughts Upon Slavery" V.6, *Wesley's Works* (Jackson) 11:79.

white supremacy:[10] "Certainly," Wesley insists, "the African is in no respect inferior to the European."[11]

There is a third assumption that, while not as evident in *Thoughts Upon Slavery*, had profound implications for Wesley's Methodists. Christian perfection, as Brendlinger so clearly demonstrates, is incompatible with slavery. With regard to the slave, Brendlinger argues, how can "one justify enslaving and degrading a person who has the potential of bearing the very image of God?" It is not possible for a theology of Christian perfection to "co-exist with an institution that reduces human beings to the image of a beast."[12] Thus no true Wesleyan could be a slave owner.[13]

With regard to the Christian growing in sanctification and seeking Christian perfection, works of mercy are necessary as both expressions of increasing love and means of grace for further growth. Holding persons as slaves is actively inflicting misery on others, the complete opposite of love. "On the contrary," Brendlinger insists, "to take seriously the works of mercy would require the believer to minister to the needs of the slave."[14] Although many Methodists in early-nineteenth-century America would seek to envision a purely "spiritual" sanctification that would ignore or accept the reality of slavery, many others would find they could not escape the Wesleyan logic and would be impelled to act to abolish slavery.

If there is an echo of Christian perfection in *Thoughts Upon Slavery*, it is in the prayer with which Wesley concludes it. There, addressing the God in whose image we were created, and to whom by grace we can be restored, Wesley prays, "O thou God of love, thou who art loving to every man, and whose mercy is over all thy works; thou who art the Father of the spirits of all flesh, and who art rich in mercy unto all; thou who hast mingled of one blood all the nations upon earth; have compassion upon these outcasts of men. . . . Are not these also the work of thine own hands, the purchase of thy Son's blood?"[15] Here creation and christology witness to God's love, and thereby to the love that is meant to be our governing motivation as well. Here too is a critical principle that exposes slavery as radically opposed to God's love.

10. Brendlidnger, *Social Justice Through the Eyes of Wesley*, 68.

11. John Wesley, "Thoughts Upon Slavery" IV.8, *Wesley's Works* (Jackson) 11:74.

12. Brendlinger, *Social Justice Through the Eyes of Wesley*, 118.

13. Ibid., 119.

14. Ibid.

15. John Wesley, "Thoughts Upon Slavery" V. 7, *Wesley's Works* (Jackson) 11:79.

While Wesley is clear as to the goal of eliminating slavery, he evolved in his understanding of the means. In *Thoughts Upon Slavery* he argued that addressing either the general public or Parliament would be ineffectual, so he made his exhortation directly to the consciences of the slave captains, merchants, and plantation owners.[16] But by 1787 he was endorsing efforts to have Parliament outlaw the slave trade, and soon urged readers of the *Arminian Magazine* to sign petitions to that effect.[17] Famously, the last letter of his life was to William Wilberforce, encouraging him in his efforts to make trading in slaves illegal. Wesley had come to see that while persons freeing their slaves was certainly good, the institution of slavery itself remained resistant to change. He had, Brendlinger argues, "underestimated the strength of social structures to perpetuate themselves and co-opt unsuspecting individuals in furthering abuse."[18] He would not be the last Wesleyan to do so. But at the same time, Wesley's emphasis on the transformation of persons remained at the center of his approach to social change. It is, after all, only persons who are motivated by love that organize to combat evil, and then mount campaigns to mobilize public opinion and effect political change. This approach to social change would be more readily chosen by many of Wesley's nineteenth-century followers in both England and America.

Methodists in America early on expressed opposition to slavery in conference. Many like Freeborn Garretson had freed their slaves upon conversion, and leaders like Bishops Thomas Coke and Francis Asbury actively preached against it, even in the South. While by no means free of white racism itself, early Methodism was one of the most egalitarian institutions in America, and quickly gained a large African American membership.

But the explosive nature of the issue was evident even in these early decades. In 1780, Asbury records, he "spoke to some select friends about slave keeping, but they couldn't bear it: this I know, God will plead the cause of the oppressed, though it gives offence to say so here."[19] Over time, this intense reaction against the antislavery argument led to an accommodation with Southern critics in the denomination. White northern church leaders, adamant in their desire not to split the denomination,

---

16. Ibid., V. 1, 75–76.

17. Brendlinger, *Social Justice Through the Eyes of Wesley*, 143.

18. Ibid., 144.

19. Cited in Wigger, *American Saint*, 124.

began to embrace gradualist approaches such as plans to return black Americans to Africa through colonization.

The emergence of the Holiness movement in the 1830s inspired a new generation of opponents to slavery to challenge that gradualism. One strand of holiness abolitionists were those allied to or influenced by Charles Finney. As Donald Dayton has shown, for Finney the growth of reform movements such as for temperance and abolition of slavery were necessary consequences of a revival of religion. But this "conjunction of reform and revival was also reversible. Finney not only argued that revivals should produce reforms, but also that resistance to reform was one of the great 'hindrances of revival.'"[20]

Convinced by 1832 that slavery was a national sin, Finney rejected colonization and embraced abolition, albeit of a moderate sort. His actions and words concerning slavery were indeed radical: as pastor at Chatham Street chapel he "refused to serve communion to slaveholders," and "preached against slavery in vivid terms."[21] Yet racism took him another decade to overcome. While welcoming black members at Chatham Street he maintained segregated seating, disappointing some of his more egalitarian financial backers. His aversion to interracial seating was not fully overcome until 1841, where he and his colleagues decisively put an end to segregated seating at Oberlin College.[22]

Finney's grand vision of national reform, as David Weddle has shown, rested "upon two premises: first, that all societal evil is the result of the selfishness of individuals; second, that the coming of the kingdom of God will be the result of the gradual increase of moral government in the world by means of revival preaching.[23] Sanctification of persons, which entails commitment to disinterested benevolence, was the motivation for reform; the moral law of God served as a critical principle to expose what in society is in need of reform. As Roger Green notes, this optimism of grace naturally fit with his postmillennial eschatology, which "provided the goal which drew the saints into such vigorous efforts at social reformation as temperance crusades and the abolitionist movement, and also provided the theological motivation for such efforts."[24] Indeed,

---

20. Cited in Dayton, *Discovering an Evangelical Heritage*, 18.

21. Hambrick-Stowe, *Charles G. Finney*, 142.

22. Ibid., 142, 199.

23. Weddle, *Law as Gospel*, 255.

24. Green, "Charles Grandison Finney," 19.

while Finney himself saw reform as a byproduct of holiness revival, many of his followers made social change through political means their central concern.

A second strand of holiness activism against slavery emerged within Methodism itself, led by New England preacher Orange Scott. Born in poverty in 1800, Scott was converted at age 21 and entered the Methodist ministry, becoming a Presiding Elder in 1830. But after reading William Lloyd Garrison's newspaper *The Liberator* and studying the slavery issue for a year, Scott became an abolitionist, and by 1836 had enlisted a large number of his fellow Methodist preachers in the cause. Defeated at and denounced by the General Conference of 1836, Scott's bishop demoted him for failing to give up his abolitionist activism. By 1842, Scott and other disaffected ministers across the north withdrew to form a new denomination, the Wesleyan Methodist Connection.[25]

Scott argued that their reasons for separation were consistent with the exception John Wesley made in his sermon "On Schism," that is, that when remaining in a denomination becomes an obstacle to holiness, then one must leave. The basis for that assessment is in the immorality of slavery itself, an immorality Wesley had recognized. "The principle of slavery," Scott insisted, "is morally wrong,—or in other words, that it is a sin. . . . No hand could sanctify it—no circumstances could change it from bad to good."[26] Once this evil has been recognized holiness requires Christians to work for its abolition.

As Timothy Wood has shown, Scott sought "to reintroduce a sense of social responsibility into the Christian vision of holiness." While Scott's *The True Wesleyan* was filled with articles emphasizing "a personal relationship with Christ," that relationship is only authentic if it responds to the sufferings of others.[27] "The real reforms of the age," wrote Scott, "though in a sense subordinate to vital godliness, are nevertheless so closely allied to it that the advancement of the latter is essential to the progress of the former. They are but the application of Christian truth to existing evils."[28]

Scott resisted the idea that social reform was optional for Christians. As Wesley had held, salvation by grace could not be understood as

25. On Scott's story, see Dayton, *Discovering an Evangelical Heritage*, 74–76, and Wood, "Parting Ways," 148–52.

26. Cited in Wood, "Parting Ways," 157.

27. Ibid., 160.

28. Ibid.

negating the command to love God and neighbor; rather it is the means of inscribing that law upon the heart. Thus, says Scott, "the doctrines of justice are as much a part of the gospel as those of grace."[29] When a denomination turns its back on holiness by accommodating a great moral evil such as slavery, separation is not only permitted but required. "We cannot stay in a pro-slavery church," Scott argued, "without doing what God's word forbids, leaving undone what it enjoins; hence . . . we are bound to leave such churches."[30]

Wesleyan Methodists occupied a middle ground between what Douglas Strong calls "institution supporting" abolitionists who "felt that slavery was merely an evil blemish that needed to be removed from a generally healthy society," and "nonresistant" abolitionists who saw human institutions in themselves as impediments to God's reign, and sought abolition by appealing to conscience rather than through politics.[31] Wesleyan Methodists and their allies in a number of other holiness-influenced denominations and churches had a more comprehensive vision of social reform than the institutionalists, but unlike the nonresisters were committed to working through politics and institutions to achieve it.

The Wesleyan Methodists only gradually came to this position. Tracing the trajectory of "ecclesiastical abolitionists" in upstate New York, Strong notes that in the 1830s the Wesleyans and their allies focused on the entire sanctification of individuals as the means to reform society. But it soon "became obvious that the attainment of personal holiness could occur only if sanctified persons operated from the foundation of sanctified organizations—purified churches and political parties." This led to increased attention to institutions in local communities. By the 1840s "their experiences with the power of large, nationally based institutions exposed them to structural evil, and to the need for a comprehensive reform that went beyond that of individuals and of local organization." They "combined the evangelical emphasis on transforming individuals with an emphasis on transforming oppressive structures."[32] This became embodied politically in the Liberty Party, which moved from being simply focused on antislavery to recognizing that all oppressions are both interrelated and embedded in society.[33] Thus they became champions

29. Cited in ibid., 161.

30. Cited in ibid., 155.

31. Strong, "'Right Use of Appropriate Means,'" 89–93.

32. Strong, *Perfectionist Politics*, 164.

33. Ibid., 165.

of women's rights, as well as opponents of racial discrimination—what Luther Lee, writing in *The True Wesleyan* in 1843, called "Colorphobia."[34]

William Goodell expressed well this more mature position. While still holding to the "old remedy of regenerating the man individually, before he can be regenerated socially," Goodell did not want "to take the old error that too commonly went with it, the error of forgetting that man individually, is a social being, with a moral nature socially defined, with social relations binding him in every direction . . . with social duties pressing every where upon him, as the condition of his individual existence and well being."[35] Sanctified persons were necessary but not sufficient; for society to approximate the millennial reign of God society itself must be perfected as well.

Thus the Wesleyan Methodists trod the path toward political action and institutional change that Wesley had followed decades earlier on the issue of slavery. Yet they went even further down that path, developing a deeper understanding of the social embeddedness of persons and a more comprehensive vision of a society that would reflect heaven below.

The Finneyites and Wesleyan Methodists did not, however, speak for the entire Holiness movement. Most notably, Phoebe Palmer, although personally opposed to slavery, did not publicly address the issue nor would she permit it and other political issues to be discussed in the Tuesday Meeting,[36] perhaps echoing the position of establishment Methodists like Nathan Bangs. Unlike Orange Scott and B. T. Roberts, she never saw abolitionism as a necessary correlate to holiness of heart and life. At the same time, in contrast to many whites even within the antislavery movement, Palmer did not believe in the racial inferiority of African Americans.

We have seen in the stories of Wesley, Finney, Scott, and their followers a common set of interrelated elements. First, through the sanctifying grace of God, love increasingly came to govern and direct their motivations and desires. Second, they become aware of an evil such as slavery, exposed as such by its contradicting the love of God. Coupled with this is a vision of society as it could be, more fully reflecting God's love in this present age. Aware of the evil, guided by the vision, and motivated by love, the question remaining was the means to effectuate the necessary change. On this they all grew in their understanding as they sought to live

34. Kaufman, *"Logical" Luther Lee*, 130.

35. Cited in Strong, *Perfectionist Politics*, 165.

36. White, *Beauty of Holiness*, 228; and Raser, *Phoebe Palmer*, 223.

out that love in the world, moving from only changing human hearts and understandings to confronting sin embedded in institutions and society. We'll see similar patterns with regard to ministry with the poor.

Visit the Poor

From its inception Methodism had a special focus on the poor. Impelled by obedience to God and a desire for perfect love, John and Charles Wesley made concern for the poor a central feature of their ministries while still at Oxford in the 1730s. It remained an emphasis as the movement took form and developed in the decades ahead. John Fletcher shared this commitment as well. His determination to settle in Madely, Barrie Trinder notes, "was dictated by his wish to engage with the social consequences of the growth of mining and iron making," the new and dangerous occupations which employed many of his parishioners.[37]

As Richard Heitzenrater has shown, John Wesley, like many in the eighteenth century, commonly defined the poor as "those who lacked the necessities of life." That is, they were those who "did not have enough good food to eat, decent clothes to wear, or a suitable place to live," conditions that "were the result of underemployment, unemployment, illness, age, or misfortune."[38] Many, as in Fletcher's parish, were working poor living on subsistence wages and without long term job security. Such poor constituted a significant portion of the membership of the Methodist Societies.

Wesley sought to address their needs through a wide range of ministries. As enumerated by Douglas Meeks, these included "feeding, clothing, housing the poor; preparing the unemployed for work and finding them employment; visiting the poor sick and prisoners; devising new forms of health care education and delivery for the indigent; distributing books to the needy; and raising structural questions about an economy that produced poverty."[39] These ministries were funded by collections received at class and society meetings, as well as at the Lord's Supper. On one occasion, Wesley's zeal in receiving these collections at the London Society—seven in four days—even exasperated Charles Wesley, who wrote his wife that his brother would soon turn giving poor into receiv-

37. Trinder, "John Fletcher's Parishoners," 29.

38. Heitzenrater, *Poor and the People Called Methodists*, 27–28.

39. Meeks, "Introduction: On Reading Wesley with the Poor," in Meeks, *Portion of the Poor*, 9–10.

ing poor.[40] But it should be said that while Methodism reached out to those outside the movement, it has a special concern to care for the poor within its own ranks.

As Meeks observes, John Wesley's concern "was not simply *service of* the poor, but more importantly *life with* the poor."[41] This was not only a concrete expression of love for neighbor, but a work of mercy through which we grow in that love, by actually becoming acquainted with the poor and increasingly aware of the conditions of their lives. Wesley made this a constant practice of his own ministry. He records in 1753 that "on Friday and Saturday I visited as many as I could find. I found some in their cells underground, others in their garrets, half starved both with cold and hunger, added to weakness and pain. But I found not one of them unemployed who was able to crawl about the room. So wickedly, devilishly false is that common objection, "They are poor only because they are idle." If you saw these things with your own eyes, could you lay out money in ornaments or superfluities?"[42] To visit the poor and come to know them removes false perceptions that impede sanctification, and leads to changes in lifestyle that enable persons to more readily live out holiness of heart.

But the role of visiting the poor as a means of grace was more critical than even this implies. Without this connection to the poor, Wesley finds it difficult to conceive of someone maturing in sanctification, much less attaining Christian perfection. As Wesley observes: "One great reason why the rich in general have so little sympathy for the poor is because they so seldom visit them. Hence it is that . . . one part of the world does not know what the other suffers. Many of them do not know, because they do not care to know: they keep out of the way of knowing it—and then plead their voluntary ignorance as an excuse for their hardness of heart."[43] This voluntary ignorance has devastating consequences for their own spiritual condition. By this they seal themselves off from having the love that is the content of both sanctification and the kingdom of heaven, that is, the love that is in Christ. As Randy Maddox aptly observes, Wesley "recognized that failure to visit was the major contributing cause of the lack of compassion that lay behind withholding aid."[44]

40. Lloyd, "Eighteenth-Century Methodism and the London Poor," 126.

41. Meeks, "Introduction: On Reading Wesley With the Poor," 10.

42. John Wesley, *Journal* (February 8, 1753), *Wesley's Works* 20:445.

43. John Wesley, "On Visiting the Sick" I. 3, *Wesley's Works* 3:387–88.

44. Maddox, "Visit the Poor," 77.

This is the reason for the insistence of Wesley's appeal in a series of letters to Miss J. C. March, a wealthy member of the Methodist movement. When she wrote Wesley that she struggled with associating with those of a "lower character," Wesley sought to redirect her understanding. In one of his letters he urges, "Go and see the poor and sick in their own poor little hovels. Take up your cross, woman! Jesus went before you, and will go with you. Put off the gentlewoman; you bear a higher character. You are an heir of God and joint-heir with Christ!"[45] Sadly, Miss March replied with a series of objections, and Wesley eventually despaired in her ability to grow much in holiness.[46] But his point is emphatic: being a disciple of Christ, bearing the image of God, loving as God loves, gives us a higher character than that recognized by society, indeed an eschatological character.

Charles Wesley was equally insistent on ministry to and with the poor:

> The poor as Jesus' bosom-friends,
>> The poor he makes his latest care,
> To all his successors commends,
>> And wills us on our hands to bear;
> The poor our dearest case we make,
>> Aspiring to superior bliss
> And cherish for our Savior's sake,
>> And love them with a love like his.[47]

Thus, Charles implores God in the following words:

> Help us to make the poor our friends,
>> By that which paves the way to hell,
> That when our loving labor ends,
>> And dying from this earth we fail,
> Our friends may greet us in the skies
>> Born to a life that never dies.[48]

---

45. John Wesley, "Letter to Miss March" (June 9, 1775), cited in ibid., 78.

46. For a detailed analysis of this correspondence see Maddox, "Visit the Poor," 77–79.

47. Cited in Kimbrough, "Charles Wesley and the Poor," 156.

48. Cited in Kimbrough, "Perfection Revisited" 115.

Early Methodists, themselves motivated by love, not only emulated the Wesleys and Fletcher but initiated their own ministries to the poor. In 1785, with John Wesley's approval, John Gardner along with others in the City Road Methodist Society established the Strangers' Friends Society. Relying from the start "on lay initiative and leadership," the Society's Visitors" sought out the poor in their miserable attics and cellars in the surrounding districts of Spitalfields and East End.[49] The idea soon spread to other cities. We read in chapter 8 how Thomas Fildes, a member of the Methodist Society in Manchester, was a founding member of the SFS in that city.

Visiting the poor to this extent could not help but raise questions in John Wesley's mind as to *why* they are so poor. While not providing a full-scale economic theory, Wesley does engage in economic analysis in his *Thoughts on the Present Scarcity of Provisions*, published in 1773. That food had become scarce was commonly acknowledged, and was verified by Wesley's own experience as he traveled throughout England. Dissatisfied with partial answers, Wesley sought to provide a more comprehensive analysis of the problem.

"Why," he asks, "are thousands of people starving, perishing for want, in every part of the nation?" They have nothing to eat, he says, "because they have no work," and this because "the persons that used to employ them cannot afford to do it any longer." The former employers cannot, as they no longer have a market for their products, the cost of food being so high "that the generality of people are hardly able to buy anything else."[50]

What follows is an analysis of why the cost of food had risen dramatically in recent years. Wesley argues that because immense amounts of corn and wheat are consumed by distilleries, this drastically reduces the amount available to the general public. That "four times as many horses" are now kept "for coaches and chaises," means a much greater percentage of oats is needed to feed them, raising the price of oats as well. And because raising horses is now more lucrative, both for purchase by gentlemen with carriages and export to France, farmers have turned from keeping cows and sheep to breeding horses, thereby raising the cost of beef and mutton. Add to this the enclosure of lands, which evicted small farmers whose financial need made them happy to send bacon,

49. Macquiban, "Friends of All?" 132.

50. John Wesley, "Thoughts on the Present Scarcity of Provisions" I.1–2, *Wesley's Works* (Jackson) 11:53–54.

pork, poultry, and eggs to market, leaving only "gentlemen-farmers" who "breed no poultry or swine, unless for their own use; consequently they send none to market."[51]

What Wesley calls the "most terrible" cause of scarcity is the luxury and waste in the households of the "nobility and gentry," who acquire more than they need. Moreover, in order to continue to live in luxury "as they have been accustomed to do," and to offset the rising cost of food, they are forced to raise rents on their land, further depleting the resources of small farmers.[52]

Additionally, Wesley also blames "the enormous taxes, which are laid on almost everything that can be named," used to service the national debt. "To sum up the whole," he says, "thousands of people throughout the land are perishing for want of food. This is owing to various causes, but above all, to distilling, taxes, and luxury."[53]

What then is the remedy? Clearly the price of food must drop in order for there to be a demand for other goods that will enable persons to go back to work. In order to bring down the cost of food Wesley advocates the prohibition of "the bane of health, that destroyer of strength, life, and virtue,—distilling"; reducing the number of horses through a tax on carriages and exports; limiting the size of farms; repressing luxury, by law or example; and reducing the national debt by half.[54]

Among the Poor

While this kind of social analysis was not prevalent among those who came after Wesley, neither was it uncommon. We have already seen how Wesleyan Methodists came to see the structural nature of sin and developed a comprehensive social vision. Later B. T. Roberts, in Howard Snyder's words, "was constantly trying to push the meaning of holiness into life in the public spheres," including his "explicitly political involvement" in helping form the Farmer's Alliance,[55] one of the major elements of what became the Populist movement. The gospel, Roberts wrote in 1890, "is revolutionary in character," producing "radical changes in soci-

51. Ibid., I. 3–6, 11:54–56.

52. Ibid., I. 6–7, 11:56–57.

53. Ibid., I. 9, 11:57.

54. Ibid., II. 1–8, 11:57–59.

55. Snyder, *Populist Saints*, 743.

ety," and it tends "to unsettle every false foundation in the social edifice."[56] This optimism that social reform could enable society itself to increasingly reflect holiness marked the entirety of Roberts' ministry.

But the focus of subsequent Wesleyanism was on visiting the poor. It certainly was a feature of early American Methodism. In the 1780s, as Nathan Hatch notes, Francis Asbury was insistent "that a ministerial calling required that one lay aside all trappings of a gentleman—the dress, the deportment, and the financial security."[57] "We must suffer *with* if we labor *for* the poor," Asbury said.[58] The example of Bishop Asbury and his preachers in turn shaped the ethos of early Methodism in America.

The story of the nineteenth century Holiness movement cannot be adequately told without reference to its commitment to the poor. Here we will highlight three of the more significant examples, beginning with Phoebe Palmer. It was her evangelistic work and involvement in the relief work of the Female Assistance Society that brought Palmer into contact with the poor of New York City.[59] What she discovered were working poor crowded together in cheap housing in slums such as the notorious Five Points. The huge numbers of the poor and their desperate need had long outgrown the capacity to be met by existing agencies.[60]

It was during her trip to Greenwood Cemetery to bury her father that Palmer developed the idea of the Five Points Mission.[61] In one sense Palmer's idea presupposed the model of evangelical humanitarian work that Methodists and others had already practiced, combining evangelism, relief work, and moral reform.[62] Yet her plan to actually locate the mission in Five Points was innovative, and would lead to the first successful urban mission. The Ladies' Home Missionary Society of the Methodist Episcopal Church was cool to the idea, given that several prior ventures had failed. But, according to Charles White, Palmer was "convinced that the Lord was guiding her," and after three years the Society, "worn down by her persistence and encouraged by her pledge of one hundred dollars," agreed to start the work.[63]

56. Roberts, "Gospel Reforms," cited in Snyder, *Populist Saints*, 740–41.

57. Hatch, *Democratization*, 85.

58. Asbury, *The Arminian Magazine* 7 (London, 1784), 681, cited in ibid.

59. White, *Beauty of Holiness*, 220–21.

60. Ibid., 218–19.

61. Ibid., 64.

62. Ibid., 220.

63. Ibid., 217.

The work of the mission was led by a missionary hired by the Society. While its early years was marred by controversy, the mission was increasingly successful in providing education for children, adoptive parents for impoverished children, and employment for many without work. It is unclear, however, how effective the mission was in achieving its evangelistic purpose of eliciting conversions.[64]

There are two features of the Five Points Mission that deserve emphasis. First was the "involvement of the women of the society in its daily work." As White notes, the women "did not pay a missionary to go places they would not go and do things they would not do, but rather worked alongside him . . . to reach the people of Five Points."[65] Thus these women from respectable middle-class backgrounds did indeed "visit the poor." But secondly, the mission itself marked a transition from not only visiting the poor but living among them. Eventually the Missionary Society built a mission house containing apartments for both the missionary and the poor. "By moving into the slums," White observes, "the workers became more available to the poor and more vulnerable to the ills the needy suffered."[66]

Inner city missions like Five Points became common in the work of evangelicals, especially those with Wesleyan and Holiness leanings. One such was the Peniel Mission, an independent holiness ministry in Los Angeles in the 1880s that attracted the attention of Phineas Bresee, a prominent Methodist minister and leader in the Holiness movement. In the recent past Bresee had built urban "tabernacles," only to see their ministry compromised when Bresee was moved to a new appointment. By being independent, as Carl Bangs notes, Peniel "promised to be an urban auditorium where the poor could be reached, where persons throughout the entire southern California region could gather, and where Methodist polity could not hand it over to strangers."[67] Bresee requested to be appointed to the Peniel Mission, but the conference declined its approval,[68] instead granting him "location" (that is, no longer remaining an itinerant

64. Ibid., 221–26.

65. Ibid., 64–65.

66. Ibid., 229.

67. Bangs, *Phineas Bresee*, 187.

68. Ibid., 188–89. While some have speculated that the Conference was unsympathetic to Bresee's holiness theology, Bangs argues that the actual reason was that Peniel Mission was not an appointment within the Methodist Episcopal Church.

minister under appointment). Bresee was then free to join the work at Peniel Mission.

Within a year, for reasons that are unclear, Bresee's relationship with the Peniel Mission was terminated by his colleagues (Bangs speculates that Bresee's ardent Wesleyanism was in conflict with their more Keswick version of holiness).[69] With Bresee now without a place of ministry, holiness laity took the initiative, renting a small lodge hall in Los Angeles as the as the location for a new congregation to be led by Bresee and his colleague J. P. Widney. It was Widney who came up with the name "Church of the Nazarene,"[70] a name that, according to the new church's original Articles of Faith and General Rules, symbolized "the toiling, lowly mission of Christ." Their mission field was explicit: "The neglected quarters of the cities."[71]

Theirs would be a church whose work would be among the poor: "We want places so plain that every board will say welcome to the poorest. We can get along without rich people, but not without preaching to the poor. . . . Let the Church of the Nazarene be true to its commission; not great and elegant buildings; but to feed the hungry and clothe the naked, and wipe away the tears of sorrowing; and gather jewels for His diadem."[72] As the church in Los Angeles linked with others to form a new denomination, initially called the Pentecostal Church of the Nazarene, it stayed true to this vision. In fact, as Donald Dayton notes, significant "parts of the denomination in the Southwest consisted of little more than chains of inner-city missions."[73] The Texas Nazarene paper *Highways and Hedges* in 1906 said that while "Steeple-house church people are busy chasing dollars," the Nazarenes would "open up a chain of missions in all our large cities where real mission and slum work will be pushed; and the poor and destitute looked after."[74]

Arguably the most radical form of inner city mission was that of the Salvation Army. William and Catherine Booth, who founded the Salvation Army, were English Methodists significantly shaped by John Wesley's theology of salvation as well as the revivalist and holiness teachings of

---

69. Ibid., 191.

70. Ibid., 195–97.

71. Cited in Dayton, *Discovering an Evangelical Heritage*, 113.

72. Cited in Ibid., 114.

73. Ibid.

74. Cited in ibid.

Charles Finney, James Caughey, and Phoebe Palmer. Unable to fulfill his calling as an itinerant evangelist in the Methodist New Connexion, with Catherine's urging William left that denomination for an independent ministry. By this time Catherine had developed a reputation as a dynamic preacher in her own right. When in 1865 the Booths settled in London, William began drawing large crowds at a three-week revival he was preaching in East London. Here he found his calling: tens of thousands of working people living in poverty and vice, who would never attend a church or chapel but desperately need the gospel of Jesus Christ.[75] The Booths founded the East London Christian Mission, which expanded throughout England and became known in 1878 as the Salvation Army.

From the very beginning, even before adopting a military-style polity and uniforms, the Christian Mission was distinctive. Most evangelical ministries and missions "began," in Pamela Walker's words, "with the assumption that the values and aspirations of the urban working class led to poverty and disorder,"[76] and sought as best as they could to instill those they assisted with the values and behavior of the middle class. This was not the approach of the Christian Mission. In Walker's succinct summary, "The authority it granted women, its emphasis on holiness theology and revivalist method, its growing independence, and its strict hierarchical structures were all features that sharply distinguished it from its contemporaries. The Christian Mission was created in the midst of the working-class communities it aimed to transform. It fashioned an evangelical practice from the geography and culture of the working-class communities it sought to convert. It was a neighborhood religion."[77] The Christian Mission went beyond visiting the poor or even being with the poor—it was of the poor.

Thus unlike existing denominations, the Christian Mission organized by neighborhoods.[78] While most Christians in the middle-class remained separate from those aspects of working-class culture deemed immoral, the Christian Mission "held services in music halls, sang hymns in front of public houses, and appropriated the language and much of the style of commercial entertainment."[79] Their preachers and members, hav-

75. Walker, *Pulling the Devil's Kingdom Down*, 35–42.

76. Ibid., 99.

77. Ibid., 42.

78. Ibid., 57.

79. Ibid., 58.

ing come from the working-class, spoke the idiom of the people, much as early Methodist preachers had done. In short, their strategy was not to save people out of the culture but to take the fight to the devil on his own turf.

The goal was not only the salvation of persons but the transformation of neighborhoods. At the annual conference of 1876, William Booth described a mission station not as "a building or a chapel or a hall; it is not even a society but a band of people united together to mission, to attack, to Christianize a whole neighborhood or town."[80] The vision, then, was not to make working-class neighborhoods middle-class, but to make them Christian.

The theological ground for this vision is shown by Roger Green's analysis of Booth's 1890 book *In Darkest England and the Way Out*. Green argues that Booth sought a path between those Christians who believed the kingdom of God to be other-worldly, having "no relation to the actual lives of people in their daily struggle for existence," and those who sought this-worldly social reform on grounds other than the gospel.[81] Booth was a postmillennialist, and insisted the millennium would be inaugurated in this world by God through God's people, most especially the Salvation Army. It would be marked, in Green's words, "by the overthrow of the forces which were in rebellion against God, by universal submission to God and his laws, and by the setting up of the kingdom of God on earth.[82] This righteousness will be both personal and corporate, and include within its scope the practices of government, business, and families. Self-sacrificing love will govern the hearts and lives of all, and human happiness will be universal, including an end to misery and suffering.[83] Much as Wesley saw his Methodists, William Booth understood the Salvation Army as instrumental to the new world God is bringing about. It was an optimism of grace that anticipated heaven below.

80. Cited in ibid., 57.
81. Green, "Theological Roots of *In Darkest England and the Way Out*," 90.
82. Ibid., 88.
83. Ibid., 91.

CHAPTER 14

Envisioning Heaven Below

Whosoever will reign with Christ in heaven,
must have Christ reigning with him on earth.

—JOHN WESLEY[1]

ANTICIPATING HEAVEN BELOW IS never uncontested. It implies living a new life of holiness in the midst of a world governed by the old, looking with new eyes at all that is taken for granted, having new expectations for the presence and power of God in the world, and new desires to join God in the work of making all things new. We have seen again and again how the culture resists, its norms reassert themselves, and accommodation to culture undermines holiness. But in addition to accommodation there is also the danger of despair, of coming to believe neither the sin in our hearts nor the injustices in the world will change until Christ returns. We will look at both of these issues in turn, and then conclude with a final look at the interplay of an optimism of grace with anticipating heaven below.

Living as Citizens of the Kingdom

We have seen how many who began by seeking to live out sanctification in their personal lives came to advocate changing society itself. These efforts led to their participation in antislavery, temperance, women's rights,

1. John Wesley, "A Blow at the Root, or, Christ Stabbed in the House of His Friends" 1, *Wesley's Works* (Jackson) 10:364.

and populist movements, among others. For some it was simply a matter of correcting those aspects of society not in accord with the will of God; for others it was in service to a more thoroughgoing societal transformation, often guided by a vision of the millennial reign of Christ.

What also must be said is that while longing for a social order governed by God's holy love, they found themselves already as members of that new order. This meant not only that their hearts were changed, but as a result they sought to live and act in accordance with the kingdom of heaven, all the while doing so in a world operating on quite different assumptions and expectations. They became living witnesses to a new reality. We have already seen in previous chapters how uncomfortable this could be with regard to race, and how intense are the pressures to accommodate to the prevailing culture. We can explore that witness and those pressures by examining the role of men and women in society.

Dee Andrews has argued that "the real power of Methodism for Americans" in the revolutionary period "lay in the spiritual egalitarianism of the revival: in its capacity to transcend conventional social distinctions and create new men and women."[2] A. Gregory Schneider has described those conventional distinctions as a "culture of honor," and contrasted it with the "culture of experimental religion" inhabited by early Methodists. In the culture of honor one's "moral worth and identity came from blood and the family name," whose honor must be preserved. The symbols of the culture of honor "were home and property," with home as an inner space distinct from and over against the world. It therefore must be kept from outside intrusion, under the control of the male head of household; otherwise it would bring shame upon the man and dishonor upon the family.[3]

In the culture of experimental religion the key distinction was not between the home and the world, but the individual and society. Whereas in the culture of honor initiative lay only with the male husband and father, here initiative was with each person, whether male or female. The goal in this culture was not the preservation of the family name but something much greater: usefulness in and sacrifice for God's purposes in the world. The honored male figure in the culture of experimental religion was the circuit rider, who had no property, no home, and often no wife or children—the inverse of who was esteemed in the culture of

2. Andrews, *Methodists and Revolutionary America*, 243–44.
3. Schneider, *Way of the Cross*, 120.

honor.[4] Andrews observes that these "itinerants were a serious threat to a social order in which distinctions of wealth were widely touted and exhibitionist displays were regular features of male culture."[5] Women who were honored were those who, in order to follow God, took initiative and made decisions, placing them in conflict with societal expectations of female passivity.

Schneider provides an example of this by relating a story from an Indiana camp meeting. There "a woman of 'good reputation' . . . came to the altar and was converted." As she "began to loudly praise God," her husband "rushed into the altar, and dragged her violently to the rear of the encampment where he began to abuse her for 'disgracing the family.'" Local preacher James Jones first tried to reason with the man, then when that failed demanded the husband "get down on his knees and pray." According to the account, when the husband "laughed and cursed the preacher,"[6] the preacher responded, "'But you shall pray,' . . . and seizing him, he brought the fellow to his knees, then flat on his face, and seated himself upon his back. . . . 'I will not pray,' said he, 'if I go to hell the next moment.' 'But you must pray or you cannot arise from this place,' said the preacher." Then the preacher, wife, and others began to earnestly pray. Soon the husband's muscles began to relax, then he started to weep, crying out, "God be merciful to me a sinner." Then came the shout of victory, with the couple now praising God together.[7]

Schneider argues that the purpose of such accounts as these was not to change the social order. It was simply to insist that each person needed to encounter God and "struggle through on his or her own to a saving faith in an affectionate heavenly father." The husband, Schneider says, had "been conquered by the grace of God in his heart that gave him victory over himself. It was the sort of victory the denizens of the culture of honor would have scorned as weak and feared as emasculating. The husband, however, had had a new order revealed to him, an order with no room for his self-assertive motives of pride, anger, and violence. The new order demanded instead a personal, self-abnegating love of God and humankind."[8] That love then extended to his marriage, now "founded

---

4. Ibid., 64–65.

5. Andrews, *Methodists and Revolutionary America*, 157.

6. Schneider, *Way of the Cross*, 76.

7. Cited in ibid.

8. Ibid.

on this mutual love that came from God." The husband still retained his authority in the home given to him by society, now "governed not by honor's conflicting demands of deference and self-assertion but by the mutual affection mandated by the way of the cross."[9]

This new order can be described as entering into an eschatological existence in the here and now, or more precisely, everyday existence in this age being reshaped by the age to come. It is the reality of the kingdom of heaven breaking in, though not its fullness. In chapter eight we saw how empowerment by the Spirit enabled women, racial minorities, and working class men to assume roles as preachers and leaders in violation of cultural norms. Here we see that the personal initiative involved in responding to God's offer of salvation itself required women to violate those norms, and both men and women to enter into a new way of living and relating.

We see something similar in the work of the Salvation Army in England. Holiness for Salvationists, says Pamela Walker, "required intense struggle," not only with "their own sinful nature" but also "against the powerful enticements to sin that surrounded them." But this "re-making of the self" had different implications for working-class men and women.[10]

For men it was a struggle with what Walker calls the "sins of the body," associated with their common leisure activities such as music halls and pubs. Drink, in particular, was a dangerous vice, as it made men violent and led them to waste money better spent on food or clothes.[11] Yet drink was inextricably tied to a whole host of activities—"the congeniality of the pub," sports, and gambling—that brought working-class men together, and spending money on such activities was a sign of their independence, indeed, their manliness.[12] Conversion in effect redefined both masculinity and the nature of male community. When "Salvationist men gave up drinking, they claimed they were more manly for 'it takes a man, with God's help, to sign the pledge and keep it, any fool or donkey can drink.'"[13] To march through the streets, "preach on street corners,"

---

9. Ibid., 76–77.

10. Walker, *Pulling the Devil's Kingdom Down*, 75.

11. Ibid., 77.

12. Ibid., 120.

13. Cited in ibid., 92.

and lead hymns were all seen as elements of an active and vigorous life.[14] Most notable, perhaps, was those men who no longer abused their wives, a practice strongly denounced by the Salvation Army.[15]

While sins of drink do figure prominently in the conversion stories of some Salvationist women, much more typically their sense of sin "was not because they thoughtlessly disregarded God but because they were painfully aware of their inability to do what they knew was required of them." Conversion and sanctification involved peace with God as well as a calling to active discipleship.[16] As "femininity was closely associated with religiosity in Salvationist theology," conversion enabled women to become their truest selves, and to do so while withstanding "the struggles of urban working-class life."[17]

Thus conversion and sanctification transformed Salvationist men and women, not to take them out of their world, but to enable them to engage it in new ways. In spite of an egalitarianism marked by women preachers and leaders, gender distinctions remained. They were able to radically challenge the culture of the urban working-class precisely because they were of that culture, remaining working-class yet having been transformed by the grace of God.

To varying degrees the entire nineteenth century Holiness movement manifested these same tendencies. Early Pentecostals would inherit this tradition. However, as Grant Wacker has shown, as least as far as the roles of women were concerned, Pentecostals were conflicted from the start. Wacker identifies this tension as between a "primitivist impulse" that "emboldened some women to flout conventional restrictions in order to pursue a vocation of active ministry," and a "pragmatic impulse" which called for "an orderly accommodation to American social expectations" as well as "a more traditional reading of Scripture" and listening to the Holy Spirit.[18]

There is no question that the primitivist impulse had a powerful impact on Pentecostal ministry and spirituality. Inheriting the radical evangelical tradition of women in public ministry, Wacker argues that "Pentecostals pressed these trends" even further. At their founding, in

14. Ibid., 120.

15. Ibid., 126.

16. Ibid., 82–83.

17. Ibid., 92–93.

18. Wacker, *Heaven Below*, 158.

both the Assemblies of God and the International Church of the Four-square Gospel, one third of their pastors were women,[19] and even in denominations that restricted their roles, women often preached or had other public ministries in defiance of social conventions.

With regard to male spirituality, Wacker notes what we have already seen: when nineteenth-century "evangelical men gave their hearts to Christ, they readily relinquished brawling, drinking, swearing, gambling, and philandering," seeking to replace "those habits with stereotypically female ones of gentleness, peaceableness, sobriety, and fidelity." "Pentecostals," says Wacker, "did all that and more. They made public weeping—scorned among men, esteemed among women—not simply acceptable but a criterion of the success of a Holy Ghost meeting."[20] Like the early Methodist and Salvationist men before them, early Pentecostal men were ridiculed as effeminate; they insisted they had discovered what true masculinity is. This phenomenon of radically changing the assumptions and behavior of male converts continues today as an aspect of Holiness and Pentecostal movements across the globe as David Martin, for one, has shown.[21]

"In its purist form," Wacker concludes, "the primitivist impulse pulled men and women away from inherited assumptions and thrust them outward" into ministry.[22] Yet at the same time, the pragmatic impulse to accommodate to societal restrictions on women's roles was also at play, fueled by reactions against the rapid culture changes of the time, such as women entering the workforce and changing their patterns of dress. Moreover, among evangelicals the Phoebe Palmers and Catherine Booths were increasingly seen as exceptions rather than the norm.[23] As a result, debates over the status of women emerged even in those Pentecostal denominations that had been most open to their ministries. The right of women to speak publicly was never itself in question; it was their doing so in an officially authorized position that for many contradicted traditional understandings of Scripture as well as natural distinctions between the sexes.[24]

19. Ibid., 160.

20. Ibid., 161–62.

21. See Martin, *Pentecostalism*, in which this is a recurring theme.

22. Wacker, *Heaven Below*, 164.

23. Ibid., 165.

24. Ibid., 171.

Thus, Wacker concludes, while "the primitivist impulse drove them to defy worldly conventions, the pragmatic impulse reminded them that defiance was costly." The struggle, he says, everywhere "raged back and forth, between traditions, within traditions, and inside the hearts and minds of individuals."[25]

With some caution, I believe Wacker's two impulses can be reframed in this way: the primitivist impulse results in the gospel reshaping culture, while the pragmatic seeks to contextualize the gospel within culture. The caution is two-fold. First the Pentecostals were not that interested in transforming culture. What they sought to do is live as witnesses to the gospel and faithfully proclaim that gospel to the world. Second, the primitivist impulse is itself not context-free, finding some cultural reinforcement even if facing much cultural opposition.

That said, the challenge of living already as citizens of heaven in a "not yet" world cannot but be marked by both defiance of and accommodation to culture. Transformation and contextualization are not exclusive choices but form the two sides of the path of faithful living and fruitful ministry. Heaven below, after all, is both truly heavenly and truly below, the life of the future lived out under the conditions of the present age. The tensions we find ourselves in will ultimately have an eschatological resolution; for now they require pneumatological power and discernment.

Apocalyptic Spirituality

Throughout most of the nineteenth century, evangelicals of all kinds were primarily postmillennialists, that is, believers that Jesus Christ would establish his millennial reign on earth in and through the church, at the end of which he would personally return in glory. Largely ignored throughout the medieval period, postmillennialism was revived and ardently taught by English Puritans, including their American descendents like Jonathan Edwards. John Wesley's own position was complex and evolved over time, but it is clear that in his later writings he had abandoned much of his inherited Anglican amillennialism (which denied a literal thousand year reign of Christ on earth) for something close to a postmillennial view that looked forward to a great expansion of Christ's reign on earth prior his second coming.[26] Using the Puritan language of "latter-day glo-

---

25. Ibid., 176.

26. For a fuller account of Wesley's evolving views, see Maddox, *Responsible Grace*,

ry," Wesley understood this to be the extension of holiness and happiness throughout the entire world through the power of the Holy Spirit.

This was an exceedingly optimistic eschatology, and in early nineteenth century America none of its adherents were more optimistic than the Holiness Movement. That hope for the millennium was severely challenged by the reality of the Civil War, which ended slavery not through the spread of holiness but the devastation of war. While most in the Holiness movement retained their postmillennialism, it was coupled now with a more chastened outlook. Many were open to new eschatologies. D. S. Warner's movement that would become the Church of God (Anderson, IN) adopted amillennialism. But the main challenger to the reigning postmillennialism was a newly resurgent premillennial eschatology.

Premillennialism tends to be more apocalyptic in orientation, often envisioning the future as becoming worse rather than better, until at a time known only to God, Christ will suddenly return and establish his millennial kingdom. It fit the cultural mood of the times, especially among evangelicals. However, it could be a challenge to an optimism of grace that looked for anticipations of heaven in this world.

Both Donald Dayton and William Faupel illustrate this dramatic shift in eschatological vision with two quotes,[27] one each from the two great revivalists of nineteenth century America. The first is from Charles Finney:

> Now the great business of the church is to reform the world—to put away every kind of sin. The Church of Christ was originally organized to be a body of reformers. . . . The Christian church was designed to make aggressive movements in every direction . . . to reform individuals, communities, and governments, and never rest until the Kingdom and the greatness of the Kingdom under the whole heaven shall be given to the people of the saints of the most high God—until every form of iniquity shall be driven from the face of the earth.[28]

Finney's postmillennial vision is in contrast to the premillennialism of his late nineteenth-century successor, D. L. Moody:

236–42; Collins, *Theology of John Wesley*, 314–16; and Dayton, *Theological Roots of Pentecostalism*, 149–50.

27. Dayton, "Pentecostal/Charismatic Renewal and Social Change," 8–9, and Faupel, *Everlasting Gospel*, 77.

28. Finney, "Letters on Revivals No. 23," 11.

I look upon this world as a wrecked vessel. God has given me a life-boat, and said to me, "Moody, save all you can." God will come in judgement and burn up this world, but the children of God don't belong to this world; they are in it, but not of it, like a ship in the water. The world is getting darker and darker; its ruin is coming nearer and nearer; if you have any friends on this wreck unsaved you had better lose no time in getting them off. . . . No, grace is not a failure, but man is. . . . Man has been a failure everywhere, when he has had his own way and been left to himself. Christ will save his church, but he will save them by finally taking them out of the world.[29]

Premillennialism does not necessarily require this degree of pessimism—historically it has been compatible with an inaugurated eschatology, to draw upon the term used for Wesley's eschatology in chapter three—but the kind of premillennialism that captured the imaginations of many late nineteenth century evangelicals was not open to a present inbreaking of the kingdom. Developed by John Nelson Darby in England, this new dispensational premillennialism was strongly Calvinistic, dividing history into rigid dispensations, and arguing that the millennium would be preceded by a time of tribulation, before which believers would be taken from the earth in the rapture. This order of end time events was established by God, and could not be altered; one could only hope to be among those who escape the tribulation by being taken up in the rapture. This eschatology was popularized by the *Scofield Reference Bible*, became a definitive element of Protestant Fundamentalism, and continued to have widespread influence among conservative Protestants in the second half of the twentieth century through Hal Lindsey's *The Late Great Planet Earth* and the Left Behind series.

Given its stark Calvinism, it is no wonder that many of the Wesleyans in the Holiness movement initially resisted this new dispensational brand of premillennialism. Yet beginning with non-Methodists like A. B. Simpson and A. J. Gordon, premillennialism came to be adopted by influential voices in the movement like Martin Wells Knapp, Seth Cook Rees, and H. C. Morrison. Though never fully supplanting postmillennialism, by the end of the century premillennialism had become the dominant eschatology of the Holiness movement,[30] and a defining belief of early Pentecostals.

29. Quoted in Daniels, *Moody*, 475–76.
30. Dieter, *Holiness Movement of the Nineteenth Century*, 254.

Some thought the Holiness debate over millennial theories was a distraction from rather than an explication of the gospel. Remarking on articles in the *Free Methodist* promoting competing eschatologies, B. T. Roberts noted, "Now but few read these long continued articles touching the millennium. They are nothing but opinions, and prove nothing; therefore of what use can they be? . . . Will the millennial theory as ventilated help us to comfort the sick and afflicted ones among us? Will the idea of a Christ coming one thousand years sooner, or later, assist us to lead souls to the Christ who came 1888 years ago?"[31]

Yet for all Roberts' protest, proponents on both sides believed much was at stake. As Melvin Dieter observes, defenders of postmillennialism like Daniel Steele believed "the biblical and doctrinal bases of . . . premillennialism were foreign to the optimism inherent in the Wesleyan understanding of the gospel and the work of the church in the world." But for its proponents, premillennialism, with its promise of "a dramatic moment of divine intervention" to remedy the problems of the world, fit easily with the Holiness emphasis on "the direct intervention of the Holy Spirit in cleansing the hearts of Christians and establishing them in perfect love in the crisis of sanctification."[32]

This indicates why the shift to premillennialism was difficult for some in the Holiness movement, and easier for others. As both Donald Dayton and William Faupel argue, the perfectionist emphasis on entire sanctification in persons correlates well with the postmillennial vision for society, while the pentecostal emphasis on the Baptism of the Spirit is a more fitting correlate to premillennialism.[33] As Dayton notes concerning Spirit baptism, for "both the personal and eschatological vision the key idea is 'descent' and a 'breaking in' from beyond, more characteristic of the apocalyptic mindset and somewhat at odds with the more gradual, growth-oriented patterns of postmillennialism or development toward perfection."[34] The integration of instantaneous and gradual aspects of salvation so strongly insisted upon by Wesley tends to fracture into competing visions when applied to eschatology.

31. Roberts, "Suggestions to Contributors," 106, cited in Snyder, *Populist Saints*, 809.

32. Dieter, *Holiness Movement of the Nineteenth Century*, 254.

33. Dayton, *Theological Roots of Pentecostalism*, 151–52; Faupel, *Everlasting Gospel*, 104.

34. Dayton, *Theological Roots of Pentecostalism*, 152.

So premillennialism was a thinkable alternative in light of Spirit baptism. The theological issue this raises is critical: in adopting premillennialism, were the later Holiness and early Pentecostal movements abandoning a Wesleyan optimism of grace and its anticipation of heaven below, at least with regard to the social order? Was this world, as Moody said, a wrecked vessel to be saved out of rather than an arena for Spirit-led reform?

Certainly there was a loss of optimism. William Kostlevy argues that a new generation of holiness evangelists, especially on the radical wing of the Holiness movement, promoted a "new chialistic perfectionism" that "looked for God's direct intervention in history," replacing "the older teaching that had once urged the faithful to experience a foretaste of heaven this side of the millennium."[35] Critical in understanding this shift are the reasons premillennialism seemed more plausible to them, and the nature of millennial vision they proclaimed.

For radicals like Knapp, Rees, and the Metropolitan Church Association, as well as more mainstream Southern Holiness Methodists like H. C. Morrison and L. L. Pickett, premillennialism was in part a response to the dashed hopes of the Populist movement and distrust of the elitist proposals of Progressivism. For the Southerners in particular, "the plummeting of farm prices in the late 1880s, the devastating depression of the early 1890s," and the defeat of William Jennings Bryan in 1896 "signaled a repudiation of the evangelical-based moral economy" Bryan had represented.[36] For Holiness radicals in the north, the hope for a "heavenly city" established through Christ's second advent "spoke to the tragic realities of the clerks, domestics, housewives, and workers, many of them immigrants, whose experiences" in all too earthly cities like Chicago "had undermined any hope in a temporal social salvation as espoused by radicals, reformers, and elite clergy."[37] In short, the radical Holiness "critique of middle-class evangelicalism, especially Methodism, was profoundly colored by their own non-Marxist preferential option for the poor."[38]

That this concern for the deteriorating conditions of farmers and workers contributed significantly to the plausibility of premillennialism is confirmed by their vision of the millennium itself. L. L. Pickett wrote

35. Kostlevy, *Holy Jumpers*, 75–76.

36. Ibid., 14.

37. Ibid., 70.

38. Ibid., 71.

that those with "two houses, needless horses, or extra farms" would have their property redistributed in the coming millennium.[39] Thus for Pickett, "the object of hope in the second coming was not "pie in the sky in the bye and bye" but a "renewed earth."[40] While the "wealth and power of the world is very largely in the hands of those who use it for selfish purposes" he wrote, "on the day of His triumph, the humble-hearth poor shall be the possessors of the kingdom, the glory, the honor and wealth of nations."[41] Likewise, his colleague H. C. Morrison predicted that in the new millennium "the earth will not be owned and dominated by a few people of vast wealth but will be amicably divided up among the people and they will possess it in peace and plenty.[42] More radical movements like the Metropolitan Church Association, as Kostlevy has amply shown, sought to practice this vision communally in anticipation of the return of Christ.

This does not sound like a movement yearning to leave this earth behind. These Holiness premillennialists have less in common with the eschatological sensibility of Moody, and much more with their antebellum postmillennial precursors. As Kostlevy concludes, these premillennialists "anticipated a fundamentally altered social order," a "radical reordering of economic, social, and political institutions."[43]

This same vision was carried forth by many early Pentecostals. Frustrated by the failure of Populism to achieve reform through political means, Charles Parham, in James R. Goff's words, "determined that real justice could come only through divine intervention."[44] Parham argued that the old order has been upheld by nationalism and patriotism, which has led to war and misery. "The ruling power of this older order has always been the rich, who exploited the masses for profit or drove them en masse to war, to perpetuate their misrule."[45] While a sharp critic of capitalism, Parham was not a socialist. The "cry of socialism," he insisted,

---

39. Pickett, *Our King Cometh*, 56, cited in Kostlevy, *Holy Jumpers*, 91.

40. Pickett, *Renewed Earth*, 30–31, cited in Kostlevy, *Holy Jumpers*, 15.

41. Pickett, *Renewed Earth*, 37–38, cited in Kostlevy, *Holy Jumpers*, 91.

42. Morrison, *Will God Set Up a Visible Kingdom on Earth?* 75–76, cited in Kostlevy, *Holy Jumpers*, 15.

43. Kostlevy, *Holy Jumpers*, 8–9.

44. Goff, *Fields White Unto Harvest*, 156.

45. Parham, *Everlasting Gospel*, 27–28, cited in Goff, *Fields White Unto Harvest*, 155–56.

"is the heart-cry to see Jesus";[46] Parham believed that the only solution to this evil order will be the new order established when Christ returns.

Thus the anticipation of heaven below in terms of a social order governed by holiness was deferred, but not abandoned; and given their common belief that Jesus was returning soon, it would not be deferred for long. The vision of new creation infused with holy love remained as a critical principle that exposed where God's will was not done in the world, and as the content of the hoped-for millennium. They didn't all agree on the details, and some, like Parham, were sadly blinded to its implications for racial equality. But the hunger for heaven below remained.

Not only was the vision of the millennium for many Holiness and early Pentecostal adherents similar to that of earlier postmillennialists, they also frequently altered premillennialism itself, diluting its Darbyite Calvinism in favor of more Arminian and/or Wesleyan emphases. Dayton in fact argues that Pentecostal eschatology is less a variant of Darby's dispensationalism than a parallel development.[47] Its emphasis on the "latter rain" as a new Pentecost, restoring spiritual gifts to the church, fits poorly within the dispensational framework of a Darby-Scofield system, and directly contradicts their Calvinist claim that miraculous gifts of the Spirit were only for the apostolic age. In addition, Dayton notes that Pentecostals "adopted different (generally tripartite) periodizations of human history" (more in the tradition of John Fletcher's Trinitarian dispensations than Darby's seven dispensations), applied "Old Testament promises to the church," and appropriated texts like the Lord's Prayer and the Sermon on the Mount as of present relevance while dispensationalists relegated them only to the millennial kingdom.[48]

Larry McQueen further develops this argument for a distinctive "latter rain" premillennialism through his analysis of the accounts of Azusa Street in *The Apostolic Faith*. Pentecostals, he argues, did not just modify dispensationalism, but transformed it "in the light of the holistic and apocalyptic nature of early Pentecostal spirituality."[49] At Azusa Street eschatology was embedded in spirituality,[50] an integration of sanctification, Spirit baptism, and anticipation of attending the future marriage

46. Parham and Parham, *Selected Sermons*, 2, cited in Goff, *Fields White Unto Harvest*, 156.

47. Dayton, *Theological Roots of Pentecostalism*, 147.

48. Ibid., 146.

49. McQueen, "Early Pentecostal Eschatology," 153.

50. Ibid., 141.

supper of the Lamb. This integrated spiritual experience was consistently described in terms of direction: "Sanctification required '*going down*' into spiritual humility, forsaking all claims of self-identity; Spirit baptism resulted from '*coming through*' into a new spiritual identity, thus becoming a member of the bride of Christ; and future hope anticipated '*rising* up' into spiritual fulfillment to meet the Lord in the air to go to the marriage supper."[51]

McQueen's research expands Dayton's list of differences between Pentecostal premillennialism and dispensationalism. Unlike dispensationalists, Pentecostals did not compartmentalize the Old Testament but viewed it as a rich source of types for contemporary soteriology and eschatology. Likewise, "images in the book of Revelation were not relegated to the future, but had contemporary importance for the spirituality of the believer." The rapture was not central but supplementary to the image of the church as the bride of Christ and the hope of attending the marriage feast of Christ. The true bride of Christ would indeed come from out of the church in the rapture, but in contrast to dispensationalism Jesus would continue to care for the portion of the church that remained on earth during the tribulation. Finally, the millennium was seen not as fulfilling a promise to the Jews but as a time faithful Christians would reign with Christ.[52] McQueen shows that even when Pentecostals and dispensationalists used similar language, they often meant quite different things.

But more significant for our purposes than this difference in definition is the spirituality out of which it comes, and which it in turn has shaped. Theirs was an apocalyptic spirituality in which "the realms of heaven and earth were often perceived to be intermingled." While believing "in heaven as a future state," McQueen notes, Pentecostals "also experienced an immediate sense of 'heaven below.'" The language of the kingdom as present was common to their accounts of dreams and visions, but even more so "with the baptism of the Holy Spirit as 'the earnest of our inheritance' or as 'a foretaste of heaven.'" Indeed, McQueen cites Joseph Grainger who viewed his time at Azusa Street as "a foretaste of the glad millennial day."[53]

51. Ibid., 146. McQueen's italics.
52. Ibid., 153–54.
53. Ibid., 150–51.

This apocalyptic spirituality lends credence to Steven Land's distinction between "good" and "bad" apocalyptic. Land describes the "apocalyptic faith" of early Pentecostals, grounded in the baptism of the Spirit, as a "break," a "turning point" in church history. The hope this evoked was not in "the present world order that is passing away" but in the coming of Jesus Christ to make all things new. This hope did not demean the world, but was rather hope for the world. Their spirituality was governed by a passion for Christ and his kingdom, marked by an "awareness of being involved in a cosmic struggle with powers and principalities." "Pentecostalism, "says Land, "lived and lives in an apocalyptic existence made existentially palpable by the presence, manifestations and power of the Holy Spirit.[54]

It is no wonder that, especially "in times of cultural rejection and persecution," Pentecostals would succumb to "bad apocalyptic," seeing "God as only over against the world," and "prophecy as fate." By this lapse into a premillennial future predetermined in detail, the larger vision inherited from the Holiness movement is reduced to only "preaching the gospel to all nations."[55]

Yet for Land that was not Pentecostal spirituality at its most vibrant and faithful. To believe in the coming of the kingdom of Christ "is to walk according to the nature, will and goal of the king." It is to "become a partaker of God's nature, a citizen of the present and coming kingdom, and a participant in a world-historical process whose end was assured, because God was working in all things for good." This is the "good apocalyptic" which Land sees at the heart of Pentecostal spirituality, a living out of the life of God, a life governed and motivated by love.[56] Such a spirituality is indeed an anticipation of heaven below, and a spirituality which, as Charles Wesley says, "owns that love is heaven."

Anticipating Heaven Below

We have seen how Wesleyan, Holiness, and Pentecostal movements are marked by an expectant faith rooted in an optimism of grace. Compared to most other Protestant traditions, theirs is an expanded vision of what

54. Land, *Pentecostal Spirituality*, 65–66.

55. Ibid., 70–71.

56. Ibid., 70.

God has promised in this present age, coupled with an intense longing to receive it. What they envisioned and expected was heaven below.

Foundational to this vision of heaven below was holiness, or Christian perfection, a present restoration of persons to the image in which they were created, enabling them to love as God loves. Holiness necessarily produced a deeper communion with God, and a more intense concern for others. This inaugurated eschatology was then readily extended to other areas: the presence of God, healing, church and society.

To live as those already belonging to the coming kingdom of God often put them at odds with prevailing culture. As they received and lived out their new eschatological identity they came to see themselves differently, defined not by their surrounding culture but by the kingdom of God. Women, lower class men, and African Americans all took on a new dignity and initiative bestowed by the love and calling given to them by God in Jesus Christ.

It was this holiness that also enabled them to envision renewed churches and a reformed social order, in which God's will is done on earth as it is in heaven. Believing that the Spirit was already transforming persons and communities, they were highly motivated to participate in the work. Yet it should be noted, and even underscored, that their very existence as Christian communities witnessing to an alternate eschatological reality in itself had a transformative effect on the larger society. Their central desire was holiness in heart and life, but as that holiness was lived out in relationships, in churches, and in acts of compassion it significantly impacted the wider society. It was also as they lived out these new desires and motivations that they came to see the needs of others more clearly, leading them to establish compassionate ministries or call for social reform.

Of course, we have also seen how difficult it is to maintain that witness, not only due to the active opposition of others, but from necessarily being a part of their culture in this present age. Being in the world while seeking to faithfully live as those not of the world is no easy task, and is beset by confusion, compromise, and contradiction at best. By recalling their struggles we can find wisdom for our own.

Chief among these was navigating the tension between the "already" and the "not yet," a tension that is only intensified by their anticipating heaven below. There has always been a danger in these movements of an overly realized eschatology, whether claiming an "angelic" Christian perfection, complete freedom from sickness, or an infallibly pure church.

This is often tied to an enthusiasm that sees intensity of feeling as the evidence for attaining purity or power. Unmediated and miraculous experiences are often privileged over encountering God in a less dramatic fashion. In addition, heaven below is sometimes guaranteed through a set formula—that your holiness or healing, for example, has already been accomplished on the cross, and you only have to obtain it through faith. This turns expectant faith into presumption, and seeks to insure God's immediate and automatic faithfulness by denying God's freedom.

The reaction to these excesses is predictable: denial that persons can be renewed in the image of God in this life, or healed through prayer, or that the church can truly be marked by holiness. Eschatological hope is limited to the age to come, and Christianity becomes largely a waiting for that day. This denial of heaven below is not only a common way to reject enthusiasm, but also marks later generations who, perhaps being more respectably middle-class, seek to distance themselves from the theology and spirituality of their forebears.

From Wesley to Seymour, the wisest theologians sought to maintain the tension between the "already" and "not yet." While we can certainly question how well they did so in this or that instance, we do well to emulate them in the attempt. This means maintaining a pessimism of nature even as we proclaim an optimism of grace, avoiding a formulaic understanding of God's faithfulness by insisting on God's freedom, and guarding against presumption even as we encourage expectancy.

A second theological tension is that between Christ and the Spirit, and with it the relation of holiness and power. Perhaps the most significant theological contribution of these movements is their emphasis on the presence and power of the Holy Spirit. In so doing, they have also restored a dynamic Trinitarianism to Protestant theology and spirituality. For centuries Western Christianity had placed its soteriological emphasis on the cross, repentance and forgiveness, and attaining a happy afterlife. Drawing on Puritan and Pietist roots, Wesley and his successors add Pentecost to the cross, sanctification to justification, and heaven below to the life to come.

A common critique of this tradition is that they overemphasize the Spirit at the expense of Christ. But I would suggest, in both the Holiness and Pentecostal movements, there is often if not more so an intensified focus on Christ. Either way, to emphasize one member of the Trinity at the expense of the other loses the Trinitarianism that characterizes them at their best. But the danger that I believe is more prevalent is an emphasis on power—whether through the work of the Spirit or by calling on the name of Jesus—at the expense of holiness. The focus on power can take the form of a preoccupation with the miraculous or of exercising gifts of the Spirit. But when power is severed from holiness as its motivation and guiding principle, both self-deception and harm to others results. On this Seymour speaks well for the entire tradition: power rests on the sanctified life; gifts of the Spirit rest on fruits of the Spirit, and the greatest of these is love.

This is also the clue to the nature of the Trinitarian relationship between Christ and the Spirit. Jesus Christ embodies love at its deepest and most profound, revealing both the heart of God and the image to which we are to be restored. The Spirit enables us to experience that love, and is the power by which we are restored to holiness and enabled to then live it out in effective service. In this Trinitarianism neither Christ nor the Spirit are subsumed to one another, nor are they separated.

Another recurrent issue has to do with the manner of God's presence and power. The heightened expectancy of these movements has drawn some to a spirituality that privileges the immediate experience of God over the mediated, and the miraculous over the everyday. Wesley was just the first of many who strongly warned against this tendency. God, they remind us, can be present in both ordinary and extraordinary ways, at the Lord's table as well as in awakening phenomena like falling to the ground, in Scripture and sermon as much as in dreams and visions, in healing through medicine along with healing through the prayer of faith. While enthusiasts sought the unmediated and formalists insisted on mediation, Wesley sought to transcend the dichotomous thinking of both by insisting that God is immediately present, most normally through means. He recognized and welcomed the extraordinary without demeaning the power of the ordinary ways we encounter the reality of God, a way of understanding God's presence that has always characterized these movements at their best.

Finally, there is the tension already mentioned, of living as citizens of the kingdom while being very much immersed in and shaped by their culture. Their doing this is one of the great strengths of these movements. From early Methodist circuit riders and class leaders on, participants in Wesleyan, Holiness and Pentecostal movements spoke the idiom of the people around them because it was from the everyday people that they had come, yet at the same time lived and thought in such a way as to challenge cultural assumptions, often radically.

Their love for neighbor and desire to share the gospel led many to cross cultural barriers of race and class. It was often through "visiting the poor" that they were able to at least in part break free of inherited cultural stereotypes by seeing for themselves the condition in which others lived, and hearing them tell their stories. It was through these experiences that God enlarged their vision of the world as it is, and also as it might become.

We can in almost every case look back and see how the prejudices and ignorance embedded in their culture compromised the ministries of many. So it will be when people look back on us from the vantage point of a changed future. What is heartening, even astonishing, is how often they did break free to see beyond their culture, to come to know persons and evaluate society from the standpoint of the kingdom of heaven. This, through the grace of God, is our possibility as well.

We began this study with the claim that both grace and love were central to Wesleyan identity, and remained central to the Holiness and Pentecostal movements that followed. We have come to see that theirs was an optimism of grace, an expectancy that through the power of the Holy Spirit God can and does transform lives, renew churches, and re-form society, all in ways that more faithfully mirror the life of the coming kingdom. The key word to describe that eschatological life is love, revealed most fully in the life and death of Jesus Christ for the redemption of the world. While all else may pass away, love never will, for the crucified Jesus is risen and coming again. When the kingdom of heaven is fully established, that love will reign supreme. But it has and continues to reign even now, in human hearts and lives, in communities that mirror the love of Christ in their worship and ministries, and wherever it is expressed through acts of compassion and cries for justice. This love is a present as well as a future hope. It is a real anticipation of heaven below.

Bibliography

Alexander, Estrelda. "Conversion and Sanctification in Nineteenth-Century African American Wesleyan Women." In *Conversion in the Wesleyan Tradition*, edited by Kenneth J. Collins and John H. Tyson, 83–100. Nashville: Abingdon, 2001.

Alexander, Kimberly Ervin. *Pentecostal Healing: Models in Theology and Practice.* Blandford Forum, UK: Deo, 2006.

Allen, Richard. *The Life Experience and Gospel Labors of the Rt. Rev. Richard Allen.* Nashville: AMEC Sunday School Union/Legacy Publishing, 1990.

Andrews, Dee. *The Methodists and Revolutionary America, 1760–1800: The Shaping of an Evangelical Culture.* Princeton: Princeton University Press, 2002.

Asbury, Francis. *Journal and Letters.* Edited by Elmer E. Clark et al. 3 vols. Nashville: Abingdon, 1958.

Baer, Jonathan R. "Perfectly Empowered Bodies: Divine Healing in Modernizing America." PhD Diss., Yale University, 2002.

Bangs, Carl. *Phineas F. Bresee: His Life in Methodism, the Holiness Movement, and the Church of the Nazarene.* Kansas City: Beacon Hill, 1995.

Barabas, Steven. *So Great Salvation: The History and Message of the Keswick Convention.* Westwood, NJ: Revell, 1952.

Barron, Bruce. *The Health and Wealth Gospel.* Downers Grove, IL: InterVarsity, 1987.

Bartleman, Frank. *Azusa Street.* 1925. Reprint, South Plainfield, NJ: Bridge, 1980.

Beaty, James M. *R. G. Spurling and the Early History of the Church of God.* Cleveland, TN: Derek, 2012.

Bebbington, David. *Holiness in Nineteenth-Century England.* Carlisle: Paternoster, 2000.

Bence, Clarence L. "John Wesley's Teleological Hermeneutic." PhD diss., Emory University, 1981.

Boardman, W. E. *The Higher Christian Life.* 1858. Reprint, New York: Garland, 1984.

Bodamer, William G., Jr. "The Life and Work of Johann Christian Blumhardt." PhD diss., Princeton Theological Seminary, 1966.

Boles, John B. *The Great Revival.* Lexington: University Press of Kentucky, 1972.

Brendlinger, Irv A. *Social Justice Through the Eyes of Wesley: John Wesley's Theological Challenge to Slavery.* Guelph, ON: Joshua Press, 2006.

Brown, Earl Kent. *Women of Mr. Wesley's Methodism.* Lewiston, NY: Mellen, 1982.

Bundy, David. "G. T. Haywood: Religion for Urban Realities." In *Portraits of a Generation: Early Pentecostal Leaders*, edited by James R. Goff Jr. and Grant Wacker, 237–54. Fayetteville: University of Arkansas Press, 2002.

———. "Gee, Donald." In *International Dictionary of Pentecostal and Charismatic Movements*, revised and expanded edition, edited by Stanley M. Burgess, 662–63. Grand Rapids: Zondervan, 2002.

Burdon, Adrian. *Authority and Order: John Wesley and His Preachers.* Burlington, VT: Ashgate, 2005.

Burton, Vicki Tolar. *Spiritual Literacy in John Wesley's Methodism.* Waco: Baylor University Press, 2008.

Callahan, Leslie. "Redeemed or Destroyed: Re-evaluating the Social Dimensions of Bodily Destiny in the Thought of Charles Parham." *Pneuma* 28:2 (2006) 203–27.

Callen, Barry L. "Daniel Sydney Warner: Joining Holiness and All Truth." In *From Aldersgate to Azusa Street*, edited by Henry H. Knight III, 141–47. Eugene, OR: Pickwick, 2010.

Carter, R. Kelso. *The Atonement for Sin and Sickness; or, A Full Salvation for Soul and Body.* 1884. Reprinted in *Russell Kelso Carter on "Faith Healing."* New York: Garland, 1985.

———. *"Faith Healing" Reviewed after Twenty Years.* 1897. Reprinted in *Russell Kelso Carter on "Faith Healing."* New York: Garland, 1985.

Chappell, Paul G. "The Divine Healing Movement in America." PhD diss., Drew University, 1983.

Chilcote, Paul Wesley. *John Wesley and the Women Preachers of Early Methodism.* Metuchen, NJ: Scarecrow, 1991.

———. *Recapturing the Wesleys' Vision.* Downers Grove, IL: InterVarsity, 2004.

Christian, Charles W. "John Wesley's Anthropology: Traditional and Innovative Elements." *Asbury Theological Journal* 59:1–2 (2004) 139–49.

Clapper, Gregory S. *John Wesley on Religious Affections.* Metuchen, NJ: Scarecrow, 1989.

Collins, Kenneth L. *The Theology of John Wesley.* Nashville: Abingdon, 2007.

Colyer, Elmer M. "Toward a Trinitarian Evangelical Theology." In *Alister E. McGrath and Evangelical Theology: A Dynamic Engagement*, edited by Sung Wook Chung, 165–94. Grand Rapids: Baker Academic, 2003.

Cone, James H. "Sanctification and Liberation in the Black Religious Tradition." In *Sanctification and Liberation*, edited by Theodore Runyon, 174–92. Nashville: Abingdon, 1981.

Coulter, Dale M. "The Spirit and the Bride Revisited: Pentecostalism, Renewal, and the Sense of History." *Journal of Pentecostal Theology* 21:2 (2012) 298–319.

Cullis, Charles. *Faith Healing.* Boston: Willard Tract Repository, n.d.

Cullum, Douglas R. "Gospel Simplicity: Benjamin Titus Roberts and the Formation of the Free Methodist Church." In *From Aldersgate to Azusa Street*, edited by Henry H. Knight III, 99–108. Eugene, OR: Pickwick, 2010.

Curtis, Heather D. *Faith in the Great Physician: Suffering and Divine Healing in American Culture, 1860–1900.* Baltimore: Johns Hopkins University Press, 2007.

Dabney, D. Lyle. "Pneumatology in the Methodist Tradition." In *The Oxford Handbook of Methodist Studies*, edited by William J. Abraham and James E. Kirby, 573–86. New York: Oxford University Press, 2009.

Daniels, David D. "Charles Harrison Mason: The Interracial Impulse of Early Pentecostalism." In *Portraits of a Generation: Early Pentecostal Leaders*, edited by James R. Goff Jr. and Grant Wacker, 255–70. Fayetteville: University of Arkansas Press, 2002.

Daniels, W. H. *Moody: His Word, Work, and Workers.* New York: Hitchcock & Walden, 1877.

Dayton, Donald W. *Discovering an Evangelical Heritage*. New York: Harper & Row, 1976.

———. "A Final Round with Larry Wood." *Pneuma* 28:2 (2006) 265–70.

———. "'Good News to the Poor': The Methodist Experience after Wesley." In *The Portion of the Poor*, edited by M. Douglas Meeks, 65–96. Nashville: Abingdon, 1995.

———. "John Fletcher as John Wesley's Vindicator and Designated Successor? A Response to Laurence W. Wood." *Pneuma* 26:2 (2004) 355–61.

———. "Pentecostal/Charismatic Renewal and Social Change: A Western Perspective." *Transformation* 5:4 (1988) 8–9.

———. "Rejoinder to Laurence Wood." *Pneuma* 28:1 (2006) 367–76.

———. "Revisting the 'Baptism of the Holy Spirit' Controversy: A Response to My Critics." In *From the Margins: A Celebration of the Theological Work of Donald W. Dayton*, edited by Christian T. Collins Winn, 149–74. Eugene, OR: Pickwick, 2007.

———. *Theological Roots of Pentecostalism*. Grand Rapids: Zondervan, 1987.

Dickerson, Dennis C. *A Liberated Past: Explorations in AME Church History*. Nashville: AME Sunday School Union, 2003.

———. *Religion, Race, and Region: Research Notes on A.M.E. Church History*. Nashville: AMEC Sunday School Union/Legacy Publishing, 1995.

———. "Richard Allen and the Making of Early American Methodism." In *From Aldersgate to Azusa Street*, edited by Henry H. Knight III, 72–77. Eugene, OR: Pickwick, 2010.

Dieter, Melvin E. "The Development of Holiness Theology in Nineteenth Century America." *Wesleyan Theological Journal* 20:1 (1985) 61–77.

———. *The Holiness Revival of the Nineteenth Century*. 2nd ed. Lanham, MD: Scarecrow, 1996.

Durham, William H. "The Finished Work of Calvary." *Pentecostal Testimony* 2 (January 1912).

———. "The Finished Work of Calvary—It Makes Plain the Great Work of Redemption." *Pentecostal Testimony* 2:2 (May 1912)

———. "Sanctification." *Pentecostal Testimony* 1:8 (Summer 1911).

Elaw, Zilpha. *Memoirs of the Life, Religious Experience, Ministerial Travels and Labours of Mrs. Zilpha Elaw, an American Female of Color*. Edited by William L. Andrews. Bloomington: Indiana University Press, 1986.

Faupel, D. William. *The Everlasting Gospel*. Sheffield: Sheffield Academic, 1996.

———. "The Everlasting Gospel: The Significance of Eschatology in the Development of Pentecostal Thought." PhD diss., University of Birmingham, 1989.

———. "William H. Durham and the Finished Work of Calvary." In *From Aldersgate to Azusa Street*, edited by Henry H. Knight III, 237–45. Eugene, OR: Pickwick, 2010.

Finney, Charles G. *Finney's Systematic Theology*. Edited by L. G. Parkhurst Jr. et al. Minneapolis: Bethany House, 1994.

———. "Letters on Revivals No. 23." *The Oberlin Evangelist* 8 (January 21, 1846).

———. *Power from on High: A Selection of Articles on the Spirit-Filled Life*. Fort Washington, PA: Christian Literature Crusade, 1944.

———. *The Promise of the Spirit*. Edited by Timothy L. Smith. Minneapolis: Bethany House, 1980.

Fletcher, John. *The Works of John Fletcher*. 4 vols. Salem, OH: Schmul, 1974.

Foote, Julia. *A Brand Plucked from the Fire.* Edited by William R. Andrews. Bloomington: Indiana University Press, 1986.

Goff, James R., Jr. *Fields White Unto Harvest: Charles F. Parham and the Missionary Origins of Pentecostalism.* Fayetteville: University of Arkansas Press, 1988.

Gordon, A. J. *The Ministry of Healing.* New York: Christian Alliance Publishing, 1882.

———. *The Ministry of Healing.* 3rd ed. Chicago: Revell, 1882.

Green, Chris E. W. *Toward a Pentecostal Theology of the Lord's Supper: Foretasting the Kingdom.* Cleveland, TN: CPT, 2012.

Green, Joel. *Reading Scripture as Wesleyans.* Nashville: Abingdon, 2010.

Green, Roger Joseph. "Charles Grandison Finney: The Social Implications of His Ministry." *Asbury Theological Journal* 48:2 (1993) 5–26.

———. "Theological Roots of *In Darkest England and the Way Out.*" In the *Wesleyan Theological Journal* 25:1 (1990) 83–105.

Gresham, John L., Jr. *Charles G. Finney's Doctrine of the Baptism of the Holy Spirit.* Peabody, MA: Hendrickson, 1989.

Gunter, W. Stephen. *The Limits of "Love Divine": John Wesley's Response to Antinomianism and Enthusiasm.* Nashville: Abingdon, 1989.

Hambrick-Stowe, Charles E. *Charles G. Finney and the Spirit of American Evangelicalism.* Grand Rapids: Eerdmans, 1996.

Hardesty, Nancy A. *Faith Cure: Divine Healing in the Holiness and Pentecostal Movements.* Peabody, MA: Hendrickson, 2003.

———. *Your Daughters Shall Prophesy.* Brooklyn: Carlson, 1991.

Harrell, David E. *All Things Are Possible: The Healing and Charismatic Revivals in Modern America.* Bloomington: Indiana University Press, 1975.

Hatch, Nathan O. *The Democratization of American Christianity.* New Haven: Yale University Press, 1989.

Heath, Elaine A. *Naked Faith: The Mystical Theology of Phoebe Palmer.* Eugene, OR: Pickwick, 2009.

Heitzenrater, Richard P. *The Poor and the People Called Methodists*, edited by Richard P. Heitzenrater, 15–38. Nashville: Kingswood, 2002.

Hempton, David. *Methodism: Empire of the Spirit.* New Haven: Yale University Press, 2005.

Holifield, E. Brooks. *Health and Medicine in the Methodist Tradition: Journey toward Wholeness.* New York: Crossroad, 1986.

Hopkins, Evan. *Hidden Yet Possessed.* London: Marshall Brothers, 1894.

Horner, R. C. *Ralph C. Horner, Evangelist: Reminiscences from His Own Pen, also Reports of Five Typical Sermons.* Brockville, ON: Standard Church Book Room, n.d.

Hoskins, Steven T. "Eucharist and Eschatology in the Writings of the Wesleys." *Wesleyan Theological Journal* 29:1–2 (1994) 64–80.

Jacobsen, Douglas. *Thinking in the Spirit: Theologies of the Early Pentecostal Movement.* Bloomington: Indiana University Press, 2003.

———, ed. *A Reader in Pentecostal Theology.* Bloomington: Indiana University Press, 2006.

Judd, Carrie F. *The Prayer of Faith.* Buffalo, NY: H. H. Otis, 1881.

Kaufman, Paul Leslie. *"Logical" Luther Lee and the Methodist War against Slavery.* Lanham, MD: Scarecrow, 2000.

Khoo, Lorna. *Wesleyan Eucharistic Spirituality.* Adelaide: ATF, 2005.

Kimbrough, S T, Jr. "Charles Wesley and the Poor." In *The Portion of the Poor: Good News to the Poor in the Wesleyan Tradition*, edited by M. Douglas Meeks, 147–68. Nashville: Kingswood, 1995.

———. "Perfection Revisited: Charles Wesley's Theology of 'Gospel Poverty.'" In *The Poor and the People Called Methodists*, edited by Richard P. Heitzenrater, 101–20. Nashville: Kingswood, 2002.

———, ed. *Songs for the Poor: Hymns*. New York: General Board of Global Ministries, United Methodist Church, 1997.

King, Joseph Hillary. *From Passover to Pentecost*. Franklin Springs, GA: Publishing House of the Pentecostal Holiness Church, 1934.

Kisker, Scott Thomas. *Foundation for Revival: Anthony Horneck, the Religious Societies, and the Construction of an Anglican Pietism*. Lanham, MD: Scarecrow, 2008.

Knight, Henry H., III. *A Future for Truth*. Nashville: Abingdon, 1997.

———. "God's Faithfulness and God's Freedom: A Comparison of Contemporary Theologies of Healing." *Journal of Pentecostal Theology* 2 (1993) 65–89.

———. *The Presence of God in the Christian Life*. Lanham, MD: Scarecrow, 1992.

———. "The Transformation of the Human Heart: The Place of Conversion in Wesley's Theology." In *Conversion in the Wesleyan Tradition*, edited by Kenneth J. Collins and John Tyson, 43–55. Nashville: Abingdon, 2001.

Kostlevy, William C. "Benjamin Titus Roberts and the 'Preferential Option for the Poor' in the Early Free Methodist Church." In *Poverty and Ecclesiology: Nineteenth-Century Evangelicals in the Light of Liberation Theology*, edited by Anthony L. Dunnavent, 51–67. Collegeville, MN: Liturgical, 1992.

———. "Holiness Church (HC)." In *The A to Z of the Holiness Movement*, edited by William C. Kostlevy, 147. Lanham, MD: Scarecrow, 2010.

———. *Holy Jumpers: Evangelicals and Radicals in Progressive Era America*. Oxford: Oxford University Press, 2010.

Land, Steven J. *Pentecostal Spirituality*. Sheffield: Sheffield Academic, 1993.

Langford, Thomas A. *Practical Divinity*. Vol. 1, *Theology in the Wesleyan Tradition*. Nashville: Abingdon, 1983.

Lee, Hoo-Jung. "The Doctrine of New Creation in the Theology of John Wesley." PhD diss., Emory University, 1991.

Lees, H. C. "The Effect on Individual Ministry." In *The Keswick Convention: Its Message, Its Method and Its Men*, edited by C. H. Harford. London: 1907.

Lloyd, Gareth "Eighteenth-Century Methodism and the London Poor." In *The Poor and the People Called Methodists*, edited by Richard P. Heitzenrater, 121–30. Nashville: Kingswood, 2002.

Lowrey, Asbury. "Is the Baptism of the Holy Ghost a Third Blessing?" *Divine Life* (September 1879).

MacArthur, William T. *Ethan O. Allen*. Philadelphia: Office of the Parlor Evangelist, n.d.

Macchia, Frank D. *Baptized in the Spirit*. Grand Rapids: Zondervan, 2006.

MacIntyre, Alasdair. *After Virtue*. Notre Dame: University of Notre Dame Press, 1981.

Mack, Phyllis. *Heart Religion in the British Enlightenment*. Cambridge: Cambridge University Press, 2008.

Macquiban, Tim. "Friends of All? The Wesleyan Response to Urban Poverty in Britain and Ireland, 1785–1840." In *The Poor and the People Called Methodists*, edited by Richard P. Heitzenrater, 131–60. Nashville: Kingswood, 2002.

Madden, Deborah. *"A Cheap, Safe and Natural Medicine": Religion, Medicine and Culture in John Wesley's Primitive Physic.* Amsterdam: Rodopi, 2007.

————. "Saving Souls and Saving Lives: John Wesley's 'Inward and Outward Health.'" In *"Inward and Outward Health": John Wesley's Holistic Concept of Medical Science, the Environment and Holy Living,* edited by Deborah Madden, 1–14. London: Epworth, 2008.

Madden, Edward H., and James E. Hamilton. *Freedom and Grace: The Life of Asa Mahan.* Metuchen, NJ: Scarecrow, 1982.

Maddox, Randy L. "John Wesley on Holistic Health and Healing." *Methodist History* 46:1 (2007) 4–33.

————. "Nurturing the New Creation: Reflections on a Wesleyan Trajectory." In *Wesleyan Perspectives on the New Creation,* edited by M. Douglas Meeks, 21–52. Nashville: Abingdon, 2004.

————. "Reclaiming the Eccentric Parent: Methodist Reception of John Wesley's Interest in Medicine." In *"Inward and Outward Health": John Wesley's Holistic Concept of Medical Science, the Environment and Holy Living,* edited by Deborah Madden, 15–50. London: Epworth, 2008.

————. "Reconnecting the Means to the End: A Wesleyan Prescription for the Holiness Movement." *Wesleyan Theological Journal* 33:2 (1998) 29–66.

————. *Responsible Grace: John Wesley's Practical Theology.* Nashville: Kingswood, 1994.

————. "'Visit the Poor': John Wesley, the Poor and the Sanctification of Believers." In *The Poor and the People Called Methodists,* edited by Richard P. Heitzenrater, 59–82. Nashville: Kingswood, 2002.

————. "Wesley's Understanding of Christian Perfection: In What Sense Pentecostal?" *Wesleyan Theological Journal* 34:2 (1999) 78–110.

Martin, David. *Pentecostalism: The World Their Parish.* Oxford: Blackwell, 2002.

Matthaei, Sondra. "Transcripts of the Trinity: Communion and Community in Formation for Holiness of Heart and Life." *Quarterly Review* 18:2 (1998) 123–37.

Matthews, Rex D. "Religion and Reason Joined: A Study in the Theology of John Wesley." ThD diss., Harvard University, 1986.

McConnell, D. R. *A Different Gospel.* Peabody, MA: Hendrickson, 1988.

McGee, Gary B. *Miracles, Missions, and American Pentecostalism.* Maryknoll, NY: Orbis, 2010.

McMullen, Joshua J. "Marie B. Woodworth-Etter: Bridging the Wesleyan-Pentecostal Divide." In *From Aldersgate to Azusa Street,* edited by Henry H. Knight III, 185–93. Eugene, OR: Pickwick, 2010.

McQueen, Larry. "Early Pentecostal Eschatology in Light of *The Apostolic Faith,* 1906–1908." In *Perspectives in Pentecostal Eschatologies: World Without End,* edited by Peter Althouse and Robby Waddell, 139–54. Eugene, OR: Pickwick, 2010.

Meeks, M. Douglas, ed. *The Portion of the Poor: Good News to the Poor in the Wesleyan Tradition.* Nashville: Kingswood, 1995.

Miskov, Jennifer A. *Life on Wings: The Forgotten Life and Theology of Carrie Judd Montgomery (1858–1946).* Cleveland, TN: CPT, 2012.

Mix, Mrs. Edward. *Faith Cures and Answers to Prayer.* 1882. Reprint, Syracuse, NY: Syracuse University Press, 2002.

Moon, Tony G. "J. H. King's 'Expansive' Theology of Pentecostal Spirit Baptism." *Journal of Pentecostal Theology* 21:2 (2012) 320–43.

Morrison, H. C. *Will God Set Up a Visible Kingdom on Earth?* Louisville: Pentecostal Publishing Company, 1934.

Mullin, Robert Bruce. *Miracles and the Modern Imagination.* New Haven: Yale University Press, 1996.

Newman, Richard S. *Freedom's Prophet: Bishop Richard Allen, the AME Church, and the Black Founding Fathers.* New York: New York University Press, 2008.

Noll, Mark A. *America's God: From Jonathan Edwards to Abraham Lincoln.* New York: Oxford University Press, 2002.

Oh, Gwang Seok. *John Wesley's Ecclesiology: A Study in Its Sources and Development.* Lanham, MD: Scarecrow, 2008.

Palmer, Phoebe. *Faith and Its Effects.* New York: Foster & Palmer, Jr., n.d.

———. *Incidental Illustrations of the Economy of Salvation.* New York: Foster & Palmer, Jr., 1855.

———. *The Promise of the Father.* Shoals, IN: Old Paths Tract Society, 1859.

———. *The Way of Holiness, with Notes on the Way.* 1867. Reprint, New York: Garland, 1985.

Parham, Charles Fox. *The Everlasting Gospel.* Baxter Springs, KS: Apostolic Faith Church, 1911.

———. *Kol Kare Bomidbar: A Voice Crying in the Wilderness.* 1902. Reprint, Baxter Springs, KS: Robert L. Parham, 1944.

Parham, Charles Fox, and Sara E. Parham. *Selected Sermons of the Late Charles F. Parham and Sara E. Parham.* Compiled by Robert L. Parham. Baxter Springs, KS: Apostolic Faith Bible College, 1941.

Pickett, L. L. *Our King Cometh.* Louisville: Pentecostal Publishing Company, 1903.

———. *The Renewed Earth; or the Coming and Reign of Jesus Christ.* Louisville: Pickett, 1903.

Rack, Henry D. *Reasonable Enthusiast: John Wesley and the Rise of Methodism.* London: Epworth, 1989.

Rankin, Stephen W. "The People Called Methodists." In *From Aldersgate to Azusa Street*, edited by Henry H. Knight III, 36–44. Eugene, OR: Pickwick, 2010.

Raser, Harold E. "Holding Tightly to 'the Promise of the Father': Phoebe Palmer and the Legacy of the Fletchers of Madely in Mid-Nineteenth-Century Methodism." In *Religion, Gender, and Industry: Exploring Church and Methodism in a Local Setting*, edited by Geordan Hammond and Peter S. Forsaith, 173–88. Eugene, OR: Pickwick, 2011.

———. *Phoebe Palmer: Her Life and Thought.* Lewiston, NY: Mellen, 1987.

Rattenbury, J. Ernest. *The Eucharistic Hymns of John and Charles Wesley.* London: Epworth, 1948.

Reeve, James Howard. "Holiness and the Holy Spirit in the Thought of Charles G. Finney." PhD diss., Fuller Theological Seminary, 1990.

Richey, Russell E. *Early American Methodism.* Bloomington: Indiana University Press, 1991.

Riss, Richard M. "John Wesley's Christology in Recent Literature." *Wesleyan Theological Journal* 45:1 (2010) 108–29.

Robeck, Cecil M., Jr. *The Azusa Street Mission and Revival: The Birth of the Global Pentecostal Movement.* Nashville: Nelson, 2006.

Roberts, B. T. "Gospel Reforms." *Earnest Christian* 59:5 (May 1890) 133–36.

———. "Suggestions to Contributors." In *Pungent Truths, Being Extracts from the Writings of the Rev. Benjamin Titus Roberts, A.M., While Editor of "The Free Methodist" from 1886 to 1890*, edited by W. G. Rose. Chicago: Free Methodist Publishing House, 1912.

Robinson, James. *Divine Healing: The Formative Years: 1830–1890.* Eugene, OR: Pickwick, 2011.

Runyon, Theodore. *Exploring the Range of Theology.* Eugene, OR: Wipf and Stock, 2012.

———. "The New Creation: A Wesleyan Distinctive." *Wesleyan Theological Journal* 31:2 (1986) 5–19.

———. *The New Creation: John Wesley's Theology Today.* Nashville: Abingdon, 1998.

Rupp, Gordon. *Principalities and Powers: Studies in the Christian Conflict in History.* Nashville: Abingdon-Cokesbury, 1952.

Ruth, Lester. *A Little Heaven Below: Worship at Early Methodist Quarterly Meetings.* Nashville: Abingdon, 2000.

Sánchez-Walsh, Arlene. "Henry C. Ball, Francisco Olazábal, Alice E. Luce, and the Assemblies of God Borderlands Mission." In *From Aldersgate to Azusa Street*, edited by Henry H. Knight III, 266–74. Eugene, OR: Pickwick, 2010.

———. *Latino Pentecostal Identity: Evangelical Faith, Self, and Society.* New York: Columbia University Press, 2003.

Sanders, Paul S. "The Sacraments in Early American Methodism." *Church History* 26 (1957) 355–71.

Sanders, Rufus G. W. *William Joseph Seymour: Black Father of the Twentieth-Century Pentecostal/Charismatic Movement.* Sandusky, OH: Alexandria, 2002.

Sandford, Frank. "Morning Lessons in the Classroom at the Bible School." *Tongues of Fire* (February 1, 1899).

Schmidt, Leigh. *Holy Fairs: Scottish Communions and American Revivals in the Early Modern Period.* Princeton: Princeton University Press, 1989.

Schneider, A. Gregory *The Way of the Cross Leads Home: The Domestication of American Methodism.* Bloomington: Indiana University Press, 1993.

Shaw, Jane. *Miracles in Enlightenment England.* New Haven: Yale University Press, 2006.

Simmons, Dale H. *E. W. Kenyon and the Postbellum Pursuit of Peace, Power, and Plenty.* Lanham, MD: Scarecrow, 1997.

Simpson, A. B. *Earnests of the Coming Age and Other Sermons.* New York: Christian Alliance, 1921.

———. *The Four-Fold Gospel.* New York: Christian Alliance, 1925.

———. *Friday Meeting Talks or, Divine Prescriptions for the Sick and Suffering.* 2 vols. Nyack, NY: Christian Alliance, 1894–99.

———. *The Gospel of Healing.* New York: Christian Alliance, 1915.

———. *The Lord for the Body.* New York: Christian Alliance, 1925.

———. *The Self Life and the Christ Life.* South Nyack, NY: Christian Alliance, 1897.

Smail, Tom, Andrew Walker, and Nigel Wright. *The Love of Power or the Power of Love.* Minneapolis: Bethany House, 1994.

Smith, Amanda. *An Autobiography: The Story of the Lord's Dealings with Mrs. Amanda Smith, the Colored Evangelist.* Chicago: Myer, 1893.

Smith, Jennie. *Valley of Baca: A Record of Suffering and Triumph.* Cincinnati: Hitchcock & Walden, 1877.

Smith, Ted A. *The New Measures: A Theological History of Democratic Practice.* Cambridge: Cambridge University Press, 2007.

Snyder, Howard A. "B. T. Roberts' Early Critique of Methodism." *Wesleyan Theological Journal* 39:2 (2004) 122–46.

———. *Populist Saints: B. T. and Ellen Roberts and the First Free Methodists*. Grand Rapids: Eerdmans, 2006.

———. *Signs of the Spirit: How God Reshapes the Church*. 1989. Reprint, Eugene, OR: Wipf and Stock, 1997.

Snyder, Howard, with Joel Scandrett. *Salvation Means Creation Healed: The Ecology of Sin and Grace*. Eugene, OR: Cascade, 2011.

Stanley, Susie C. *Holy Boldness: Women Preachers' Autobiographies and the Sanctified Self*. Knoxville: University of Tennessee Press, 2002.

Stanton, R. L. *Gospel Parallelisms: Illustrated in the Healing of Body and Soul*. Buffalo, NY: Office of Triumphs of Faith, 1884.

Steele, Richard B., ed. *"Heart Religion" in the Methodist Tradition and Related Movements*. Lanham, MD: Scarecrow, 2001.

Stephens, Michael S. *Who Healeth All Thy Diseases*. Lanham, MD: Scarecrow, 2008.

Stephens, Randall J. *The Fire Spreads: Holiness and Pentecostalism in the American South*. Cambridge: Harvard University Press, 2008.

Stevens, Abel. *The Life and Times of Nathan Bangs, D.D.* New York: Carlton & Porter, 1863.

Stevick, Daniel B. *The Altar's Fire: Charles Wesley's 'Hymns on the Lord's Supper, 1745'.* London: Epworth, 2004.

Streiff, Patrick. *Relunctant Saint? A Theological Biography of Fletcher of Madely*. London: Epworth, 2001.

Strong, Douglas M. *Perfectionist Politics*. New York: Syracuse University Press, 1999.

———. "'The Right Use of Appropriate Means': The Debate Over Strategy and Goals among Nineteenth-Century Evangelical Reformers." *Asbury Theological Journal* 56:1 (2001) 87–100.

Synan, Vinson. *The Holiness-Pentecostal Tradition*. Grand Rapids: Eerdmans, 1997.

Synan, Vinson, and Charles R. Fox, Jr. *William J. Seymour: Pioneer of the Azusa Street Revival*. Alachua, FL: Bridge-Logos Foundation, 2012.

Taves, Ann. *Fits, Trances, and Visions*. Princeton: Princeton University Press, 1999.

Thornton, Wallace, Jr. "God's Trustee: Martin Wells Knapp and Radical Holiness." In *From Aldersgate to Azusa Street*, edited by Henry H. Knight III, 148–57. Eugene, OR: Pickwick, 2010.

Thuston, L. F. "C. H. Mason: Sanctified Reformer." In *From Aldersgate to Azusa Street*, edited by Henry H. Knight III, 227–36. Eugene, OR: Pickwick, 2010.

Trinder, Barrie. "John Fletcher's Parishoners: Reflections on Industrial Revolution and Evangelical Revival in Severn Gorge." In *Religion, Gender, and Industry: Exploring Church and Methodism in a Local Setting*, edited by Geordan Hammond and Peter S. Forsaith, 25–37. Eugene, OR: Pickwick, 2011.

Tyson, John R. *Charles Wesley on Sanctification: A Biographical and Theological Study*. Grand Rapids: Asbury, 1986.

———, ed. *Charles Wesley: A Reader*. New York: Oxford University Press, 1989.

Van De Walle, Bernie A. *The Heart of the Gospel: A. B. Simpson, the Fourfold Gospel, and Late Nineteenth-Century Evangelical Theology*. Eugene, OR: Pickwick, 2009.

Vickers, Jason E. "Charles Wesley and the Revival of the Doctrine of the Trinity: A Methodist Contribution to Modern Theology." In *Charles Wesley: Life, Literature, Legacy*, edited by Kenneth G. C. Newport and Ted A. Campbell, 278–98. Peterborough, UK: Epworth, 2007.

———. "Christology." In *The Oxford Handbook of Methodist Studies,* edited by William J. Abraham and James E. Kirby, 554–72. New York: Oxford University Press, 2009.

Wacker, Grant. *Heaven Below: Early Pentecostals and American Culture.* Cambridge: Harvard University Press, 2001.

Wainwright,Geoffrey "Why Wesley Was a Trinitarian." In *Methodists in Dialogue,* edited by Geoffrey Wainwright, 261–74. Nashville: Kingswood, 1995.

Walker, Pamela J. *Pulling the Devil's Kingdom Down: The Salvation Army in Victorian Britain.* Berkeley: University of California Press, 2001.

Watson, David Lowes. *The Early Methodist Class Meeting: Its Origin and Significance.* 1985. Reprint, Eugene, OR: Wipf and Stock, 2002.

Webster, Robert. "'Health of Soul and Health of Body': The Supernatural Dimensions of Healing in John Wesley." In *"Inward and Outward Health": John Wesley's Holistic Concept of Medical Science, the Environment and Holy Living,* edited by Deborah Madden, 213–32. London: Epworth, 2008.

Weddle, David L. *The Law as Gospel: Revival and Reform in the Theology of Charles G. Finney.* Metuchen, NJ: Scarecrow, 1985.

Wesley, Charles. *Hymns for Our Lord's Resurrection.* Madison, NJ: Charles Wesley Society, 1992.

———. Published Verse. Center for Studies in the Wesleyan Tradition, Duke Divinity School. http://divinity.duke.edu/initiatives-centers/cswt/wesley-texts/charles-wesley.

Wesley, John. *Explanatory Notes Upon the New Testament.* London: Epworth, 1950.

———. *The Letters of the Rev. John Wesley.* Edited by John Telford. London: Epworth, 1931.

———. *The Works of John Wesley.* Edited by Albert C. Outler. Bicentennial ed. Nashville: Abingdon, 1984–. [*Wesley's Works*]

Vol. 1: Sermons I. Albert C. Outler, ed. 1984.

Vol. 2: Sermons II. Albert C. Outler, ed. 1985.

Vol. 3: Sermons III. Albert C. Outler, ed. 1986.

Vol. 4: Sermons IV. Albert C. Outler, ed. 1987.

Vol. 7: A Collection of Hymns for the Use of the People Called Methodists. Franz Hildebrandt and Oliver S. Beckerlegge, eds. 1983.

Vol. 9: The Methodist Societies. Rupert E. Davies, ed. 1989.

Vol. 10: The Methodist Societies: The Minutes of Conference. Henry D. Rack, ed. 2011.

Vol. 11: The Appeals to Men of Reason and Religion and Certain Related Letters. Gerald B. Cragg, ed. 1987.

Vol. 19: Journals and Diaries II (1738–1743). H. Reginald Ward and Richard P. Heitzenrater, eds. 1990.

Vol. 21: Journals and Diaries IV (1755–1765). H. Reginald Ward and Richard P. Heitzenrater, eds. 1992.

Vol. 22: Journals and Diaries V (1765–1775). H. Reginald Ward and Richard P. Heitzenrater, eds. 1993.

Vol. 23: Journals and Diaries VI (1776–1786). H. Reginald Ward and Richard P. Heitzenrater, eds. 1995.

———. *The Works of John Wesley, M. A.* Edited by Thomas Jackson. 14 vols. [*Wesley's Works* (Jackson)]

Whaling, Frank, ed. *John and Charles Wesley: Selected Prayers, Hymns, Journal Notes, Sermons, Letters and Treatises.* New York: Paulist, 1981.

White, Charles Edward. *The Beauty of Holiness*. Grand Rapids: Zondervan, 1986.

Wigger, John H. *American Saint: Francis Asbury and the Methodists*. New York: Oxford University Press, 2009.

———. *Taking Heaven by Storm: Methodism and the Rise of Popular Christianity in America*. New York: Oxford University Press, 1998.

———. "Where Have All the Asburys Gone? Francis Asbury and Leadership in the Wesleyan, Holiness, and Pentecostal Traditions." In *From Aldersgate to Azusa Street*, edited by Henry H. Knight III, 63–71. Eugene, OR: Pickwick, 2010.

Williams, Colin W. *John Wesley's Theology Today*. Nashville: Abingdon, 1960.

Wood, Laurence W. "An Appreciative Response to Donald W. Dayton's 'Review Essay.'" *Pneuma* 27:1 (2005) 163–72.

———. "Can Pentecostals Be Wesleyans? My Reply to Don Dayton's Rejoinder." *Pneuma* 28:1 (2006) 120–30.

———. "Historiographical Criticisms of Randy Maddox's Response." *Wesleyan Theological Journal* 34:2 (1999) 111–35.

———. *The Meaning of Pentecost in Early Methodism*. Lanham, MD: Scarecrow, 2001.

———. "Pentecostal Sanctification in John Wesley and Early Methodism." *Wesleyan Theological Journal* 34:1 (1998) 24–63.

Wood, Timothy L. "Parting Ways: The Separatist Impulse in the Theology of Orange Scott." *Wesleyan Theological Journal* 39:2 (2004) 147–66.

Wright, N. T. *Surprised by Hope: Rethinking Heaven, the Resurrection, and the Mission of the Church*. New York: HarperOne, 2008.

Wynkoop, Mildred Bangs. *A Theology of Love*. Kansas City: Beacon Hill, 1972.

Yong, Amos. *Spirit of Love: A Trinitarian Theology of Grace*. Waco: Baylor University Press, 2012.

———. *The Spirit Poured Out on All Flesh*. Grand Rapids: Baker, 2005.

———. "Wesley and Fletcher—Dayton and Wood: Appreciating Wesleyan-Holiness Tongues, Essaying Pentecostal-Charismatic Interpretations." In *From the Margins: A Celebration of the Work of Donald W. Dayton*, edited by Christian T. Collins Winn, 179–90. Eugene, OR: Pickwick, 2007.